THE GREEN HOUR

THE GREEN HOUR

A DAILY DOSE OF NATURE FOR HAPPIER, HEALTHIER, SMARTER KIDS

TODD CHRISTOPHER

 TRUMPETER | BOSTON & LONDON | 2010

TRUMPETER BOOKS
An imprint of Shambhala Publications, Inc.
Horticultural Hall
300 Massachusetts Avenue
Boston, Massachusetts 02115
www.shambhala.com

9 8 7 6 5 4 3 2 1

FIRST EDITION
PRINTED IN CANADA

⊗This edition is printed on acid-free paper that meets the
American National Standards Institute Z39.48 Standard.
♻This book was printed on 100% postconsumer recycled paper.
For more information please visit www.shambhala.com.

Distributed in the United States by Random House, Inc.,
and in Canada by Random House of Canada Ltd

Library of Congress Cataloging-in-Publication Data
Christopher, Todd.
The green hour: a daily dose of nature for happier, healthier, smarter kids / Todd Christopher.
—1st ed.
p.   cm.
Includes bibliographical references.
ISBN 978-1-59030-756-4 (pbk.: alk. paper)
1. Outdoor recreation for children. 2. Children and the environment.
3. Parent and child. I. Title.
GV191.63.C57 2010
796.083—dc22
2009034552

For Elijah and Leila, my companions for many happy green hours

Come forth into the light of things,
Let Nature be your teacher.

—WILLIAM WORDSWORTH, 1798

CONTENTS

PREFACE

Let me tell you something about acorns. They fit ten to a pocket—twenty if you're a grownup, thirty if you really stuff them in. They come in a wide assortment of shapes and sizes, and they are a delightful combination of textures—smooth, woody shells and rough, checkered caps—that feel just right in your hand.

I remember all of this from childhood, of course, but I am reminded of these little wonders by my young son and daughter who now collect them by the dozens, turning the shells and caps into crafts and creations and—best of all—the shrillest whistles imaginable.

Luckily, my children are blissfully unaware that acorns have, of late, fallen out of fashion.

You see, a while ago, I stumbled upon a rather telling bit of information on the website of the *Daily Telegraph*—that, in its most recent edition, the *Oxford Junior Dictionary* had dropped numerous nature words in favor of increasingly technological terms.[1]

If we are to accept at face value this updated—and ostensibly upgraded—version of the *lingua franca* for seven-year-olds everywhere, then the ABCs no longer include *acorn, beaver,* or *clover. Blackberry*—the natural kind—is gone, with *blog* taking its place. *Violets* have been traded for *voice mail. Dandelion* is out; *database* is in.

Perhaps just as telling is the addition of two words with environmental overtones—*biodegradable* and *endangered*—the inclusion of which might sound like a progressive and well-intentioned decision. But words like these arguably drive deeper the wedge between today's children and the actual, physical, joyful experience of the natural world; they describe a natural environment young children now speak of *saving,* whether or not they first have the opportunity to *know* it, much less come to love it.

But simply taking those first steps of being in, of discovering, of knowing the natural world—something that has been slipping away from the overscheduled, media-driven childhood of today—is of critical importance for a young person's complete and healthy development.

As a child who once learned about the world by experiencing its natural wonder on a small scale—and as the nature-loving parent of two children who now do the same—I am privileged to be part of the movement to heal the separation of childhood and nature. I have had the good fortune to wed my professional life with my personal convictions by creating the National Wildlife Federation's original GreenHour.org website, a source of inspiration and information for parents to keep their children—and themselves—connected to nature in small but meaningful ways. This book has grown out of that effort, exploring in greater depth the ways in which parents can overcome the barriers keeping their families from nature and offering tried-and-true activities, ideas, and advice for beginning—and making the most of—their discovery together.

But perhaps the most satisfying result of that work has been to watch the community of parents and caregivers—many of them first inspired by the 2005 book *Last Child in the Woods*—that continues to rally and grow out of a shared passion for keeping the nature-child bond alive and well. In that watershed book, author Richard Louv called attention to the growing disconnection between children and nature, coining the term *nature-deficit disorder* to describe it.

If that book raised the alarm for the need to reunite children and nature, it is the goal of this book to encourage parents to do so by making a "green hour" part of their families' lifestyle—a time to reconnect with nature, and with each other, where children can explore and discover the natural world with their minds, bodies, and spirits, becoming happier, healthier, smarter souls along the way.

I hope you find this book useful, interesting, and enjoyable. I hope it brings back a few fond memories—or encourages you to make new ones together—and invites the eight-year-old inside you to come out and play. But above all, I hope it inspires you to get outside with your child, simply to enjoy the wonder of it all. Chasing fireflies, catching snowflakes, picking berries, puffing dandelions—these may seem like little things today, but they'll stay with your child forever.

Now . . . have you had your green hour today?

ACKNOWLEDGMENTS

Jennifer Urban-Brown for sowing the seeds of this book and all at Shambhala Publications for giving them such rich soil.

John Dawson for drawing a fine line.

Craig Tufts for always sharing his boundless knowledge and love of nature.

Bethe Almeras, Kevin Coyle, Mary Dalheim, Becky Garland, Kate Hofmann, Anne Keisman, Cindy Lewin, and Anne Senft of the National Wildlife Federation.

Gail Ross for her guidance.

Melissa, Elijah, and Leila for their love, patience, and understanding, and my entire family for their encouragement.

THE GREEN HOUR

INTRODUCTION

Somewhere around the age of five, my son became fascinated by the concept of a time that existed before he did. He had somehow stumbled upon the word *old-fashioned* and rather charmingly began to apply it to anything and everything that obviously predated the world as he knows it: steam engines, antique cars, Victorian houses. Perhaps not quite as charming, at least to my wife and me, was when he would point to family photos from when we were children and explain to all who would hear that these, too, were artifacts from "the old-fashioned days."

Our feigned indignation and slightly bruised egos aside, those images, just a generation old, capture a basic truth. The world we knew as children is not the same world today's children know. In some ways, the disparities are simply the benign indicators that progress marches on. For children who have known only mobile phones and digital music players in their lifetime, rotary phones and record players are relics that reveal as many similarities as they do differences between us.

But what worries me—and, I believe, a growing number of parents, caregivers, and concerned adults—is the extent to which childhood itself has undergone fundamental changes in that relatively short time.

Only a generation ago, kids spent long days fully engaged in outdoor play and discovery. Curiosity was our guide, wonder our reward. Our minds and bodies were engaged, our senses alive. We interacted with the world around us—learning about it, and ourselves, in the process—and were endlessly challenged and delighted by doing so.

I'm not simply romanticizing an idyllic childhood. I grew up in a place—perhaps you did, too—remarkable only for being unremarkable; it lay equidistant between city and wilderness, without being either. But even that place was more than adequately endowed with the landscape of childhood: dirt and stone, grass and trees, butterflies and birds, flowers and bees. And while we certainly cherished our own diversions and distractions, it was not within our nature to be removed from nature. A glorious day would begin with the bang of the door shutting behind us and would luxuriously unfurl to the languid evening, until the streetlights came on and we, at last, would return home.

That all has changed. We have reached the point where the children of today spend significantly less time at play outdoors than the previous generation.[1] And when they do go outdoors it is less frequently, and for markedly shorter periods of time. University of Maryland researchers have found that outdoor and nature-based activities—from walking to camping—now comprise less than one-half hour per week of a child's time.[2] And, even though many parents recognize the benefits of outdoor time for their children—and themselves—we are nonetheless in the midst of a generation-long shift away from nature-based recreation as a whole.[3]

At the same time, several alarming and interrelated trends have emerged. Children have increasingly withdrawn from the fundamental and formative experiences of nature in their own neighborhoods, leading lives more sedentary, more structured, and more saturated by media than their parents, as children, did. Not coincidentally, the rates of childhood obesity have risen dramatically, attention-deficit and emotional disorders have been diagnosed with alarming frequency, and the virtual world presented on a screen has become more meaningful to young people than the natural world right outside their doors.

That lack of real, direct experience in and with nature has caused many children to regard the natural world as mere abstraction, that fantastic, beautifully filmed place rife with endangered rainforests and polar bears in peril. This hyperbolic, often fictionalized version of nature is no more real—and yet no less real—to them than the everyday nature right outside their doors, waiting to be discovered in a child's way, at a child's pace. Consider the University of Cambridge study which found that a group of eight year-old children was able to identify substantially more Pokémon characters than common wildlife species.[4] One wonders whether our children's inherent capacity to recognize, classify, and order information about their environment—abilities once essential to our very survival—is slowly devolving to facilitate life in their increasingly virtualized world. It's all part of what Robert Pyle first called "the extinction of experience."

This should ring alarm bells for parents and

caregivers, because that direct experience in nature, we now understand, is nothing short of vital to our children's intellectual, emotional, physical, and spiritual development.[5] Mounting research demonstrates that, at this most critical time in life, interaction with nature affords children the pleasurable multisensory experiences that challenge their minds, invigorate their bodies, restore their spirits, and sharpen their focus. And, as we will explore, it is perhaps a parent's first and best medicine for addressing that trio of decidedly modern maladies endemic to childhood today: obesity, attention deficit, and media addiction.

GENERATION MEDIA

Imagine for a moment that a child could be transported through time, from a generation ago to the present day. Looking at the world around him, what would he think? What would she say?

I wonder whether it would be this simple question: "Where is everybody?"

For that child searching the backyards, parks, woodlands, and meadows of today for other kids might have a much harder time finding them. The days of children exploring the natural world around them at their own pace, in their own way, have largely given way to full schedules and highly structured activities. But even more notable is the fundamental shift in how children and youth now spend their free hours—"green time" has been replaced by "screen time" to an astounding degree.

The Kaiser Family Foundation's study *Generation M: Media in the Lives of 8–18-Year-Olds,* found that young people today spend an average of 5 hours and 43 minutes per day with electronic screen media—television, computers, and video games. Add CDs and MP3 players to the mix, and their average time spent with all electronic media adds up to an astonishing six and a half hours per day.[6] It would be hard to underestimate the impact and influence of these media on their lives. According to Common Sense Media's 2008 report *Media and Child and Adolescent Health: A Systematic Review,* children today, on average, spend nearly as much time with media as they do with parents and in school combined.[7]

But these children, in all likelihood, are simply following the precedent already being set at home. In the 2003 study *Zero to Six: Electronic Media in the Lives of Infants, Toddlers, and Preschoolers,* the Kaiser Family Foundation found that an alarming number of young children live in TV-centered households. For two-thirds of these children, the television set is constant background noise, left on at least half of the time whether or not anyone's actually watching; for a third of them, it is simply left on most, if not all, of the time.[8] And, incredibly, a third of all children under the age of seven have a television in their bedrooms.[9]

At best, electronic media demonstrate the power of information and communication unfettered by the constraints of space and time. At worst, they blur the line between improving and consuming our lives.

But the media and devices are only what we make of them, what we allow them to be. What gives me pause is the prevailing attitude that so easily, so readily, weaves them into the fabric of our—and our children's—lives. And I mean fabric both metaphorically and literally; we recently bought a child's jacket that turned out to have dedicated interior pockets for both a cell phone and a media player, not to mention integrated loops for managing earphone cords. I now have the cold comfort of knowing that my eight-year-old son's garment is equipped to protect him from the elements of wind, rain, snow—and, heaven forbid, being without portable electronics.

It's a small example, but it draws the big picture: for today's youth, media are *everywhere*. The Kaiser Family Foundation study *Generation M* revealed that young people today not only spend an average of six and a half hours per day with media, they also pack the equivalent of eight and a half hours of media use into that time, frequently using more than one medium simultaneously.[10] For an adult culture that by and large praises multitasking as a sign of increased efficiency, if not effectiveness, this should come as no surprise. But it should be cause for concern; the more media young people consume, the less they may be able to discriminate among the messages they carry. In an age where marketing to children has become more pervasive and more aggressive, this is no small matter.

In an interview in *Multinational Monitor,* Susan Linn, author of *Consuming Kids: The Hostile Takeover of Childhood,* said that "comparing the marketing of yesteryear to the marketing of today is like comparing a BB gun with a smart bomb."[11] And it's not just because of the amount, though jaw-dropping, spent on marketing to children, an annual figure that has increased from roughly $100 million to about $17 billion over the past twenty-five years.[12] It's in part because of the hyper-targeted nature of marketing campaigns aimed at kids, which reach across media and mix their messages with the content. In parlance closer to the devices that have become the medium: the signal-to-noise ratio for today's kids

is pretty bad—and there are no signs of it getting any better.

Many parents and researchers alike have long wondered what effect this overexposure to media would have on our children. To conclusively answer that question, researchers from the National Institutes of Health, Yale University School of Medicine, and California Pacific Medical Center conducted a comprehensive review of 173 studies of media exposure and children's health. The resulting report, *Media and Child and Adolescent Health,* demonstrates a strong correlation between greater media exposure and long-term negative effects on the health of children and teens. The outcomes range from increases in childhood obesity and early sexual behavior to substance use and low academic achievement.[13]

Even computers, ostensibly a boon to our children's academic progress, seem to present hazards of their own. In the Alliance for Childhood's report *Fool's Gold: A Critical Look at Computers in Childhood* (2000), a number of health risks are tied to children's computer use: repetitive stress injuries, eyestrain, obesity—even damage to their physical, emotional, or intellectual development.[14] Some of the casualties are less obvious but no less costly; computers, the report posits, "undermine the sense of wonder and reverence that young children typically bring to their encounters with the real world of rocks, bugs and stargazing."[15]

For immediate gratification, that world of rocks, bugs, and stargazing may not be able to compete with the world that flashes by on the screen of a television, computer, or video game. But the real danger in that latter world lies in how quickly children can be seduced into passivity and inactivity, their senses bombarded, overwhelmed, and ultimately diminished. Most sadly, it is the sense of wonder that seems to be first to go.

MEDIA'S EFFECTS ON LIFESTYLE

In 1999, the U.S. surgeon general David Satcher observed that "we have the most sedentary generation of young people in American history." Today, that trend continues, if not worsens. As a result, of all developed nations, the United States has the highest prevalence of obesity, and obesity in its children and youth has reached epidemic proportions. Between the growing demands on their time and the seductions that lead them into an increasingly indoor-dwelling, media-focused lifestyle, remaining active and fit has largely fallen by the wayside for the youth of today.

The statistics are staggering. The 1999–2000 National Health and Nutrition Examination Survey found that the number of overweight or obese children and youth had tripled since the 1960s.[16] Figures from the National Center for Health Statistics indicate that, just four years later, one in six young people between the ages of two and nineteen was overweight, and nearly one in three adults was obese.[17] By 2008, the number of overweight youth between the ages of six and nineteen had seen a 45 percent increase in the span of just one decade.[18] Up to four out of five obese youth continue the unhealthy trend into adulthood,[19] fostering a household environment where the cycle would, in all likelihood, continue.

Yet, interestingly enough, many of today's overweight and obese youth are being raised by parents who are themselves active and fit. A 2005 article in the *New England Journal of Medicine* analyzed data related to obesity and longevity and made a startling prediction: we are raising the first generation of American children whose life expectancy may be shorter than that of their parents.[20] In the span of a single generation, the children who wore out the knees of their own pants have become the parents of children who wear out the seats of theirs.

Providing children access to safe outdoor spaces—and the encouragement to explore and play in them—is an obvious remedy. Even in urban settings, the impact of the natural environment can be great. A study published by the *American Journal of Preventive Medicine* found that city children living in "greener" neighborhoods gained less weight than their counterparts living in areas with less green space.[21] Whether you reside in an urban, rural, or suburban setting, switching off the TV or computer is a sensible first step. A study conducted by researchers at the State University of New York at Buffalo found that children who reduced their screen time—cutting TV and computer use by half—ate less and lost weight accordingly.[22] And evidence suggests that these children would enjoy benefits beyond their increased physical fitness.

It is estimated that some two million school-aged children are affected by attention-deficit/hyperactivity disorder, or ADHD. This figure makes it the most common neurobehavioral disorder of childhood, but one need only examine the production and consumption of methylphenidate—commonly marketed as Ritalin—to piece together the story. The first and most popular prescription drug to treat ADHD in children, methylphenidate production and prescriptions skyrocketed in the 1990s, with some estimates placing the increase over the decade as high as 700 percent.[23] A disorder unheard of a generation ago, ADHD vaulted to almost routine diagnosis and, as often seems to be the case, medication. In fact, United Nations figures indicate that the United States alone produces, and consumes, about 85 percent of the world's methylphenidate.[24]

The steep rise in ADHD coincides with that of childhood obesity, and it's difficult to imagine the two as completely unrelated. At a minimum, they both share a connection to the continued increase in television use and electronic media consumption by children and youth. The effect of television viewing on sedentary bodies is plain to see; the effect on children's neurological health was initially less so. A wave of research, including two separate studies published by the journal *Pediatrics*, confirms that early exposure to television is indeed associated with attention problems later in childhood,[25] and that childhood television viewing is associated with attention problems in adolescence[26]—the American Academy of Pediatrics now recommends that children under the age of two see no television at all.

So what's the connection between nature and attention disorders? The argument that children who are disconnected from the natural world are somehow more susceptible to ADHD is inferential, but logical. If they are not engaged in traditional outdoor play and discovery, how do those children occupy their time? If it is with television and electronic media, they certainly are at greater risk for developing problems with attention and concentration.

But more compelling are what appear to be the powerful restorative effects of nature on children affected by attention disorders. In a groundbreaking national study published by the *American Journal of Public Health* in 2004, Frances E. Kuo and Andrea Faber Taylor found that "green" outdoor settings appear to reduce ADHD symptoms in children; even in individuals not diagnosed with an attention disorder, time in nature had the effect of reducing ADHD-like symptoms such as inattention and impulsivity.[27] In a carefully controlled test in a follow-up study, they found that children professionally diagnosed with ADHD enjoyed greater levels of attention and concentration after twenty-minute nature walks in green settings. Remarkably, the effects were similar to and as effective as methylphenidate, suggesting that a "dose of nature" could become a potent alternative in managing ADHD symptoms.[28] Taken alongside the earlier work of the Cornell researcher Nancy Wells—which found that nature in and around the home increases both a child's attention and psychological well-being[29]—it makes a strong argument for the importance of a daily connection to the natural world in our children's lives.

THE NEED FOR A GREEN HOUR

This growing body of research clearly indicates what parents have known for generations—that time outdoors is essential to the healthy development of young minds, bodies, and spirits. The studies point to the problems invited by children and youth leading a lifestyle disconnected from nature—as well as the intellectual, physical, and psychological benefits to be enjoyed by those given the chance to explore, to play in—simply to spend time in—the natural world.

But knowing does not necessarily mean doing. Many parents today—even those who enjoyed a childhood full of nature play and discovery themselves—now raise children who are over-scheduled, overexposed to media, and essentially disconnected from the natural world in any meaningful way. And we now see the first wave of parents who themselves missed out on those formative experiences and opportunities to learn and grow in nature; consequently, they do not have them to draw upon now as they raise children of their own.

Fortunately, this is a challenge that all families can tackle together, and one with a solution that benefits children and parents alike: reclaiming a "green hour" a day for play and discovery in the natural world. And that natural world begins right outside your door; it doesn't matter whether you spend time in a wilderness setting or in your own backyard—a valuable experience can be had in both. A green hour is simply a time for families to unplug, unwind, and recharge as they reconnect to the natural world—and to each other. It is an opportunity for parents to strengthen family bonds as they guide the natural experiences that foster happier, healthier, smarter children.

ABOUT THIS BOOK

Whether you led a childhood full of outdoor experiences or you will be learning alongside your children as you go, this book is full of information and inspiration to get your family outside and to help you make the most of your time there.

The opening sections identify and break down the barriers that keep many children—and families—from making a meaningful connection to the natural world, offering advice and practical tips for making a green hour a rewarding part of your family's routine.

The remainder—and the majority—of the book leads the way to the wonder that begins just outside your back door, whether you live in the city, the country, or somewhere in between. From your own backyard to open fields and hiking trails to the heavens above, it explores nearly two dozen starting points for discovery, filled with activities, facts, science lessons, projects, and resources—focusing on the most accessible and universal experiences—all with an eye toward helping parents to guide the exploration, while letting children discover their world at their own pace.

It is the modest proposal of this book that we strive to provide our children a green hour a day to keep that most vital connection between children and nature alive. And, if we can join them to share in the discovery and the wonder—to invigorate family ties as we invigorate ourselves—so the better. In the chapters that follow, we'll explore how parents and caregivers can put this idea into practice.

DISCOVER TOGETHER

I am struck by the fact that the more slowly trees grow at first, the sounder they are at the core, and I think that the same is true of human beings. We do not wish to see children precocious, making great strides in their early years like sprouts, producing a soft and perishable timber, but better if they expand slowly at first, as if contending with difficulties, and so are solidified and perfected. —HENRY DAVID THOREAU

It's eight o'clock in the morning, and the SUV in front of us is in warp drive. Or, at least, its occupants are. At the helm, a mother drives with one hand and cradles a mobile phone with the other, punctuating her conversation with animated head movements. In the passenger seat, a preteen girl bobs her head in time with the song playing on her portable music player. In the backseat ride two younger children wearing headphones, each of them entertained by the cartoon flickering on the screens built into the headrests of the seats in front of them. (I wonder: is the radio on, too?) The traffic light ahead turns yellow and the mother brakes, thinks the better of it, and revs up the engine, hurtling through the intersection a split second before the light turns red. What a tableau of our hurried, modern life they present!

To be fair, the gadgets themselves are only what we make of them. Mobile phones and pocket-sized music players have become everyday conveniences of our digital culture. And goodness knows that a kid-friendly movie makes for a relatively harmless way to pass some time on a long drive or a family road trip.

But it's a weekday morning and I can only assume that this parent, just like me, is simply making her family's daily commute to school and to work—part of that precious fraction of time the average parent and child get to spend together each day. At a time and in a place seemingly made for conversation, this family is instead conspicuously plugged in to their devices, sitting mere feet apart but tuned into anything but each other.

At home, at work, even in transit, we've become quite adept at filling every quiet or empty space with . . . well, what is it, exactly? Most of us, thinking of the pace of our lives, surely would describe them as full. But are they fulfilling?

More and more, it's hard to avoid the conclusion that today's children, following their parents' example, are leading lives where they are overbooked, overstructured, and overstimulated. And now, more than ever, they need the restorative balm that only time spent in nature can provide them.

The light turns green, and we're on our way.

THE IMPORTANCE OF FREE TIME

In the Alliance for Childhood report *Fool's Gold: A Critical Look at Computers in Childhood*, there's a remarkable observation—that childhood is our evolutionary edge.[1] What species, besides humans, enjoys such a protracted period for the physical, cognitive, and social development of its young? We are wired not for rapid growth but for deliberate development, inspired by an innate curiosity and informed by our physical interaction with the world around us.

"Childhood takes time," the report suggests. "And many children are simply not being given the time to be children."[2]

Indeed, many children today live life at the same manic pace as their parents, shuttling from task to task, speeding from milestone to milestone, all in an effort to get by, if not to get ahead. Unfortunately, in the wake, it's the most joyful experiences of childhood that often get left behind.

It's a difficult tide to turn. As a society, we somehow have become obsessed by the notion of time as a commodity but have seemingly lost sight of how to use it wisely. We value it, without necessarily understanding its value. Even our language for it evokes basic economics—we speak of saving, spending, even of investing time, as though it will accrue to some eventual reward. Time, it might seem, is our currency in trade. But what seems to be lost is the notion that time is currency in an absolute sense—nothing more than a succession of moments. Is there any better way to spend time than to be fully, completely, in each current moment as it comes?

If you've ever watched a child digging on a sandy beach, collecting flowers, or building a fort made of sticks, you might agree that being completely in the moment is an inherent human capacity—and, regrettably, one that many of us lose as we grow into adulthood. Time spent in free play outdoors is a golden time when children are fully engaged— mind, body, and spirit. What might look like nothing . . . well, it really is something.

However, children's free playtime has been on the decline for a generation, dropping 25 percent between 1981 and 1997 alone.[3] What's filling the void? In large part, it is the rise of structured activities for children. Certainly, these organized activities, such as youth athletic programs, do have their positive aspects—especially in light of the current epidemic of childhood obesity.

But they do not, and cannot, take the place of children's free play outdoors—those freely chosen activities that delight a child's mind, body, and senses. No less an authority than the United Nations High Commission for Human Rights, in its 1989 Convention on the Rights of the Child, recognized the right of every child to play.[4] And the American Academy of Pediatrics describes play not only as vital to children's cognitive, physical, and social development, but also as an ideal way for parents to strengthen family bonds of affection and to serve as role models for their children.[5] The family that plays together stays together.

And the family that stays together stays strong. Consider the results of the Columbia University survey which found that teens who regularly participate in family dinners were more likely to do well in school and less likely to drink alcohol, smoke cigarettes, or try marijuana.[6] The magic bullet could be nothing more than the fact that these families, even if it's only for the duration of one meal together each day, put everything else on hold to connect, to communicate, and to reaffirm for each other that first things still come first.

In that regard, the notion of reclaiming some time for outdoor play and discovery each day—for your children, if not for your entire family—joins the swelling movement to slow down, to simplify, and to savor life: family, friends, food, culture, the wonders of the world around us. It's a commitment to live life in an authentic, meaningful way,

in tune with the rhythms of our hearts, our minds, and of nature itself.

TIPS FOR RECLAIMING FREE TIME

For our children, there's no better antidote to the noise of modern life than to unplug from its trappings, slow down, and retreat to the steadfastness of the outdoors. There, they can move, explore, and grow at their own pace, reconnecting with all of their senses, including their sense of wonder.

To those who take the time to discover it—and to discover themselves in it—the natural world yields many benefits: a fitter body, a keener mind, a soaring imagination, an uplifted spirit, and greater powers of concentration. And when families take the time to do so together, the effect is that much stronger.

Here are some suggestions for parents who want to bring balance and harmony to family life by slowing down, unplugging, and playing together:

- Examine your own media use. Which are essential? Which are helpful? Which are taking time away from the people and pursuits that are most important to you?
- Draw clear lines between the different demands on your time, and you'll better be able to give each the full attention it deserves.
- Make outdoor time a priority, and part of your family's routine. Consider it a chance to unplug, unwind, and recharge, even as you reconnect with each other.
- Play. Laugh. Repeat. The world outside is full of surprise and delight.
- Be patient with your children, and with yourself.

Remember that while childhood takes time, it is precious and fleeting.

"Don't blink." So my wife and I will sometimes whisper to each other when we sense the impermanence of that occasional perfect moment with our children. It's a sentiment that the Baha'i writer George Townshend expressed most poignantly when he wrote these lines: "Childhood is but for a day. Ere you are aware it will be gone with all its gifts forever." The meaning is clear. Take the time to be in, and to savor, those moments with your children, and the joy of those gifts will never fade.

THE BENEFITS OF LESS MEDIA

In order to navigate our busy lives, we often turn to electronic media and devices and their promise of convenience. But instead of freeing up time for living life more fully, these media have a way of working themselves into every quiet corner of our lives, whetting our appetite for more.

The next time you're around a group of young children—say, at a birthday party—get them to pose for a photograph. After they see the flash, almost invariably, at least one of them will head straight for you, eager to see the image displayed on the camera's LCD screen. To them, that's just what cameras are: devices that take, and display, photographs *instantly*. I know it's all that my children, in their lifetime, ever have known them to be.

Like so much of our modern electronics and media, they are both marvelous and convenient. But, less obviously and perhaps a bit insidiously, they also reinforce for our children the unsustainable expectation of instant gratification.

It'd be hard for them not to. Consider the world of devices a child sees today. Digital cameras produce images instantly. Wireless phones provide instant communication from virtually anywhere by voice, text, and photographs. Music, videos, and movies can be downloaded instantly to computers or handheld media players, some small enough to clip on to your clothing. Pocket-sized gadgets in our automobiles—which have themselves evolved to resemble mobile movie theaters —tell us, turn by turn and street by street, precisely where we're going and how to get there. And there always seems to be a dizzying array of new devices that connect wirelessly to the Internet or communicate with global positioning satellites. You can have it all—and take it with you—without waiting. But once you can take it all with you, do you ever really leave it all behind?

TIPS FOR UNPLUGGING YOUR FAMILY

Parents understand intuitively that there are no shortcuts here; the passive pleasures of electronic media might make for an easy short-term alternative, but they do little for a child's long-term well-being. Still, pulling the plug can be difficult—TV and computer games were cited by more than five out of six surveyed mothers in a national study as the primary reason for their children's lack of outdoor play time.[7] But for a family determined to trade screen time for green time together, it can be done.

Here are some suggestions for keeping your family's media consumption under control:

- Talk with your children about your family's electronic media use and set clear expectations and limits together.
- Model sensible media use for your children.

Show them that you can hang up the phone, put down the laptop, or switch off the TV.

- Consider a "no screen time on weekdays" policy for your family. Or start by designating one "turnoff" day each week.
- Avoid arguments by using timers. Even better, have your child set his or her own timer at the start of screen time.
- Remember that the American Academy of Pediatrics recommends no television viewing for children under the age of two.
- Consider allowing older children to "earn" screen time by offsetting it with time spent more productively—reading, exercising, being of service.
- Keep tabs on content and online safety by limiting electronic media use to the common or family areas of your home.
- Demystify screen media by using it wisely with your children. Playing your child's favorite video game together or having a family movie night provides an opportunity to model sensible media use—and helps to keep screen time from turning into forbidden fruit.
- Most importantly, offer engaging family activities and outdoor time as an alternative to electronic media.

You may or may not agree with Edward O. Wilson's theory of biophilia: that we humans have evolved with—and because of—a connection to and an affinity for nature and other living things. Still, anyone who has watched the genuine, spontaneous reactions of children discovering and interacting with the natural world around them surely would find it a difficult notion to discount altogether. There's simply no greater, or more delightful, proving ground for young minds, bodies, and spirits.

It's entirely possible that we may never again see the day where children and nature are truly inseparable. Too much has changed, too fast. But this book is predicated on the notion that we cannot accept that possibility as a foregone conclusion. The importance of the natural world to a child's healthy development—as playground, laboratory, classroom, and refuge—simply remains too great to let the connection fade away.

THE JOYS OF DISCOVERING NATURE TOGETHER

If you could design the perfect learning environment for children, what would it be like?

Certainly, it would need to be engaging—stoking the fires of fascination while at the same time extinguishing boredom. It would invigorate not just the intellect but the whole child—mind, body, and spirit. It would activate all of the senses and reward a child's curiosity with discovery and wonder. And it would instruct intimately while conveying lessons at a grand scale.

Such a place exists, and it can be found in a nearby park, on a local trail, or even in your own backyard. The tuition is quite reasonable—even free.

The natural world, of course, offers all of these things, and more.

For nature is that uncommon place in children's lives that asks them not merely to react, but instead allows them to truly reflect. It also is that increasingly uncommon place that still has the capacity to surprise them.

I have observed, with some sadness, that the

notion of surprise seems to be disappearing from modern childhood. Given that surprise so easily leads to delight—real, wide-eyed, jaw-dropping delight—this is a particularly unfortunate development. More and more, the lives of today's children seem to be scripted, with outcomes safely predetermined at the outset of any given undertaking. Even their play and their playthings have become hyper-realistic, usually requiring batteries but leaving little to the imagination.

In nature's classroom, the rules change. The natural world improvises a limitless number of variations, even on familiar themes. But to the patient observer and willing participant, nature will unfailingly reveal the order in what initially might appear to be chaos. From seemingly random or unrelated pieces, larger patterns and unifying concepts inevitably emerge.

In the best sense of the words, the natural world holds great mystery and suspense. At the same time, that uncertainty leads inexorably, reassuringly, to a familiar conclusion. The child who becomes accustomed to nature's rhythms and patterns will be endlessly comforted and confirmed by them, living a life in tune with spring flowers and summer storms, autumn leaves and winter skies.

TIPS FOR ENJOYABLE OUTINGS

Here are some suggestions for parents who want to provide positive outdoor experiences for their children and make the most of their opportunities to discover the natural world together.

Keep It Simple

Wonder unfolds at a child's scale and pace, which are necessarily smaller and slower than an adult's.

Childhood, after all, is a succession of first experiences, so expect frequent stops—and questions. Remember that even familiar objects can be made "new" by seeing them with a fresh perspective or by appreciating them with all of your senses.

Keep It Positive

The wonder of nature may lie in its almost inexhaustible capacity to offer new discoveries, but the joy of nature comes from the outdoor experience itself. The time you and your child spend together outdoors is its own reward. Knowledge is a terrific goal—and there certainly is a lifetime of lessons to be learned from nature—but remember that it often arrives at the heels of wonder. And knowledge isn't a prerequisite for exploration. There's nothing at all wrong with saying "I don't know." Even better is to turn it into "Let's find out," which becomes an invitation for you and your child to investigate together. Remember, too, as you encounter the unfamiliar (or, as the case may be, the familiar) to avoid negative reactions or showing fear, something we may unintentionally teach our children.

Keep It Flexible

Nature wouldn't be nearly so magical if it were completely predictable. Expect—and make the most of—the unexpected. Whenever possible, let your child lead, and let learning follow. Watch for teachable moments and take advantage of them. Ask questions to affirm your child's expectations or experience, or to lead them to the next level of understanding. Resist the temptation to share everything you might know, instead guiding your child toward independent discovery whenever possible. Read your child's signals so that you can offer more guidance, or allow more independence, as needed.

Tips for Making Learning Fun

For parents and caregivers who want to dig a bit deeper, there are several well-established theories of learning and development that may be helpful, at least in part, for making your child's time outdoors a positive learning experience. Here are a few of them:

Montessori Method

Based on the work of the Italian educator Maria Montessori, this approach values child-directed activity as the basis for learning. Focused primarily on early childhood, it fosters the development of cognitive and physical abilities through discovery and active, multisensory experimentation. Montessori philosophy outlines several inherent tendencies of humans that inform the way we interact with, and learn about, the world around us. They include orientation (our desire to understand our environment and to find our place within it), order (our preference for organization, stability, and predictability over chaos), and exploration (our disposition to use our senses to investigate and to satisfy our curiosity).

How might you apply these concepts?

- Let the child's interests guide the activity.
- Encourage children to use all of their senses to discover the world around them.
- Remember that younger children often learn best when engaged both physically and intellectually.

Multiple Intelligences

In his 1983 book *Frames of Mind: The Theory of Multiple Intelligences,* Harvard psychologist Howard Gardner set forth one of the most intriguing and controversial learning theories of the last century. Gardner challenged the traditional view of intelligence by introducing the concept of "multiple intelligences," which loosely describe the diverse cognitive strengths and learning styles of different people. Especially for the parents of children who struggle with traditional methods, this framework can offer insight into new approaches and strategies to reach and to inspire all kinds of learners.

The original list of multiple intelligences includes:

- linguistic intelligence
- logical-mathematical intelligence
- musical intelligence
- bodily-kinesthetic intelligence
- visual-spatial intelligence
- personal intelligence (interpersonal and intrapersonal)

It is important to note that the multiple intelligences are not mutually exclusive, but instead function much like several passageways leading to the same place. Ideally, they provide touchstones for the caregiver who would adapt an activity for an individual child's learning style.

Consider how this concept might inform one's approach to, say, the study of backyard birds. A visual-spatial learner might make sketches of the birds he observes, noting their anatomical differences. A musical learner might listen to and learn to distinguish the songs of different species. And a logical-mathematical learner might collect and analyze data on the species that visit her backyard feeder.

How might you apply these concepts?

- Determine which learning style(s) your child seems to have.
- Tailor activities to your child's strengths and interests.
- Remember that there can be many different ways to experience or to understand the same thing.

Bloom's Taxonomy

In 1956, the University of Chicago cognitive psychologist Benjamin Bloom helped to change the way we think about thinking. His *Taxonomy of Educational Objectives*—more commonly known as Bloom's Taxonomy—outlined a succession of progressively more sophisticated intellectual processes associated with learning outcomes. The continuum moves from the retention and comprehension of information to the synthesis and evaluation of larger concepts. Over the years, Bloom's original classifications have been revised or renamed, but the core tenets have remained essentially the same. Here's an overview of the six levels, from lowest to highest, with an example of each:

1. Knowledge: recalling basic information. *A young child is able to identify a stick.*
2. Comprehension: interpreting and explaining basic concepts. *A child understands that sticks are twigs or branches that have fallen from a tree.*
3. Application: using or organizing information. *A child discovers that sticks are useful for poking, digging, drawing in dirt, and (when nobody's looking) personal defense.*
4. Analysis: examining and differentiating pieces of information. *A child determines that smooth, green sticks are more flexible and less rigid than rough, brown sticks.*
5. Synthesis: pulling together pieces of information into a meaningful whole. *A child designs and builds a small fort made of sticks.*
6. Evaluation: making comparisons and defending value judgments. *A child decides that stout maple sticks make a good frame for a fort, while green sassafras sticks and pine boughs are useful for the roof and walls.*

How might you apply these concepts?

- Assess your child's level of understanding of a given concept.
- Ask leading questions to encourage thinking at the next level.
- Remember that learning is an iterative and ongoing process.

Childhood and nature, quite simply and quite perfectly, go together. So it's been since time immemorial, and so we hope it will always remain. But now it just might be that childhood and nature, for their continued survival, need each other more than ever.

We've already examined the alarming trends that have been fundamentally reshaping childhood. And even the casual observer is aware of the myriad threats that confront the environment today, to say nothing of the perils that unchecked climate change may bring tomorrow.

But the combined forces of childhood and nature may be allies powerful enough to preserve and to protect each other in the face of these challenges. In the children who enjoy formative experiences outdoors, the natural world not only fosters vibrant minds, bodies, and spirits—it also finds its future champions. Cornell University researchers have found that children's participation in nature activities is positively associated with the development of pro-environmental attitudes as adults. And for children who have deeper, "wilder" experiences—such as hiking, camping, or playing in the woods—that positive relationship extends to both pro-environmental attitudes and behaviors alike.[8] The researcher Nancy Wells suggests that "when children become truly engaged with the natural world at a young age, the experience is likely to stay with them in a powerful way—shaping their subsequent environmental path."[9] Likewise, in an article titled "Learning to Love the Natural World Enough to Protect It," Louise Chawla finds two significant factors common to adults who have chosen to work in defense of the environment: having positive outdoor experiences as a child, and being taken outdoors by a parent or caregiver.[10]

These outcomes are confirmation that this is, indeed, powerful stuff. They also serve as gentle reminders that we, as parents, simply need to provide our children with plentiful opportunities to discover and to know the natural world—and their love will follow, naturally. Even well-intentioned caregivers who are too preachy or pedantic can inadvertently muddle the purity of their children's experiences in nature. David Sobel in *Beyond Ecophobia* said it perfectly: "If we want children to flourish, to become truly empowered, let us allow them to love the earth before we ask them to save it."[11] Whatever path they follow as adults, they'll be the better for these experiences and will hold a lifelong respect for themselves, for others, and for the wondrous world around them.

SAFETY FIRST

When asked to the name the things that keep them and their children indoors, many parents place the potential hazards and discomforts of the great outdoors at the top of their lists. The litany is familiar—bug bites, bee stings, an itchy rash or two—but, in actual fact, most of the bugaboos are more inconvenient or annoying than they are dangerous. And the ones that justify legitimate concern seem to take on a life of their own in our popular culture, to the point where the *perception* of such dangers arguably could be more hazardous in the long run than the dangers themselves, as millions of children—and their families—miss out on the physical, intellectual, and emotional benefits of time spent exploring the natural world together. A feedback loop is created: the less one experiences and knows nature, the more intimidating it may seem, making one even less likely to experience and to know nature, and so on.

But is the natural world of trees and meadows, trails and streams, somehow more dangerous to our children than the man-made environment of jungle gyms and ball fields, busy streets and swimming pools? Every parent is keenly aware of the risks posed by the latter. Perhaps more parents should consider the benefits offered by the former.

Ultimately, common sense and balance prevail. How many parents would deny their children education for fear of the potential childhood maladies—head lice, chicken pox, the common cold—that might await them at school? How many would trade their children's physical fitness for the reassurance that their kids never will suffer a bump, bruise, or sprain from playing youth sports? The benefits in each case, of course, outweigh the risks, and the same holds true for a child's time spent exploring and discovering the natural world.

While it's true that spending time outdoors could possibly expose you and your family to potential health hazards, it's also true that, for every concern, there are safeguards to keep you from harm, and that a little information and preparation can prevent most problems before they arise. Talk openly and in an age-appropriate manner with your children about safety and precaution. You'll empower them to understand and assess risks and to make intelligent decisions to help minimize them.

Here's an overview of those outdoor bugaboos, with some tried-and-true advice for tackling them head-on and preventing them from ruining your family's time outdoors.

POISON IVY AND FRIENDS

The warmer months bring plants flush with sap and people baring more of their skin, and it's not always a good combination. Poison ivy—along with its close cousins, poison oak and poison sumac—is the quintessential summer bummer, though it's best to steer clear of it at any time of year. Nearly five out of six people will develop an itchy, blistery rash within a day or two if their skin comes into contact with the plant; the lucky remainder are seemingly unaffected by the mostly colorless, odorless oil—called *urushiol*—found in poison ivy, oak, and sumac alike. The rash, more properly called *urushiol-induced contact dermatitis,* typically clears up on its own within two weeks, though a variety of treatments to ease the itch and dry the blisters can bring relief faster. In rare cases, severely allergic individuals will require immediate medical attention, and they may be given an antihistamine or corticosteroid as part of their treatment.

The best strategy for dealing with poison ivy's rash, as anyone who has experienced it firsthand

Poison ivy

will attest, is not to get it in the first place. It is the first plant that I taught my own children to identify, and with good reason—poison ivy thrives in the so-called edge habitat to be found at the perimeters of housing developments, parks, and fields and frequently can be found alongside roads, trails, and streams. (And there are indications that a changing climate, with higher temperatures and greater concentrations of atmospheric carbon dioxide, creates more favorable growing conditions for poison ivy.)

But identification sometimes can be tricky. The old folk wisdom—"leaves of three, let it be"—aside, poison ivy is highly variable in form, sometimes appearing as a ground cover, a shrub, or a vine. The leaves themselves can range from deep to light green, and from glossy to dull, but the arrangement of three leaflets is generally consistent. The center leaflet typically has a longer stem than its partners, which often display a subtle notch or thumb along the outer edge, giving the triad a somewhat symmetrical appearance—even if the plant itself is more unruly in its arrangement. The presence of clustered white berries, brilliant scarlet-colored fall foliage, and reddish-brown "hair" on old stems and woody vines are other good field marks. But if there's any doubt at all, don't touch!

It is worth pointing out that while it's important to avoid the plants themselves, it's imperative to avoid contact with the urushiol—the resinous oil in the plants—to prevent an allergic reaction. There are plenty of cases of individuals getting a rash from touching tools, equipment, clothing—even pets—that previously had brushed against poison ivy and come into contact with urushiol. And, because the oil is persistent, even in dead or dried-out vines and plants, one should be very careful when gathering firewood. As an extra measure of protection, older children and adults may wish to try a lotion containing *bentoquatum,* which creates a barrier that inhibits the penetration of the skin by urushiol.

Even if exposure to poison ivy is suspected, acting quickly can prevent an allergic reaction. First and foremost, the urushiol oil should be washed from the skin. Rinse—but don't scrub—thoroughly with whatever water is available to you, whether it's a garden hose, water bottle, or stream. Gently swabbing the area with rubbing alcohol is effective at removing the oil and helping to draw

Did You Know?

THE NOTION THAT POISON IVY'S RASH CAN "SPREAD" IF THE BLISTERS ARE SCRATCHED OPEN IS A MYTH. A RASH THAT SEEMS TO WORSEN OVER SEVERAL DAYS IS LIKELY CAUSED BY THE URUSHIOL TAKING EFFECT AT DIFFERENT RATES—THIN SKIN IS MORE LIKELY TO BE AFFECTED FIRST—OR BY REPEATED EXPOSURE TO THE OIL THAT WASN'T FULLY WASHED AWAY. (HELPFUL HINT: USE A STIFF BRUSH FOR CLEANING UNDER FINGERNAILS.)

it out of the skin. Taking a warm, soapy shower—not a bath—as soon as possible should wash away any remaining oil.

Should a rash develop, the best remedy is to ease the itch and to dry the blisters. Hydrocortisone cream, calamine lotion, oatmeal baths, and cool showers all are effective ways to provide temporary relief. Especially for children, preventing scratching—and, therefore, possible secondary infection—is the key to dealing with the itchy rash, which, left untreated, should resolve itself within two weeks. But it can be a long two weeks . . . so best to avoid it altogether.

Quick Tips:
- Practice identifying poison ivy, oak, and sumac.
- Use a barrier cream containing bentoquatum.
- Wear long pants and long sleeves.
- Stay on established trails.
- Avoid vines, tangles, and thick underbrush.
- Never burn poison ivy or wood covered with its vines.
- Rinse hands often, especially after possible exposure.
- Avoid touching or rubbing your eyes and face.
- Carry wipes moistened with rubbing alcohol.
- Take a warm, soapy shower when you return home.
- Wash clothing in hot water and rinse well.

BEES AND WASPS

Although bees and wasps are decidedly beneficial to humans—whether producing honey, pollinating native plants and agricultural crops, or preying upon pest insects—it's easy to forget that, should you find yourself on the wrong end of their sting-

ers. The bad news for outdoor lovers is that these familiar insects are capable of delivering painful stings, when disturbed. The good news is that the vast majority of stings can be prevented and, except for highly sensitive individuals, are not dangerous.

Yet a sting, when it happens, really smarts—and can be a scary experience for younger children. But by understanding the behavior of bees and wasps and taking a few simple precautions, you and your children can enjoy countless outdoor hours without worrying about them.

Unless you bother or come into direct contact with them, bees and wasps generally will be content to go about their own business—gathering pollen and nectar, hunting other insects—and leave you alone. (However, it should be noted that even otherwise docile bees and wasps can become dangerous when they are in the vicinity of their hives or nests. Always stay clear of beehives and wasps' nests.) Most situations where a sting might occur can be avoided simply by not attracting bees and wasps to you. There's a good reason why flowers smell sweet and are brightly colored—it makes them attractive to pollinators. Unfortunately, wearing bright, floral colors and strong fragrances or perfumes will make *you* attractive to bees and wasps, too. If you're going to be around them, stick to drab solid colors—and long sleeves and long pants help, too.

Like many creatures, wasps can become more problematic in the presence of food. Who hasn't seen yellow jackets buzzing around garbage cans and picnic tables, scavenging for a free meal? Picnickers should consider drinking water; the only thing worse than cups of syrupy soda pop at a cookout are the soda cans that yellow jackets can

Did You Know?

WHEN TREATING BEE STINGS, SOME TIME-HONORED HOME REMEDIES—SUCH AS TOOTHPASTE, MEAT TENDERIZER, OR A PASTE MADE FROM BAKING SODA AND WATER—ACTUALLY MAY BE EFFECTIVE. THESE ALKALINE PRODUCTS CAN POSSIBLY HELP TO COUNTERACT THE VENOM, WHICH IS ACIDIC.

slip into, unnoticed. Extra care should be taken in late summer and fall, when yellow jackets become particularly aggressive scavengers.

Unlike wasps, hornets, or yellow jackets, which can sting multiple times, a honeybee can sting a person just once—leaving its slightly barbed stinger behind. Whether you remove the stinger by pinching and pulling or by scraping it with the edge of a fingernail or a credit card, the most important thing is to remove the stinger quickly. The faster the stinger is removed, the less venom will be injected, which can lessen the severity of the reaction. Once the stinger is removed, a honeybee sting should be treated like any other sting: reduce the swelling by applying ice wrapped in a cloth, and apply a topical analgesic to alleviate the pain, if necessary. Monitor the site of the sting closely, especially in individuals who never have been stung before. Allergic reactions may not show up until a second exposure, making it a good idea to keep an oral antihistamine for children on hand. A typical sting in a person with normal sensitivity should begin to feel better in a few hours and clear up in a few days.

It must be stressed that for those who are hypersensitive to stings or extremely allergic to the venom, a bee or wasp sting can be a medical emergency requiring immediate attention. Medications ranging from antihistamines to epinephrine are used to suppress the body's reaction to the sting, and individuals with such severe allergies always should carry their "sting kit" when spending time outdoors.

QUICK TIPS:
- Avoid dressing in bright, floral colors.
- Wear long pants and long sleeves, in solid white, gray, or tan.
- Avoid perfumes, lotions, or heavily scented products.
- Avoid walking barefoot, especially where clover is present.
- Avoid the trash cans and food waste that attract yellow jackets.
- Keep food covered outdoors, especially fruits and sweets.
- Stay far away from wasp nests and beehives.
- Never swat or wave your arms at bees or wasps.
- Get away from bees and wasps by moving calmly and slowly.
- Carry antihistamines or epinephrine pens for allergic individuals.
- Remove honeybee stingers as quickly as possible.

- Reduce the swelling by applying ice wrapped in a cloth.

MOSQUITOES

The mosquito is a pest that needs no introduction—though it would be more than happy to make your acquaintance. To be specific, it's the adult female mosquito that skillfully and persistently finds our skin and causes us to slap and swat all summer long. In order to produce eggs, she requires the nourishment of a blood meal, and she will seek any available warm-blooded host to bite and to feed on. That host often is a bird or a mammal, including—unfortunately—a human. Anticoagulant agents in the mosquito's saliva are introduced during a bite, and it is the reaction to the saliva that causes the raised bump, or wheal, and the characteristic itch as a result.

In many parts of the world, particularly tropical and equatorial regions, mosquitoes have long posed a serious health risk, spreading diseases such as yellow fever, malaria, and dengue fever. But in much of the Western world and more temperate regions, and until recently, the mosquito was more likely to be regarded as a nuisance than as a hazard. Today, however, there is genuine cause for concern, and for taking proper precautions to keep mosquitoes at bay.

One generation ago, the Asian tiger mosquito couldn't be found in the continental United States. Since its inadvertent introduction in 1985, this notorious invasive species has spread rapidly, especially throughout the southeast, and now can be found in almost all parts of the country east of the Rockies. Unlike their native counterparts, these black-and-white-striped mosquitoes are more ag-gressive and more likely to feed throughout the day—not the just the peak times around dawn and dusk. Mounting evidence suggests that they will become increasingly important carriers of West Nile virus—as native mosquitoes already are.

Since the appearance of West Nile virus in the United States in the summer of 1999, much attention has been given to mosquitoes as the vector for the transmission of the virus to humans. The primary cycle of transmission involves mosquitoes biting infected birds, carrying the virus, and spreading it to uninfected birds. However, a mosquito carrying the virus can spread it to a human during a bite. Humans do not pass the virus to each other.

The good news is that even when infected with West Nile virus, four out of five people will show no symptoms or ill effects. Up to one in five individuals, however, will develop a mild or moderate illness including such flu-like symptoms as headache, fever, body aches, and nausea. And, according to the Centers for Disease Control and Prevention, 1 in 150 will develop a severe illness, potentially with long-lasting neurological effects.[1] Individuals over the age of fifty are most at risk for developing severe symptoms, if infected. Though researchers are working on developing one, there is, at present, no vaccine for humans.

Since most mosquitoes don't stray far from the water source that nurtured them, an effective way to reduce the mosquito population near you is to make your home and property inhospitable to them. Mosquitoes require water to breed—but they can breed in or around a surprisingly small amount of it. Look around your home, and drain or eliminate all sources of standing water such as flower pots, wading pools, buckets, tarps, pet

Did You Know?

EVEN THOUGH WE MAKE REFERENCE TO MOSQUITO "BITES," THAT'S NOT ENTIRELY ACCURATE. MOSQUITOES LACK THE MOUTHPARTS TO DELIVER AN ACTUAL BITE. INSTEAD, THEY PIERCE THE SKIN OF THEIR HOSTS WITH A SPECIALIZED, NEEDLE-LIKE PROBOSCIS AND SUCK BLOOD THROUGH IT LIKE A STRAW.

dishes, and backyard toys. And remember to keep your gutters clean; even wet leaves in a stopped-up gutter can provide a suitable breeding ground for mosquitoes.

Most important, though, is to minimize your chances of being bitten. Limiting outdoor activity near dawn and dusk where mosquitoes are present and wearing long pants and long sleeves may help. But, since mosquitoes are naturally attracted to heat, body odors, and carbon dioxide—three things people naturally emit—a good repellant is your best line of defense.

A broad range of topical repellants is available, some with chemically synthesized active ingredients, others with those derived from natural or botanical sources. Those containing the chemical known as DEET (N,N-diethyl-m-toluamide) are particularly effective and have been deemed safe for use on children as young as three months by the American Academy of Pediatrics. Check the label for the percentage of DEET in the product; 10 percent is a reasonable amount for use on children. Repellants containing the active ingredient Picaridin also have been proven to be highly effective.

The naturally derived oil of lemon eucalyptus (para-menthane-3,8-diol) is an effective active in-gredient for those preferring to avoid synthetic ingredients. Though not quite as potent as DEET, it still is very reliable and is the active ingredient in the repellant of choice in my household. Note that it is not recommended for use on children under the age of three.

With any kind of repellant, follow the guidelines on the label carefully, including recommendations for safe application. Be sure to apply repellants only to exposed skin or clothing, and never near the eyes or mouth or on children's hands—which inevitably will end up near their eyes or mouths.

QUICK TIPS:
- Wear long pants and long sleeves.
- Apply repellant to exposed skin or clothing.
- Don't apply repellant to skin covered by clothing.
- Don't allow children to apply repellant to themselves.
- Don't apply repellant to children's hands.
- Eliminate sources of standing water around your house.
- Keep your gutters clean and clear of wet leaves.
- Keep screens on doors and windows.
- Limit your exposure to mosquitoes at dusk and dawn.
- Wash bitten areas with soap and water.

- Alleviate the itch with calamine lotion or hydrocortisone cream.

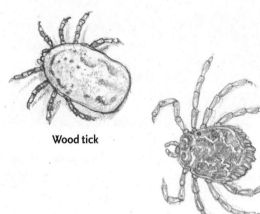

Wood tick

Deer tick

TICKS

Relative to their size, these diminutive parasites may cause more consternation than any other creature. The bane of backcountry adventurers, ticks are tiny arachnids—eight-legged relatives of spiders and mites—which, like mosquitoes, feed on the blood of their warm-blooded hosts. Unlike mosquitoes, which bite and feed quickly, most ticks feed slowly, requiring them to attach and to remain latched to their hosts, sometimes for days. They prefer to feed on animals such as deer, mice, chipmunks, and birds, but many species will target humans, when they happen upon them.

It's possible to enjoy an active outdoor lifestyle without ever encountering a tick. But, because they possibly can transmit diseases to humans, ticks should be regarded seriously and your family's exposure to them should be minimized. Fortunately, most of the diseases they carry—such

as Rocky Mountain spotted fever, erlichiosis, and Lyme disease—are treatable with antibiotics. That said, the illness in each case can be severe, especially when not diagnosed and treated promptly, and an ounce of prevention in this instance truly is worth a pound of cure.

Because of their limited mobility and their preference for particular types of habitat, ticks can be avoided with a little forethought and preparation. As a general rule, ticks favor humid environments over dry, sunny, well-drained ones. In areas where ticks are known to be present, most encounters can be prevented by staying clear of ideal tick habitat—tall grass, weeds, leaf litter, and shrubs, particularly near damp or shaded woods—and hikers should stay on marked trails to avoid brushing against these potentially tick-infested areas. Because ticks will almost always be found at grass or shrub level, long pants tucked inside socks provide an effective, if not entirely fashionable, barrier; wearing white or light-colored long-sleeved shirts and long pants makes it easier to spot ticks on your clothing.

A tick typically boards a person by clinging to the ends of tall grass, weeds, or shrubbery and climbing onto the potential host as it brushes by. This usually means hitching a ride on or near a person's feet, and then climbing upward in search of a dark or moist place—such as the groin, belt line, navel, armpits, or scalp—to attach itself. For this reason, repellants applied to shoes, socks, and pants can be effective. If your family already has a DEET-based repellant for mosquitoes, try spraying it directly onto shoes, clothing, and exposed skin before entering tick-friendly environments. Alternatively, a stronger permethrin-based repellant—which actually will kill any ticks that come into contact with it—can be applied to shoes and clothing before wearing, but care should be taken to avoid contact with the skin.

Ticks range from the size of a pinhead or smaller (as nymphs) to approximately the size of a sesame seed (as adults), which makes them difficult to detect by sight or by touch during normal activity. Therefore, the simplest, and most important, line of defense against ticks is to perform a daily tick check on your children and on yourself—and more frequently if you've spent time in known tick habitat. Pay special attention to the places a tick might gravitate toward, such as the groin, the armpits, or the scalp. And should you find one, don't panic. An unattached tick can be easily removed with a swatch of sticky tape, which then should be folded over onto itself, flattened, and discarded.

Even a tick attached to the skin, if spotted early, presents little problem. In order to transmit dangerous bacteria, like the one that causes Lyme disease to humans, a tick needs to be attached for a long time. Prompt removal is key; the Centers for Disease Control state that the risk of contracting Lyme disease from a tick attached to your skin for less than twenty-four hours is extremely small.[2]

To properly remove an attached tick, gently grasp it by the head with fine-tipped tweezers—getting as close to the skin as possible—and steadily pull the tick directly away from the skin. Be careful not to yank, twist, or crush the tick, and discard it after removal. Wash and monitor the affected area, seeking medical attention should redness, swelling, or a rash appear in the days or weeks afterward.

Quick Tips:

- Discourage ticks by keeping your lawn neatly mowed and trimmed.
- Avoid ground cover such as pachysandra.
- Create barriers of gravel or wood chips at the perimeter of your yard.
- Avoid tick habitats such as tall grass, weeds, and leaf litter.
- Wear long sleeves and long pants tucked inside socks.
- Wear hats or bandanas and pull long hair into a ponytail or bun.
- Use DEET-based repellants for skin and clothing.
- Use permethrin-based repellants for shoes and clothing only.
- Vaccinate pets and check them frequently for ticks.
- Stay in the center of marked trails and paths.
- Conduct a thorough tick check daily.
- Remove attached ticks properly and promptly.
- Wash and monitor the affected area.

Did You Know?

FORGET ABOUT THOSE OLD FOLK REMEDIES FOR REMOVING ATTACHED TICKS. TRYING TO REMOVE A TICK BY USING PETROLEUM JELLY, GASOLINE, OR A HOT MATCHSTICK IS INEFFECTIVE, AND THESE METHODS MAY DO MORE HARM THAN GOOD.

COLD WEATHER

Not surprisingly, the chill of a winter's day is enough to drive many families indoors. Yet, for those willing to bundle up, cold days can make for a wonderful time to be outside—especially for those who'd rather not share the great outdoors with stingers and biters. Bees, wasps, and mosquitoes are long gone, and even ticks become inactive once the mercury consistently drops below 40 degrees Farenheit.

And, as it turns out, one of the time-honored reasons to stay *indoors* is no reason at all. According to the National Institute of Allergy and Infectious Diseases, there is no evidence that people catch colds as the result of exposure to cold weather.[3] It's true that most colds occur in the fall and winter, coinciding with the falling temperatures. But it's more likely that the proliferation of colds at that time of year is caused by people spending greater amounts of time indoors—where they, in turn, are more likely to be in close contact with each other, spreading the viruses that easily take hold in nasal passages dried by heated indoor air.

Spending time outdoors in cold weather can help to keep your family fit at a time when it otherwise might be easy to settle into sedentary patterns. The fresh air and exposure to sunlight also can help to stave off the blues that often accompany winter's shortened days. But winter weather can be both unpredictable and extreme, so common sense and a few precautions are necessary to keep your family safe.

The essential advice is to stay warm (to avoid frostbite from exposure), dry (to avoid the danger of hypothermia), and hydrated (to offset the effects of dry, frigid air and wind).

Proper dress, of course, is of primary importance. Dressing in increasingly warm layers of comfortable clothing topped by a wind and water-resistant shell is a good approach for cold weather activity. Choose materials that not only insulate but also effectively wick moisture away from active bodies and feet. Hats, scarves, and water-resistant gloves and boots are recommended, but be careful not to bundle up *too* much. Being warm should not lead to becoming overly sweaty—being wet in frigid weather is both uncomfortable and potentially dangerous.

Remember that the parts of our bodies farthest from our hearts and lungs are the ones that feel the cold first and are most susceptible to its effects. Our bodies lose most of their heat through our heads and hands alone. And, because of their extremity and their proximity to the cold ground, our feet are particularly prone to chill. Keep in mind that children typically will cool faster than adults, but often are more active and therefore generate more body heat to compensate. When activity ceases, however, it's not uncommon for children to begin to feel colder, faster. Frequent breaks are a good idea as a matter of course, and are best taken indoors, or at least in a place sheltered from the wind and cold. Most important is to teach children to be mindful of the signals their bodies will send them—cold hands, stinging noses, tingly feet—when it's time to get inside and warm up. And, failing that, hot cider or cocoa will work every time!

QUICK TIPS:

- Dress in layers of warm, moisture-wicking clothing.
- Cover heads and hands to retain the most body heat.

Did You Know?
- -

To keep warm—and safe—in cold weather, you first have to stay dry. When your clothing gets wet, it loses about 90 percent of its insulating value. Wetness, wind, and cold can lead quickly to hypothermia, which occurs when the body loses more heat than it is able to produce.

- Avoid overdressing and heavy perspiration.
- Wear a waterproof shell, boots, and gloves in wet or snowy weather.
- Stay dry, and get inside promptly when wet.
- Pay attention to the wind chill and avoid extreme conditions.
- Drink plenty of fluids to offset dehydration from dry air and wind.
- Prevent and treat chapped lips with shea butter balm or lanolin ointment.
- Protect eyes from UV (ultraviolet) rays and glare from sun and snow.
- Keep moving for warmth and better circulation.
- Take a break at the first sign of discomfort in your extremities.

HOT WEATHER

In many ways, summer is the ideal time to be outside. Long sunny days and a world teeming with life offer no shortage of activities to occupy a family's leisure time.

But summer, as we all know, really can turn on the heat. The sun's rays are strongest, and humidity often is highest, at this time of year—and both can present possible health considerations.

Sunshine is beneficial, even essential. When we're exposed to the sun's ultraviolet rays, our bodies respond naturally by producing vitamin D. In careful moderation, unprotected exposure to the sun's rays can provide our bodies with all the vitamin D they need. But a sunburn is simply too much of a good thing—the red, swollen, painful skin that results from overexposure to ultraviolet rays. How much is too much? It depends on the amount of melanin, a protective pigment, in your skin. Everyone's skin is different, but fairer skin has less melanin, in general, and is therefore more susceptible to burning.

The midday hours bring the strongest rays and the greatest chance of sunburn. Extra care should be taken during the peak hours from 10 AM until 3 or 4 PM, when unprotected exposure to the sun should be kept to a minimum. Wide-brimmed hats and loose-fitting shirts and pants—especially those made of fabrics with a UPF (ultraviolet protection factor) rating of 15 or more—can offer great protection, but oftentimes are simply not practical.

While a good sunscreen may be the best solution for children and adults alike, there is a bewildering variety of sprays and lotions available, nearly all of them purporting to be safe, effective, and waterproof. In actual fact, the majority of sunscreen products on the market do not deliver on all three counts. In its 2008 study, the Environmental Working Group (EWG) analyzed nearly one thousand sunscreen products and found that four out of five were ineffective or contained potentially unsafe ingredients.[4] (Current reviews and sunscreen product research can be found on EWG's Cosmetic Safety Database website at www .cosmeticsdatabase.org.)

When selecting a sunscreen for your family, try to choose one with zinc oxide or titanium oxide as its active ingredient. This will offer full spectrum protection against both UV-A and UV-B rays while avoiding the harmful chemicals, such as oxybenzone, found in the products of many popular brands. Even though sprays may be more convenient, lotions make a safer choice. Spray sunscreens could accidentally be inhaled, a growing concern as more and more products contain micronized or nanoscale particles. Sunscreen should be applied to skin *before* exposure to the sun—up to thirty minutes beforehand, if possible—and should be reapplied often, especially in situations where it might be washed away by water or perspiration. When applying sunscreen, be aware that water and sand (and, in wintertime, snow) can reflect ultraviolet rays back at you, and that it's easier to burn at higher elevations. Remember that even good sunscreens will begin to break down and lose their effectiveness, and therefore should be replaced with a fresh bottle each year.

Unfortunately, once skin is burned by the sun, little can be done to speed its recovery. Over-the-counter anti-inflammatory medicines, such as ibuprofen, can help to reduce the swelling and discomfort. Lotions containing aloe can help to cool and to moisturize the skin. Sunburned skin should not be exposed to the sun again until it has healed—and has been protected by sunscreen.

When summer serves up both soaring temperatures and high humidity, the combination requires an extra measure of caution. Strenuous activity in such conditions can lead to overheating, as the heat and humidity impair the body's natural ability to cool itself by the evaporation of sweat. When the body heats up more quickly than it can cool itself, heat exhaustion can result; symptoms include headaches, dizziness, and nausea. Left unchecked, heat exhaustion can progress to heatstroke, the very dangerous situation occurring when the body's core temperature reaches 104 degrees Farenheit.

Fortunately, overheating can be prevented by avoiding overexertion and by keeping your family hydrated by consuming plenty of water or electrolyte drinks. Pay attention to your local weather forecast for reports of unhealthy air quality or an unsafe heat index. Limit strenuous outdoor activity on those days or, at a minimum, restrict your activities to the relatively cooler morning and evening hours. Most importantly, teach your children to recognize the early signs of overheating—fatigue, thirst, muscle cramps, wooziness—and to take a break to cool off and rehydrate as soon as they appear.

Quick Tips:
- Drink plenty of water (and avoid alcohol) to prevent dehydration.
- Minimize exposure to the sun's rays between 10 AM and 4 PM.
- Cover up with hats, visors, and long sleeves when possible.

- Apply sunscreen thirty minutes before exposure.
- Use a sunscreen rated at SPF (sun protection factor) 30 (or higher), reapplied often.
- Replace your sunscreen each year.
- Reduce sunburn pain and swelling with ibuprofen.
- Cool and moisturize sunburned skin with an aloe-based lotion.
- Wear sunglasses rated to block the full spectrum of UV rays.
- Protect against UV rays reflected by water and sand.
- Monitor weather forecasts for unsafe heat indices.

Though it might seem like a lot of information, much of what your family needs to know to stay safe outdoors is common-sense caution, and easy to remember once you put it into practice. And while the goal of preparedness is to avoid a negative outcome, it's much better to keep things positive—encourage your family to view taking these precautions not as a chore, but instead as a way to ensure a rewarding time outdoors for everyone.

YOUR OWN BACKYARD

FAR TOO OFTEN, the word "nature" conjures up images so majestic and idyllic that we have a tendency to imagine ourselves right out of the picture. We think of nature as a destination—a distant one, at that—and reduce the familiar to the ordinary, no matter how wonderful it might be. But in the ordinary there is great virtue; it's where discovery begins.

Even the smallest of green spaces allow children to stimulate their senses, exercise their imaginations, and engage in the exploration and nature play that aids their physical, cognitive, and emotional development. A modest suburban yard, townhouse lot, or small city park—each offers a child a vast world of wonder. While we can easily lose sight of this fact, everything children need to begin interacting with the natural world is literally right outside our doors.

And while the nature presented by those spaces may be modest in scale and in scope, it is nonetheless nature that is accessible, tangible, and approachable, and therefore rich in experiences. Especially for younger children, it is where they can begin to forge a physical and emotional connection to the world around them. It's one small step for a child, one giant leap for childhood.

And even a familiar space—for older kids, for kids at heart—holds its share of wonders when you see it with fresh eyes. All it takes is a sense of adventure and a willingness to explore.

The pages that follow are dedicated to activities and ideas to help guide your family's exploration of the backyard world of bugs and birds, dirt and trees, muddy hands and grass-stained knees. The concepts—and confidence—you build upon here can ease your family into nature and serve as a starting point for adventures farther afield.

MAKING THE CONNECTION

Right outside your door, there are discoveries waiting to be made.

Perhaps the best way for families to forge a meaningful connection to nature is simply to head into the world together—eyes wide open, senses alive, ready for wonder. Together, they can share in the joy of discovery—for children, of seeing and doing things for the first time; for parents, of experiencing them anew through their children's eyes.

It all starts by heading outside with the expectation that there *is* wonder to behold, waiting to be discovered by those willing to find it or willing simply to see the world around them in a new way.

SEEKING HIDDEN TREASURE

A scavenger hunt might seem like a quaint undertaking, an old-fashioned pursuit in the vein of mud pies and stick forts. And it is. But such games and activities, which allow children to explore and make a physical connection with the natural world, to behold it with all of their senses, fulfill a loftier purpose. They encourage children to gather and to

35

interpret information about the world around them for themselves—and thereby to begin to make meaning of it.

For younger children, this can mean simply ordering objects by size, shape, color, and texture; for older children, categorizing, classifying, and analyzing. At any age, children are able to see themselves—to *be* themselves—freely interacting with and in the context of their natural environment. As they stretch their minds and muscles, they will learn as much about themselves, their abilities, and their sensibilities as they will about the world around them. And once they've realized their capacity to find wonder and delight in the commonplace and the ordinary, the world they inhabit will always be nothing short of wonderful.

Familiar seeds, pods, and cones

Backyard Scavenger Hunt

There's probably no better invitation to explore an outdoor space than this simple, tried-and-true activity, which can easily be adapted to the season, the location, and the age of the participants.

WHAT YOU NEED:
- an outdoor space to explore
- notepads and pencils
- small reusable bags or containers

WHAT YOU DO:
1. Provide each child with a collection bag or container.

2. Create a scavenger hunt list of natural items, appropriate for the season and location, for the participants to find. To get you started, here are some suggestions:

- leaf
- twig
- stone
- berry
- cone
- stem
- bud
- sand
- shell
- flower
- feather
- bark
- acorn
- seed
- grass

Lists work well for beginning readers and older children. For younger children, create a visual checklist with a simple sketch of each item.

3. If you have a large group of children, try pairing them into teams. Consider creating a different list of items for each team, and have teams trade their lists when they've completed them.

A scavenger hunt also can encourage children to explore with their senses. Try adding list items to be observed but not collected (squirrel, bird, web, butterfly, nest, etc.). Include items that can be "found" by listening (a bird call, the buzz of an insect, rustling leaves) or by touching (rough bark, a smooth stone, something warm, something cold)—even by smelling.

For another fun alternative, create a game card for each player by drawing a large three-by-three grid on a piece of paper. In each square, write the name—or, for younger children, make a sketch—of an object to be found. Keep all of the game cards at a common starting point. As players find items on the list, they should return to their game cards and cover those items with markers such as pennies or pebbles. Play until the first player has covered three squares in a row, tic-tac-toe style, or the entire game card.

This activity lends itself well to almost limitless variation. One surefire favorite is to turn your scavenger hunt into a backyard treasure hunt. Simply use waterproof plastic containers or reusable sandwich bags to house a succession of clues and the "booty" to be found at the end of the trail on a hand-drawn map. Besides being a lot of fun, it's a good way to introduce basic map reading and orienteering skills. Bushes, trees, rocks, sandboxes, flower pots—all make good hiding places for clues along the way. And if you've got a place, such as a mulch bed, where you don't mind digging, nothing beats uncovering buried treasure at the end of the hunt. (Suggested bounty: a favorite book to read together outside, "tickets" for a trip to a favorite park or playground, or an invitation to a backyard picnic.) Older children can try their hand at hiding "treasure" of their own and creating maps and clues for caregivers and younger siblings to follow.

COLOR HUNT

This variation on the scavenger hunt theme challenges you to look at your own backyard or your neighborhood just a little bit differently.

WHAT YOU NEED:

- crayons, markers, or colored pencils
- small slips of white paper or index cards
- an assortment of sample paint chips or swatches (optional)
- a notepad and pencil

WHAT YOU DO:

1. Have each child choose several crayons, markers, or colored pencils of different colors and color a slip of paper or index card with each of them. Alternatively, have each child select several paint chips or swatches of different colors.
2. Explore your backyard, neighborhood, park, or other green space, trying to find natural objects that match the colors each child has selected.
3. Keep track of your findings on the notepad.

Afterward, compare notes. Did you find all the colors? Which colors were easiest to find? Which were hardest? Imagine living somewhere very different—the seaside, the desert, the mountains. How might that change the game? How about playing in a different season?

It's interesting to note that some things in nature are just begging to be noticed—brilliant yellow flowers, bright red berries, vivid orange and black monarch butterflies. Why do you suppose these things might want to stand out and be seen? How might that help them? Conversely, there are a great many creatures that are outfitted in colors, streaks, and patterns designed to help them blend

> REMEMBER: NEVER DIG IN AN AREA WHERE UNDERGROUND UTILITY LINES MAY BE PRESENT.

in with their surroundings. Can you think of any? What might be the advantage of creatures that can hide in plain sight that way?

COLLECTING TREASURES

Empty the pockets of your children's clothes after a day of outdoor exploration, and you'll be sure to find an assortment of treasures—acorns and cones, flowers and shells, rocks and stones. You can't keep it all, of course, but there's also no reason to discard every special find a child makes. Here's a terrific way to keep and display the ones most important to your kids.

MAKE A NATURE TABLE

By setting up a small nature table in your home, a place where these special finds are displayed, you can create a space where your family's connection to nature—and your child's contribution—is honored. And it can be more than just a collection; by refreshing or replacing the objects throughout the year, you can use your family's nature table to mark the arrival of the seasons and commemorate holidays. In that small way, keeping a nature table reinforces the notion of living even a little bit more in step with the rising and falling rhythms of the natural world.

If space is at a premium, consider creating a nature bowl instead. This makes for an attractive and inviting display of natural treasures that can't grow too large—once the bowl is full, your children will need to remove older finds to make room for the new ones. In our home, a moss-green stoneware bowl stands chock-full of little wonders, each with its own story, which my children are more than happy to recount. The dried seahorse, for instance,

is more than just an amazing artifact: it's a concrete reminder of a lucky find on a wonderful morning spent walking the white sandy shores of Florida's Gulf Coast together. When you hear a child talk about the special objects they've collected, you can't help but be humbled by the fact that they're really talking about—and sharing—pieces of themselves.

MAKING MEMORIES

Not everything your children find outdoors can be—or should be—picked up and collected. Like the best scientists and explorers, they can record many of their discoveries in ways that leave the environment just as they found it. Let them try preserving their outdoor experiences in one or more of these ways:

Making notes in a nature journal

MAKE A NATURE JOURNAL

Think of this as a nature diary. Your kids can fill it with notes about the things they've seen and done, or get creative by adding their own stories, poems, drawings, and photographs. There's no one way to keep a nature journal, but the best ones are quite personal, capturing not just the observer's notes but also how he or she feels about them. Spiral-bound notebooks with durable lined, unlined, or graph paper all work well, and invite a mix of words, images, and objects taped or glued in place, scrapbook-style.

Make a Photo Album

With digital cameras becoming ever more accessible and easier to use, creating a physical—or virtual—photo album of the world around them is a wonderful way for children to express themselves. Flowers, trees, butterflies, birds, squirrels—there are many good subjects to be found without even leaving your neighborhood.

No matter what kind of camera, and whatever the subject, here are a few basic tips to help your family get better results from your photos:

- Avoid shooting toward the sun. For best results, keep the sun behind you, or at least to the side, and remember that the best light for photography comes early and late in the day—times when nature is often buzzing with activity.
- Get as close to your subject as you can, or use your camera's zoom to fill the frame with whatever it is you're photographing. Unless the background is important to the picture, it might draw attention away from your subject.
- Position yourself so that you can take your photograph from an interesting or unusual angle. Instead of just looking down and shooting, you might decide to go eye-to-eye with a bug or nose-to-nose with a frog. You'll become accustomed to seeing things from different perspectives, and will make lots of great photos—and discoveries—along the way.

Make Sound Recordings

Does your family have a portable media player? Many of these devices have fairly sophisticated built-in or accessory microphone capabilities. Challenge your children to go outside with ears wide open and record the sounds of the natural world, from birds, frogs, and insects to wind, water, and weather. To help them identify what they've heard, compare their recorded calls of birds, frogs, and insects to those available on reference websites. Or, for a different approach, encourage them to use the device to record themselves, by describing what they see and hear in a sort of audio journal, or by narrating the action like the host of a backyard nature documentary.

More to Explore: Life Lists

Many birdwatchers keep what's known as a *life list*—a running list of all the bird species they have ever observed. And while the name might connote finality, a life list instead should demonstrate the ongoing connection with nature one has in his or her life. It's not a contest, and it's not a race—the point isn't sim-ply to fill a checklist, but instead to record and to confirm experiences.

Your child can do the same thing, whether for birds, bugs, flowers, or whatever piques his or her interest. Even children too young to write can draw things they've observed—and make them all the more real in the process.

For another kind of life list, keep a family nature log where everyone can contribute the observations they've made around your home. It fosters a special, intimate connection to a place—*your* place—and serves as a reminder that even a backyard offers plenty of wonders for young explorers to discover.

BOOK NOOK

One Small Square: Backyard
By Donald M. Silver
Age range: 7 to 12

Here's a wonderful introduction to nature from the ground up—and down. *One Small Square: Backyard* encourages children to sharpen their observation skills and use all their senses to uncover and discover the amazing, teeming natural world to be found right outside their own back doors.

GOING ON A BUG SAFARI

*It has been estimated that more than half of the life forms on
Earth are insects. If you can't beat 'em, join 'em!*

Kids just seem to be naturally drawn to bugs—they're plentiful, colorful, accessible, and endlessly fascinating to curious young observers. And, while there certainly are stingers and biters to be aware of and to avoid, the vast majority of bugs are completely harmless. What better way to appreciate them than to set out on a bug safari in your own backyard with your child?

To be accurate, we should point out that the term *bug* properly refers to a specific order of insects—sometimes called the *true bugs*—which includes species such as stinkbugs, assassin bugs, and water striders. Casually, it refers to any or all insects, arthropods, and assorted invertebrates, and it's in that spirit that we will use it here.

By any name, kids know them when they seem them. And, with some one million known species of insects on our planet—with many more yet to be described, documented, or discovered—you are sure to find a good number of insects in your backyard.

You should find a diverse range of insects, too. From a common set of characteristics—an exoskeleton and three distinct body segments—comes an incredibly varied class of life that can run, fly, swim, climb, lift, and leap in degrees that, relative to each member's size, can be mind-boggling.

They're remarkable little beings and, for most children, any fear or revulsion they might engender isn't instinctual; it's learned—from us. Even if spending time with creepy-crawlies isn't your idea of outdoor fun, try not to let that dampen your kids' instincts to explore; interacting with these deceptively simple creatures plants the seeds of respect for all living things.

ABOUT BUGS

Most—but not all—of the bugs you encounter will be insects. But insects appear in such an amazing variety of shapes and sizes, from water beetles to walking sticks, that what they all have in common may not be readily apparent.

So what exactly makes an insect an insect? First off, all insects have an exoskeleton. Unlike many animals—including people—that have an internal skeleton of bones topped by muscles and skin, insects wear their protective coating on the outside, with all of their muscles and organs on the inside.

Insects also have three distinct body parts: a head, a thorax, and an abdomen. The head, as you might imagine, is where you'll find mouthparts and sensory organs like eyes and antennae. The thorax is an insect's middle section, and it has the important job of anchoring an insect's wings and legs. Most insects have two pairs of wings, some have only one, and some have none at all. But when it comes to legs, all insects follow the same rule: three pairs of legs, for a total of six. (Any bug with more than that is not an insect.) The last section is the abdomen, which helps an insect to breathe, digest its food, and make more insects.

What about spiders? Spiders are relatives of insects, fascinating in their own right, and you will likely encounter plenty of them on your bug safaris. But spiders are *not* insects. Here's why:

	Insects	Spiders
BODY SECTIONS	3	2
LEGS	3 pairs	4 pairs
WINGS	Usually	Never
ANTENNAE	Yes	No

Spiders can be found almost any place you can find people. Many spiders hunt or make their homes near (and in) houses and buildings, some of them spinning beautiful webs. Spiders may bite, and some of them are venomous, so they are best admired but not handled.

Here's a quick look at just some of the backyard visitors you might encounter.

Insects

Ants are familiar to everyone, but have you ever stopped to watch them closely? The next time you see them, take some time to observe them. Are they swarming, or marching in a line? Are they hunting for food, or bringing it back to their colony? Remember that ants have strong jaws and can bite if they feel threatened.

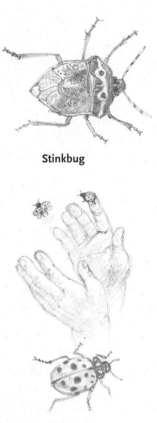

Stinkbug

Convergent lady beetle

good disguise. Cicadas are the big, bulgy-eyed insects that leave behind those familiar "bug shells," the discarded exoskeletons of cicada nymphs you often can find stuck to tree trunks, fence posts, and telephone poles. While you can see cicadas every summer, there's a certain kind of cicada that spends a very long time—either thirteen or seventeen years—maturing underground, before emerging by the thousands at the same time.

Mantids often can be found on shrubs and bushes around homes. Commonly called a *praying mantis* because of its folded front legs, this insect isn't getting ready to pray—it's getting ready for *prey*. Mantids are some of the most fearsome insect hunters around; sometimes their first meal is one of their own siblings.

Mosquitoes are not an insect you need to look for; they'll find you. (Remember to use insect repellent, especially in the late afternoon and evening.) Mosquitoes actually belong to the family

Bees can sting, but they usually do so only when defending themselves or their colony. These are extraordinarily beneficial insects. They produce honey and beeswax, and pollinate flowers, trees, and agricultural crops. From a respectful distance, you can watch bees gathering pollen. The sticky powder clings to their legs and is spread as they move from plant to plant.

Cicadas and *katydids* often are not seen, but definitely are heard. Summer just wouldn't sound the same without the high-pitched buzzing of cicadas and the raspy songs of katydids singing their names—*Ka-ty-did! Ka-ty-did-n't!* Most katydids are leafy in color and shape, giving them a

Praying mantis

of insects known as flies; those pesky insects need no introduction. Crane flies are members of the family that resemble gangly-legged, giant-sized mosquitoes. That similarity and their tendency to enter homes and garages often get them swatted, even though they are completely harmless.

Ladybugs are actually a type of beetle—lady beetle, to be precise. It's hard to imagine a more popular insect than these colorful little ladies. Look for them around bushes, flower beds, and in the garden. If you find them in the garden, be glad—ladybugs are beneficial insects that devour aphids and other destructive garden pests.

Junebugs—another type of beetle—can easily be seen and caught on early summer evenings. Just turn on your porch light, and it'll soon be buzzing with these insects. If you set up a light trap, there's a good chance they'll pay it a visit.

Stinkbugs are true bugs commonly found around houses, often climbing on walls or window screens. Sometimes called shield bugs because of their distinctive shape, they come in a range of colors from dull grays and browns to vivid red and black or bright green. If you handle a stinkbug, watch out—you just might find out how it got its name. If it feels threatened, glands on the stinkbug's underside may emit an odorous liquid, so be sure to wash up afterward.

Butterflies, moths, and *caterpillars* are among the most recognizable and most popular insects of all. We'll learn more about them, soon.

Spiders

House spiders and their messy, tangled webs can be found around windows, doors, and the outside of homes. While these familiar brownish spiders are responsible for cobwebs, they are harmless to

Wolf spider

people and actually are beneficial, preying upon a variety of pest insects. Females produce a silken egg sac; if you find one in a sheltered location and observe it over time, you can watch the baby spiders emerge.

Orb weavers are a family of spiders commonly found in gardens and around homes and other man-made structures, such as fences, to which they anchor their webs. These are the spiders that create the intricate webs, shaped like a series of spiraling rings connected by spokes, which are most noticeable from late summer to fall. Many orb weavers spin their webs in the evening; if you spot one at work, grab a flashlight and enjoy the show. Morning dew reveals webs that otherwise might have gone unnoticed—and turns them into dazzling jewels in the early light.

Jumping spiders don't spin webs; they hunt for their prey instead. These smallish, usually hairy spiders can commonly be found around, and sometimes in, houses. Though they don't spin webs, they do produce silk. When a jumping spider leaps after its prey, it releases a silken strand as a lifeline should it miss its target or fall. If you get a good look at a jumping spider's face, you might notice a pair of conspicuously large, forward-facing eyes, unusual for its kin. How do you suppose these help the spider?

Like jumping spiders, *wolf spiders* forego web spinning for hunting. These large, hairy, grayish-brown spiders sometimes can be found inside homes—perhaps lured by the warmth as temperatures fall—but they truly are ground spiders, at home among grass, mulch, or leaf litter. Night-time hunters, wolf spiders have eyes that pick up and reflect light. Because of this, one way to spot them is to stand in a grassy area at nighttime, holding a flashlight to your forehead and shining it at the ground no more than ten yards away. A wolf spider's eyes will reflect the light with an ee-rie glow, which will appear as bluish-green dots. Since they don't spin webs, wolf spiders have an-other neat trick. A female wolf spider will carry her egg sac—a white, silken, pea-sized ball—around with her; when the eggs hatch, the spiderlings will hitch a ride on their mother's back for several days before setting out on their own.

Harvestmen, sometimes known as daddy long-legs, are not actually spiders, but they are close rel-atives. These common inhabitants of woodpiles,

TIP: A GOOD FIELD GUIDE—EVEN A BEGINNER'S FIELD GUIDE—TO INSECTS IS AN INVALUABLE AID IN SORTING OUT THE MANY, MANY SPECIES TO BE FOUND. *THE PETERSON FIRST GUIDE TO INSECTS* IS A GOOD RESOURCE, AS ARE THE WEBSITES WWW.ENATURE.COM AND WWW.BUGGUIDE.NET.

leaf litter, gardens, and grassy lawns are not ven-omous, despite the urban legend to the contrary. Take care handling them—they've been known to drop a leg as means to escape danger.

BUG-CATCHING CONTRAPTIONS

Insects and their relatives can be observed al-most anywhere, anytime—but a good bug hunter

Did You Know?

BELIEVE IT OR NOT, YOU CAN EVEN FIND INSECTS IN THE SNOW. TINY *SNOW FLEAS* BELONG TO THE GROUP OF INSECTS KNOWN AS SPRINGTAILS. LOOK FOR THEM AT THE BASE OF TREES ON A MILD OR SUNNY DAY FOLLOWING A SNOWFALL. IF YOU SPOT WHAT LOOKS LIKE BLACK PEPPER, ASH, OR DUST ATOP THE SNOW, TAKE A CLOSER LOOK—IF THOSE SPECKS BEGIN TO HOP AND BOUNCE AROUND ON THE SURFACE OF THE SNOW, YOU'VE FOUND SNOW FLEAS.

can never be too prepared. Here are some helpful items for making the most of your bug safari:

- a magnifying glass
- tweezers or forceps
- clear plastic or glass jars with perforated lids
- field guides
- bug collectors and traps

Not everyone is content to wait and watch for the bugs that happen along. If you want to take

A homemade bug vacuum

your bug exploring to another level, try these special bug-catching tools and techniques.

Make a Bug Vacuum

The best way to check out bugs is by getting up close and personal with them; because of their small size, many of their incredibly detailed features could easily be overlooked from a distance. Not all bugs, however, are volunteers willing to be caught and studied, and some of them—from bees to blister beetles—really shouldn't be handled at all. A great way to get a closer look at bugs without hurting them—and without having to touch them, if you'd prefer not to—is to capture them with a bug vacuum. The proper name for this tool is an *aspirator,* though it's much more fun to refer to it by its other name: a *pooter.* A simple one can be constructed from materials you most likely already will have on hand.

What you need:
- a small, clear plastic or glass jar with lid
- two large flexible drinking straws (the wider the better)
- modeling clay or putty
- a small piece of cheesecloth, gauze, or nylon stocking
- a small rubber band
- a hammer and nail or cordless drill

What you do:
1. Punch or drill two holes into the lid. The holes should be just large enough to fit the drinking straws.
2. Stick the straws into the holes in the lid. Most flexible straws, when bent, have a short side and a long side. For best results,

stick the short side of each straw into the holes.

3. Use a bit of modeling clay or putty to seal any gaps around the straws. For your bug vacuum to work, it needs to be airtight.
4. Cover the end of one of the straws by securing the piece of cheesecloth or gauze over it with the rubber band. Be sure to seal the end of the straw under the lid—the end that will be inside the jar.
5. Screw the lid on tight.
6. The straw with the covered end is your mouthpiece. (The cheesecloth or gauze keeps bugs out of the mouthpiece.) The other straw is the collection end. Simply hold the collection end over the bug you want to capture and suck on the mouthpiece. Be sure only to vacuum bugs small enough to make it through the straw.

Your bugs will be gently drawn up and into the jar, where you can study them for a while before releasing them. If you like, you can move your specimens to a jar with a perforated lid for observation. Just unscrew the lid of the pooter and hold the jars mouth to mouth to make the transfer.

This simple version of the pooter uses common household objects. A more sophisticated version can be created by substituting flexible plastic tubing—such as aquarium tubing—for the drinking straws. This not only will make the pooter a bit easier to use, but the wider diameter of the plastic tubing will allow you to catch larger insects, ones that might be too big to be drawn through the drinking straws.

This design can be improved upon even further by using a flask or beaker with a rubber stopper.

TIP: ONE WAY TO GATHER A VARIETY OF BUGS TO STUDY IS TO PLACE AN OLD WHITE TOWEL OR SHEET ON THE GROUND BENEATH A BUSH OR SMALL TREE. GENTLY SHAKE THE BUSH OR TREE—A BROOMSTICK IS USEFUL FOR REACHING AND TAPPING TREE LIMBS—AND QUICKLY COLLECT ANY BUGS THAT FALL ONTO THE SHEET.

You can get these from scientific or school supply companies, oftentimes with holes predrilled, but you might be able to find a suitable alternative—a glass food storage jar with a rubber stopper—at a cooking or kitchen supply store. Simply drill two holes through the rubber stopper and insert the plastic tubes; the fit should be airtight, making the putty unnecessary. However, don't forget to cover the other end of the mouthpiece tube with cheesecloth or gauze, or you'll be getting a little closer to your bugs than you'd intended!

MAKE A PITFALL TRAP

Ground-crawling bugs can be attracted to, and caught with, a simple device known as a pitfall trap.

WHAT YOU NEED:

- a smooth-walled container, such as a jar, can, or cup
- a small, square piece of wood, plastic, or tile
- scraps of fruit or meat

What you do:

1. Choose a location where you might expect bugs to be present.
2. In level ground, carefully make a round hole just big enough to fit your container. When it's in place, the mouth of the container should be just even with the ground surrounding it—that way, beetles, ants, and other bugs attracted to the bait will fall right in.
3. Place a small food scrap in the bottom of the container as bait. A bit of leftover meat or ripe banana should work well.
4. Position the wood, plastic, or other material over the open mouth of the container. Place a small stone or flat rock under each corner to lift the cover. This should protect the container from the elements and lift the cover enough to allow bugs to crawl under it and into the trap.
5. Leave your pitfall trap overnight. Come back in the morning to see what you might have caught.

These instructions are for the most basic type of pitfall trap. You can improve upon the design by fashioning a funnel to rest inside the container, flush with or as close to the top as possible. A plastic cup with its bottom removed works well, as does the top part of a plastic bottle—the part that narrows to the mouth—cut off and turned upsidedown. The funnel guides the bugs into the bottom container, and also creates a barrier preventing them from flying out or crawling up the sides to their escape.

Make a Light Trap

Anyone who has turned on a porch light on a warm summer evening knows that bugs can be attracted to light. This is good news for young bug enthusiasts, who can attract a host of night-flying insects by making their own light traps.

What you need:

- a length of cord, rope, or clothesline
- a white sheet
- a bright flashlight, lantern, or work light
- a blacklight (optional)

What you do:

1. If you don't already have a backyard clothesline, tie a length of cord between two trees, fence posts, deck supports, or other structures. Try to choose a sheltered location near trees, bushes, or other insect cover.
2. Drape a white sheet over the cord or clothesline, taking care not to let it drag on the ground.
3. As evening falls, shine the light source onto the white sheet, which will act as a reflector. Use a small table or stool to raise the light source, if necessary.
4. Give your light trap some time to begin working. After a short while, come back to see whether moths, beetles, and other insects have gathered on the sheet. Collect the ones you'd like to study more closely.

Do you have access to a blacklight—the kind used for special visual effects or with fluorescent posters? If so, you can create a variation on the light trap by using a blacklight instead of a white light source. Because a blacklight emits ultraviolet light, you may find that it attracts a greater number and variety of insects than white light. (So-called bug zappers work on this principle.) As a precaution, avoid looking directly at the blacklight bulb. No matter which kind of light you choose, a light trap typically will work best on a still, dark evening and in a location with few other sources of light nearby.

More to Explore: Metamorphosis

At the beginning of their lives, many creatures look more or less like smaller versions of the adults they eventually will become. Not so with insects. Their life cycle is a series of remarkable changes known as *metamorphosis*.

All insects begin life as an egg. For some, the next stage of life is called the *nymph* stage. In this stage, the young gradually grow larger and begin to resemble the adults, but still lack characteristics such as fully developed wings. Grasshoppers and true bugs follow this life cycle, known as *gradual metamorphosis*.

Other insects pass through what is called a *complete metamorphosis*, a four-stage cycle of life that moves from *egg* to *larva* to *pupa* to *adult*. Most remarkable about this kind of metamorphosis is how dramatically different the larval and adult stages are from each other—they look nothing alike, and oftentimes are so different in diet and habitat that they seem like separate beings unto themselves. In fact, the larvae of some familiar insects are better known by common names of their own: grubs (which will become beetles), maggots (flies), and caterpillars (butterflies and moths).

LOOKING OUT FOR BIRDS

Feeding and watching birds are simple but rewarding activities that can be done almost anywhere.

From the chill of Antarctica to the sweltering heat of the tropics, from the desert to the sea, from the most remote wilderness to the bustle of city—it's hard to imagine a place on this planet where you couldn't find birds.

Closer to home, they are quite possibly the most abundant and familiar wildlife children see each day—from city pigeons to backyard robins to the many species that come and go with the seasons. They add life and color to our surroundings, cheer us with their songs, and inspire us with the marvel of their flight. And through the simple act of bird feeding, children can begin to forge a bond with nature right in their own neighborhood.

ABOUT BIRDS

The birds you might attract to your backyard or bird feeder will vary by location and season, but here's a list of just some of the most common backyard feeder visitors to watch for.

White-throated sparrow

Cardinals

These familiar birds can be seen year-round east of the Rockies. Males are distinctive with their bright red plumage and crest, black bib, and stout orange bill. Females are drab, overall, with splashes of red limited to their wings, tail, and crest. Cardinals can be quite vocal—their *birdy-birdy-birdy* and *what-cheer-cheer-cheer* songs are easy to recognize, as is their high-pitched call: *chip!*

Juncos

The arrival of these sparrow-like birds, frequent visitors to feeding stations across the country, is a sure sign of winter. You can spot the males by the even, slate-gray color contrasted by their white bellies and females by their overall grayish color, dark eyes, and light bills. Juncos will often visit feeders in groups, foraging the ground for scattered seeds such as millet.

Chickadees

These charming little birds are year-round residents in most of the United States, but are most familiar as winter feeder birds. Identify both males and females by the black cap and bib separated by a white cheek, and listen for their call: *chick-a-dee-dee!*

Goldfinches

In the summertime, a male goldfinch is hard to miss in his eye-popping yellow and black plumage. In the wintertime, however, he takes on the muted, brownish-yellow tones the female wears year-round. Goldfinches are attracted to thistle plants in the wild, but the best way to lure them to your feeder is with nyjer, a delicate black seed.

Nuthatches

These curious birds stand out from the crowd by hopping down tree trunks headfirst. There are two kinds of nuthatches in the United States, and both have bluish-gray backs and some amount of black and white on their heads. Both also have nasal calls, the most familiar one a quiet *yank!* They are fond of both sunflower seed and suet feeders—more about those, soon.

Titmice

Perky little birds, titmice are among the most common feeder visitors in the eastern United States. Identify them by their grayish color, tufted crest, and conspicuously big, dark eyes. Like nuthatches, they will visit both sunflower seed and suet feeders.

Woodpeckers

Like many year-round residents, woodpeckers appreciate an easy winter meal at a well-stocked feeding station. Hanging a suet feeder is the best way to attract them. Two look-alike species of different sizes, the downy and hairy woodpeckers, are quite common across the country and will readily visit feeders. They are quite striking, decked out in only black and white, save for the red patch on the back of the male's head. In the southeast, the red-bellied woodpecker also is a familiar sight at feeders—but the reddish tinge to its belly is much less noticeable than the red that extends from its bill to the back of its neck.

Jays

Because most feeder birds are smallish in stature, a blue jay seems all the more impressive when it pays a visit. There's no mistaking this large, crested songbird in vivid shades of blue accented with black and white. The Stellar's jay, similar to the blue jay but with a uniformly black head and shoulders, can be found in the mountainous West. Both are quite loud and loquacious.

Doves

The mourning dove, a close relative of the pigeon, is one bird that's at home almost anywhere—from cities and suburbs to farmland and forests. Once you've heard its low, mournful call, you won't forget it—and you'll understand how it got its name. Like juncos, doves that visit feeding stations often can be found on the ground, foraging for scattered grain seeds.

Sparrows

The members of this family of songbirds are so numerous—and sometimes so similar—that birders often will describe one simply as an "LBJ," an acronym for "little brown job." The sparrows that visit your backyard feeder, however, most likely will be one of just a handful of species. The tree sparrow is a frequent visitor to winter feeders, distinguished by a central dark spot on an otherwise unmarked breast. The song sparrow, a year-round resident in much of the United States, also has a central spot—but on a heavily streaked breast. Two other common winter visitors—the white-throated and white-crowned sparrows—both have crowns of dark and white stripes. The white-throated sparrow, however, has a distinctly white throat and a yellow spot before its eye, key field marks for telling the two apart. The white-throated sparrow also has one of the most recognizable songs of any songbird—*Oh, sweet Canada, Canada, Canada*—which you can hear on warmer days or if you happen to live within its breeding range.

Wrens

No list of backyard birds would be complete without wrens, those vivacious little birds with chunky bodies and short, up-tilted tails. In the East, the Carolina wren is a regular feeder visitor and common denizen of urban, suburban, and rural backyards. You may well hear this bird before you see it; it's one of the loudest songbirds, singing its *teakettle, teakettle, teakettle* song repeatedly. Our

> **TIP:** FOR HELP IDENTIFYING YOUR FEEDER VISITORS, CONSULT A FIELD GUIDE SUCH AS THE *PETERSON FIRST GUIDE TO BIRDS* OR A WEB RESOURCE SUCH AS WHATBIRD.COM. FOR A COMPREHENSIVE BIRD GUIDE ONLINE, VISIT THE CORNELL UNIVERSITY WEBSITE WWW.ALLABOUTBIRDS.ORG/ GUIDE/SEARCH.

other common wren is the house wren and, while it's not much of a feeder bird, it will take readily to a birdhouse, making it relatively easy to attract to your backyard or nearby green space.

HANDMADE FEEDERS

Bird feeding is a wonderful activity for children. There's the obvious benefit—attracting these beautiful, fascinating creatures to your own backyard, where your family can enjoy observing them. But bird feeding also teaches responsibility, and it leads children to consider the welfare of other creatures and to think about the necessities all living things require for their daily survival.

Store-bought feeders are fine, of course. But making your own bird feeders with your children is easy, inexpensive, and can be a whole lot of fun, too.

Let's start there—with some homemade bird feeders. These will likely draw bigger crowds in the colder months of late autumn and winter, when migrating and wintering birds will appreciate the convenience of an easy meal at a time when one otherwise might be more difficult to come by.

Make a Bagel Feeder

This simple feeder might be the easiest—and most fun—to make of all.

> **Tip:** If you use store-bought feeders, remember to clean them regularly, and be sure to wash your hands immediately after filling or handling your feeders.

What you need:

- a bagel
- twine
- peanut butter
- bird seed

What you do:

1. Spread peanut butter on the bagel until it's completely covered.
2. Cover the bagel by rolling it in the bird seed.
3. Pull a length of twine through the hole in the bagel, and tie the ends together.
4. Hang your bagel feeder from a tree limb.

Make a Pine Cone Feeder

Do you have an extra pine cone in your nature bowl or on your nature table? Here's a great way to turn a souvenir from a nature walk into a treat for the birds. Your backyard visitors will appreciate this high-energy recipe on the coldest winter days.

What you need:

- pine cones
- twine
- 1 cup birdseed
- ½ cup peanut butter
- ½ cup fat (lard or suet)
- 2 cups cornmeal
- ½ cup dried fruit or berries (raisins, cranberries, currants)

What you do:

1. In a saucepan, melt the fat and peanut butter together.
2. Stir in the birdseed, dried fruit, and cornmeal.

3. If the mixture seems wet, add more corn-meal until all the fat is absorbed.
4. Let the mixture cool. When cool, spread it around each pine cone, making sure to push the mixture under the scales.
5. Tie a length of twine to each pine cone and hang from a tree limb.

MAKE A SUET FEEDER

This is another wintertime favorite for many birds, especially woodpeckers and nuthatches. Because suet can spoil, it is best to use this feeder during cold weather only.

WHAT YOU NEED:

- a mesh food bag (the sort that holds onions, avocadoes, or citrus fruits)
- suet (available at butcher shops or meat counters) or store-bought suet cakes
- birdseed (optional)
- twine

WHAT YOU DO:

1. Soften the suet by gently heating it in a pan. Mix in birdseed, if you like. (Store-bought suet cakes will come ready for use.)
2. Heated suet can be molded, shaped, or simply rolled into balls. Let the suet cool and harden.
3. Place the balls or cakes of suet into the mesh bag, gathering it together at the top and tying it off with a small length of twine.
4. Tie a longer length of twine to the top of the mesh bag and hang it from a tree branch. Choose a location far enough from the ground, tree trunk, and sturdy branches to deter small animals.

MAKE A FESTIVE FEEDER

During the winter holidays, your family might enjoy decorating a bush or small tree with this simple gift for the birds.

WHAT YOU NEED:

- popped popcorn
- cranberries (fresh or dried)
- roasted peanuts in the shell
- grapes
- a large, blunt needle (such as a tapestry needle)
- yarn

WHAT YOU DO:

1. With the needle, thread a length of yarn through the popcorn, peanut shells, and fruit.
2. Drape the finished garland over the branches of a tree or bush.

MAKE A HUMMINGBIRD FEEDER

Even during spring and summer, you still can have feeder fun by attracting hummingbirds to your backyard, deck, or balcony.

> **TIP:** BLACK-OIL SUNFLOWER SEEDS ARE THE BEST BET FOR BACKYARD FEEDERS, PREFERRED BY A WIDE VARIETY OF BIRDS. FOR MORE INFORMATION ABOUT BIRD FEEDING, VISIT PROJECT FEEDER WATCH AT WWW.BIRDS .CORNELL.EDU/PFW/.

Ruby-throated hummingbird

There are many inexpensive hummingbird feeders available, but if you're feeling crafty, why not try making your own from household items? Here's one of the simplest ones.

WHAT YOU NEED:

- a small plastic water bottle
- a hammer and a big nail
- red ribbon or red craft foam
- twine or copper wire
- sugar
- water

WHAT YOU DO:

1. Bring 2 cups of water to a boil. Stir in ½ cup of sugar until dissolved. Remove from heat and cool.

2. Remove the label from a clean water bottle. Using the hammer and nail, carefully punch a hole in the center of the lid. Wiggle the nail in all directions to widen the hole (it should be ⅛ of an inch wide when finished) and to bend the plastic on the inside of the lid away from the hole. This will allow a hummingbird to safely insert—and remove—its bill.

3. Tie a big red bow around the neck of the bottle. Or, draw and cut out a large flower shape from a piece of red craft foam and slip it around the neck of the bottle. Hummingbirds are naturally drawn to red flowers.

4. Tie a length of twine, or wrap a length of copper wire, around the base and the neck of the bottle.

5. Fill the bottle to the brim with the cooled sugar water mixture and screw the lid on tightly. The leftover mixture can be stored in the refrigerator, but for no longer than two weeks.

6. Use the twine or copper wire to hang the feeder from a nearby tree branch or balcony rail, preferably in a spot that gets at least some shade. Position the bottle so that it's not quite horizontal—tip the mouth up just enough to keep the sugar water in the neck of the bottle while preventing it from dripping out.

Hummingbird feeders require a lot of attention. Be sure to empty and clean them every other

TIP: SOME PLASTIC BOTTLES, LIKE THOSE FOR SODA POP OR SOME CARBONATED AND FLAVORED WATERS, HAVE RED LIDS. IF YOU CAN FIND A RED LID THAT FITS YOUR WATER BOTTLE, IT'LL BE MUCH MORE ATTRACTIVE TO HUMMINGBIRDS. ALTERNATIVELY, YOU CAN TRY PAINTING THE LID BRIGHT RED.

day, refilling them with fresh sugar water mixture, and take them down if you'll be away or unable to tend to them. If you find that you're attracting more wasps and ants than hummers, don't be discouraged—but do try a new location. And, if you'd like to attract hummingbirds naturally, consider planting one of the many beautiful flowers—such as red columbine, cardinal flower, or trumpet honeysuckle—that provide them nectar.

BE A BIRD-WATCHER

Bird-watching is an increasingly popular hobby, and a wonderful one for children to take up—it requires no expertise to begin, while offering an almost limitless world to learn about and explore. It also fosters attentiveness and patience in children, who can exercise their powers of observation and visual discrimination, and see their efforts rewarded with glimpses of beauty and wonder.

KEEP A BIRD JOURNAL

Creating and keeping a journal is a terrific way for your child to hone his or her observation skills while enjoying the birds in your neighborhood or at your family's bird feeders. It's easy—just take some time each day to watch the feeders, and record what you see. Just as field scientists would, try to include as much information as possible: the date, the time, the weather conditions, the species observed, and so forth.

Consider this: How could you take the data you've recorded and present it on a chart? As you collect more and more data, are any patterns developing? Which birds are the most frequent visitors? What time of day seems to be the most

Did You Know?

BIRD FEEDERS ARE A GREAT WAY TO HELP YOUR FEATHERED FRIENDS, ESPECIALLY IN WINTER. BUT BY GARDENING FOR WILDLIFE YOU CAN PROVIDE THEM THE ESSENTIALS— FOOD, WATER, AND PLACES FOR THEM TO TAKE COVER AND RAISE THEIR YOUNG—TO HELP THEM YEAR-ROUND.

MANY *NATIVE* PLANTS—THOSE WHICH NATURALLY OCCUR AND BELONG IN A GIVEN ENVIRONMENT—ARE AVAILABLE AT NURSERIES AND HOME CENTERS. THESE PLANTS NOT ONLY CAN BE EASIER TO GROW AND TYPICALLY REQUIRE LESS WATER AND MAINTENANCE, BUT THEY ALSO ARE OF GREATER VALUE TO LOCAL WILDLIFE, ATTRACTIVE TO BOTH BIRDS AND HOMEOWNERS ALIKE.

TO LEARN HOW TO MAKE YOUR BACKYARD MORE BIRD-FRIENDLY, VISIT HTTP://NWF .ORG/BACKYARD.

active? Does the weather have any noticeable effect? What other information could you collect and record?

A journal is useful for capturing more than just data. Hand-drawn sketches, stories and poems, thoughts and impressions, even questions to answer later—all are valuable, and all go a long way toward personalizing each child's experience. Whatever the child's learning style, keeping such a journal can present the opportunity for critical thinking about the relationships between living things, their environment, and each other.

Need a little inspiration? Take a good look at the backyard birds you see throughout the year, and focus on the characteristics and behaviors you observe.

- Are they singing or calling? Is there a certain time of day—or time of year—when you especially notice bird songs? Is there a time when the birds seem quiet? Are there certain songs or calls you recognize? Are there birds you can identify even without seeing them?

- Are they gathering together in groups, or moving about on their own? Are some birds more likely to appear with others of the same kind? Are some more likely to be alone? Why might birds stick together? When might they want to be apart?

- Are any birds "showing off" for others? Are any birds trying to drive away others? Why might they be behaving that way? Have you noticed any birds preening or cleaning themselves? How do they do it?

- Are any birds building a nest? If so, where and how are they building it? Are there eggs or young in the nest? How do the adult birds take care of them?

- Look at the bills of the birds that visit your yard. Are they all the same size and shape? Does there seem to be a connection between the size and shape of a bird's bill and what it eats?

- What about their legs and feet? Are they long or short? Think about the many jobs different birds' feet might do: walking, perching, swimming, climbing—even hunting. Can you even see a hummingbird's feet?

Did You Know?

PHOTOGRAPHERS AND SCIENTISTS SOMETIMES USE A *BLIND* TO GET A CLOSER LOOK AT BIRDS, AND YOU CAN, TOO. A BLIND IS SIMPLY ANYTHING THAT BLENDS IN WITH THE ENVIRONMENT AND CAN HIDE AN OBSERVER. YOU CAN MAKE A SIMPLE BLIND OUT OF A BIG CARDBOARD BOX, OR OLD SHEETS AND BLANKETS DRAPED OVER LAWN CHAIRS—JUST REMEMBER TO LEAVE A SMALL OPENING TO LOOK THROUGH. PLACE YOUR BLIND NEAR YOUR FEEDER OR OTHER BIRD-FRIENDLY PLACE. SLIP INSIDE WITH YOUR BINOCULARS, CAMERA, FIELD GUIDE, AND JOURNAL AND WAIT—*VERY* QUIETLY.

More to Explore: Bird Counts

Maintaining bird feeders can bring a lot of fun and learning to your backyard. It's also a way for ordinary people to help the scientists who study bird populations.

Every year, tens of thousands of people do just that by making, recording, and sending their observations to the scientists who collect and monitor the data. These "citizen science" projects have been growing in size and popularity, and participating in them is easy, fun, and rewarding. Consider making one a family nature activity.

For more information, visit the following websites:

- Project FeederWatch: www.birds.cornell.edu/pfw/
- Great Backyard Bird Count: www.birdsource.org/gbbc/
- Christmas Bird Count: www.audubon.org/Bird/cbc/

DISCOVERING DETAILS IN THE DIRT

Out of sight, out of mind—but underfoot, there's a whole world to find.

Walk outside—into your backyard, a local park, or a favorite green space—and your first instinct just might be to look up and all around you. After all, there's probably a lot competing for your attention. What do you notice? Green grass? Blue sky? Flowers and trees? A soft-blowing breeze? The buzz of insects? The flight of birds?

Much less obvious, and often forgotten, is the world right beneath our feet. At ground level—even below ground level—nature teems with life. Here you'll find many of the little creatures who live their entire lives in the dark, damp world of dirt, rarely seeing the light of day. And even as they toil away in relative obscurity, they perform the very important, if thankless, job of creating and enriching the soil that ultimately benefits all life on our planet. Theirs is the business of dirt, of breaking down organic matter and turning what otherwise might be waste into something quite valuable. Think of them as members of nature's clean-up crew, part of the original recycling program.

Besides being fun and fascinating for children to handle and to study, these creatures also offer children a glimpse into vital natural processes that often escape our notice or consideration. (Have you ever asked a child where food comes from? Have you ever gotten "the supermarket" as an answer?) And they quietly teach an important lesson about the interconnectedness—and the value—of all life, no matter how small or insignificant it might seem.

But, perhaps best of all, mucking about in the world of dirt is nothing short of good old-fashioned fun. Roll up your sleeves and get ready to dig in. It's a dirty job, after all, but somebody's got to do it!

DIRT IS FOR DIGGING

Seems there's more to digging in the dirt than meets the eye. It turns out that good old-fashioned dirt play just might help to make children healthier and happier. Researchers at the University of Bristol in the United Kingdom have suggested that exposure to the "good" bacteria found in soil may lift one's mood by raising the levels of serotonin in the brain. Chris Lowry, lead author of the study, has said "the results leave us wondering if we shouldn't all spend more time playing in the dirt."[1]

Studies also suggest that "dirty" activities expose children to a host of microbes and microorganisms that stimulate and strengthen their immune systems—refreshing news in this era of the antibacterial soaps and hand sanitizers that actually may be helping to foster more resistant strains of bacteria.

Whatever you think of the science, history is on the side of kids and dirt finding each other, and probably always will be. After all, dirt is literally nature's unformed clay—a blank canvas for whatever strikes a child's fancy on any given day.

While you may not have any trouble encouraging your kids to play in the dirt, here's an idea to get you started.

Digging in the dirt

DESIGNATE A DIGGING STATION

A terrific way to invite this sort of imagination play is to devote a tiny corner of your yard to a digging station for your children. Simply use a garden shovel to turn over a small section of yard—make sure there are no underground utility lines nearby, first—and work the soil with a cultivator to give it a good, kid-friendly consistency; even better, have your kids pull on their boots and dig in with you. (For places where space is tight or digging in the yard isn't possible, a sandbox filled with a couple of bags of topsoil makes a suitable alternative.)

Add children and a few implements for working the soil, and let the fun begin. The tools can be simple—hand trowels, old spoons, plastic pails, cups, and watering cans—but the results can be wonderful. Who knows? In your own backyard, you just might stumble upon an archaeological dig busy unearthing dinosaur bones, a construction crew hard at work digging trenches, an artist's studio full of sculptures, or a bakery serving up mud pies.

Isopods are also known as pillbugs or roly-polies . . .

. . . and here's why

EXPLORING LIFE AT GROUND LEVEL

They are neither fleet of foot nor flashy fliers, but these denizens of the dirt can be downright fascinating to kids. Here are some ideas for taking a closer look at some of the most approachable creatures to (sometimes) see the light of day.

POKE A PILLBUG

You should be able to find *pillbugs*—completely harmless and strangely adorable—in almost any of the damp, dark, dirty places around your home. Try looking underneath bricks, stones, or splash blocks, under logs or piles of wood, in leaf litter, behind tree bark, or under planters and flower pots. So long as they have darkness, moisture, and decaying plant matter to feed on, they are quite content.

Pillbugs—you also may know them as *roly-polies* or *woodlice,* but they are more correctly called *isopods*—are not insects, though their name might imply that they are. Look closely and you'll see that instead of six legs, they have fourteen legs that move back and forth like pairs of tiny oars.

Did You Know?

THE RICH, EARTHY STUFF WE KNOW AS DIRT OR SOIL IS ACTUALLY A COMBINATION OF MINERAL SUBSTANCES (SUCH AS CLAY OR SILT) AND ORGANIC MATERIAL (THE MICROSCOPIC BITS OF PLANTS AND ANIMALS THAT ONCE WERE ALIVE).

A HANDFUL OF DIRT
BY RAYMOND BIAL
AGE RANGE: 8 TO 12

THIS LOVELY PHOTO ESSAY IS BOTH A SCIENTIFIC EXPLANATION AND A NOSTALGIC APPRECIATION OF DIRT. IN TEXT THAT IS ALMOST POETIC AT TIMES, BIAL DESCRIBES THE CYCLICAL NATURE OF THE SOIL, AND INDEED OF ALL LIFE—FROM SIMPLE MICROORGANISMS TO HUMAN BEINGS—WHICH DEPENDS ON IT. *A HANDFUL OF DIRT* MAKES A GREAT BOOK TO READ TO YOUNGER CHILDREN, OR FOR EARLY-GRADE READERS TO TACKLE ALONE.

If you find a pillbug, gently pick it up and place it in your palm. Don't worry; they don't bite—but those fourteen fast-moving legs might tickle a bit. Want to see how fast? Place a pillbug on a ruler and time it in the fifty-millimeter dash. Or try having a pillbug race with a friend.

Gently poke a pillbug with your finger and watch what happens. When disturbed, it will defend itself by rolling up into a tight little ball—not unlike a miniature armadillo. How long does it take for your pillbug to unroll?

Keeping pillbugs to observe for a short while is an easy and fun project to do with your child. Keep them in a covered, but not airtight, container with a floor of soil, leaf litter, grass clippings, or mulch. Keep your pillbug habitat damp by adding a moist sponge or paper towel or by spraying it with a mist bottle.

When you're through studying—all right, *play-ing with*—your pillbugs, be sure to return them safely to the place where you found them.

SNEAK A PEEK AT A SNAIL

Have you ever noticed dried, silvery trails on your sidewalk or patio? That's a sure sign that snails—or slugs, their close relatives without shells—have been there. The silvery trail actually is dried mu-

> **TIP:** IF YOUR PILLBUG DOESN'T ROLL UP, YOU MAY HAVE FOUND A SOWBUG INSTEAD. A SOWBUG LOOKS ALMOST EXACTLY LIKE A PILLBUG BUT IS SLIGHTLY FLATTER AND CAN'T ROLL UP COMPLETELY.

cous; snails and slugs move by secreting and gliding along on a layer of the slimy, sticky stuff.

Look for these trails first thing in the morning. (And, if you find one, follow it to its end—you just might find the snail that made it.) Like many of the creatures who live on or in the ground, snails and slugs need to stay moist and will die if they dry out. For that reason, they're often most active under the cover of darkness, and that's usually when they leave their trails.

We think of snails and slugs as slowpokes. While they may never win a footrace, you have to admire how well they get along—they've got no arms, no legs, and just a single foot to propel themselves.

Lie down on your back with your legs straight and your arms at your side. Without using your arms or legs, how would you move your body across the floor? By wriggling the muscles in your shoulders, back, and bottom, you most likely can slowly wiggle yourself along.

Snails and slugs move in much the same way, and you can see for yourself. To find them, look in damp, dark hiding places around your home, such as under rocks, boards, leaves, and stones or near pools and garden hoses. Place your snail inside a clear glass jar or on window glass, and peer through from the other side. As it moves, you should be able to see the muscles in its foot making a rippling pattern as they contract and move the snail forward. Use a magnifying glass, if you've got one, for a better view. Look closely—can you see the snail's mouth?

Snails and slugs are a kind of *mollusk* and belong to the class of creatures known as *gastropods,* which literally means "stomach foot." Do you think the name fits?

As the worm turns

NAB A NIGHTCRAWLER

Everyone has seen earthworms after a warm-weather rainfall, when the excess water in the soil drives them above ground and occasionally strands them on sidewalks and driveways. For kids interested in these wonderful wigglers, there's no easier time to gather them.

But there are other, more adventurous ways to collect worms to study. The most fun of all is to try to catch nightcrawlers.

As the name would suggest, *nightcrawlers*—those big, fat earthworms favored by fishermen—are most active after dark, when they can be found emerging from their tunnels in open, grassy areas. Look for them in the spring and summer, especially after the rain has soaked the ground—and get ready for some slippery, slimy fun.

WHAT YOU NEED:

- a grassy yard, park, golf course, or field
- a flashlight, preferably one covered with red plastic or cellophane
- a bucket or pail filled with moist dirt or potting soil
- a small can full of sawdust or flour

WHAT YOU DO:

1. Head outside to an open, grassy area after dark. Evenings after a rainfall work best, but you can coax nightcrawlers out of the ground by soaking a small patch of yard with a garden hose or a few buckets of water.

2. Walk softly and quietly. Noise or vibrations could scare the nightcrawlers back into their tunnels.

3. If you have a red-tinted flashlight, shine it onto the ground to spot nightcrawlers coming out of their tunnels. Avoid shining white light directly onto the worms—since they spend their lives below ground, they are quite sensitive to light and will retreat into their tunnels before you can catch them.

4. To catch a nightcrawler, approach it slowly and try to grab it between your thumb and

TIP: WANT TO KNOW WHICH END IS WHICH? THE DISTINCTIVE BROAD BAND ON AN EARTHWORM'S BODY, CALLED THE *CLITELLUM*, IS LOCATED CLOSER TO ITS FRONT END.

forefinger, getting as close to the ground as possible. Worms are faster than you might think; don't be surprised if the first few slip between your fingers! When you get one, don't tug—just hold on firmly, but gently. The worm's first reaction will be to pull itself back into its tunnel, but it soon will relax, allowing you to gently pull it from the ground.

5. Place the nightcrawlers in your collection bucket. Dip your fingers into the sawdust or flour to keep them dry and give you a better grip.

Take a moment to let a nightcrawler wriggle in your palm. Gently touch the length of the worm with your finger. Can you feel the tiny bristles, called *setae,* along its body? These help worms to remain anchored in place—as you might have learned from trying to pull them from their tunnels.

After collecting them, be sure to keep your nightcrawlers in a cool, dark place. If your family goes fishing, you may wish to use them for bait. If not, return them to a garden or grassy area when you've finished studying them.

Make a Worm Jar

Whether you have caught a handful of nightcrawlers or dug up some garden worms, a worm jar

TIP: If you're digging for worms to study, try using a hand cultivator instead of a shovel—you'll be less likely to injure them.

makes a fun and easy way to keep and study them for a while.

What you need:

- a large, round glass jar
- soil
- sand
- grass clippings, vegetable peels, lettuce leaves
- water
- black construction paper
- tape
- a handful of worms

What you do:

1. Moisten the soil and the sand until each is thoroughly damp (but not wet).
2. Add a one-inch layer of soil to the bottom of the jar. Top with a one-inch layer of sand, and alternate layers of soil and

Did You Know?

It's been said that every bite of food we eat has, at some point, passed through an earthworm.

sand, topping off with a layer of soil. Leave a couple of inches of space at the top of the jar.

3. Place your worms on top of the soil. Cover them with a thin layer of the leaves, peels, or clippings (or all three).

4. Wrap the construction paper around the outside of the jar, taping the ends of the paper together to create a sleeve. This will keep the interior of the worm jar dark—just the way the worms like it. Alternatively, a paper bag could be slipped over the entire jar.

5. Place your worm jar in a cool, shaded spot. Don't disturb it, but do check the soil each day, carefully adding water to dampen it if it seems dry.

After a week or so—or at least a few days, if you can't wait—remove the sleeve. (The sleeve should remain in place except for when you're observing the worms.) You may begin to notice the layers of sand and soil mixing together as the worms create their tunnels. You also may begin to notice small, dark piles appearing on the surface. Do you know what they are? You can keep and watch the worms in your jar for several weeks—just be sure to keep the soil damp and to replenish the leaves, peels, and clippings on top from time to time.

If the mouth of your worm jar is wide enough, consider placing a small, clean can or plastic cup upside-down in the bottom of the jar before you fill it with soil and sand. This will force the worms toward the walls of the jar, where you'll better be able to monitor their activity.

More to Explore: The Garden of Eatin'

Just by going about their business, worms perform an invaluable service to the earth. Their tunnels help to turn over and aerate the soil, allowing water and air to mix freely with it. Their voracious appetites allow them to gobble up prodigious amounts of organic waste and turn it into a nutrient-rich material. Worm poop—also known as *castings*—is an incredible, all-natural fertilizer prized by farmers and gardeners alike. Knowing this, some people put worms to work by *composting* with them. Forget about nightcrawlers—this is a job for a certain kind of worm known as *redworms, tiger worms,* or *red wigglers.* Simply by keeping red wigglers in a properly constructed worm bin and feeding them kitchen scraps such as coffee grounds, eggshells, and vegetable peels—most anything except for meat, dairy, or greasy foods—you can watch them turn everyday garbage into castings perfect for fertilizing the plants in your home or garden.

WORMS EAT MY GARBAGE
BY MARY APPELHOF
AGE RANGE: 12 AND UP

MAKING AND KEEPING A WORM BIN IS SIMPLE IN THEORY, BUT THERE'S STILL A LOT TO KNOW ABOUT SETTING UP A SYSTEM THAT WILL KEEP YOU AND YOUR WORMS HAPPY. THIS BOOK COVERS *VERMICULTURE*—CULTIVATING WORMS—QUITE THOROUGHLY, AND IS A GOOD CHOICE FOR FAMILIES WHO WANT TO GIVE COMPOSTING WITH WORMS A TRY.

Did You Know?

NEARLY ONE-FOURTH OF THE GARBAGE WE SEND TO LANDFILLS COULD HAVE BEEN COMPOSTED INSTEAD. WITH THE RIGHT MATERIALS AND A LITTLE PATIENCE, YOU CAN TURN FOOD WASTE AND LAWN CLIPPINGS INTO USEFUL MATERIAL IN YOUR OWN COMPOST BIN OR PILE. FOR BACKGROUND INFORMATION AND HELPFUL LINKS, VISIT WWW.EPA.GOV/COMPOSTING.

GETTING TO KNOW TREES

Take the time to take in the splendor of trees.

The Giving Tree, Shel Silverstein's venerable book, presents a wonderful parable of selflessness: a tree so loves a boy that it gives everything—literally gives itself—for his happiness.

But is that so far removed from reality? To a child who grows up in the company of trees, they can be so many things—a jungle gym, a hiding place, a playhouse, a sanctuary. And they can give so many things—sticks for building, leaves for piling and jumping in, and a bounty of fruits, seeds, nuts, and cones.

Fortunately, these marvelous beings are a fixture of the landscape of childhood, accessible to almost every child, everywhere. And, as kindred spirits to trees, all children should have the opportunity to really know them, through all of their changes and in all of their moods and seasons.

After all, children and trees are, in a way, very much alike. While you may not be able to chart the growth of trees in days, or even weeks, they do grow tremendously over a lifetime, from seeds to tender shoots to saplings

71

with the potential to transform into something of almost unimaginable stature.

A TREE FOR ALL SEASONS

The most interesting and easily observable changes in a tree's appearance are the ones that happen seasonally. Choose a tree in your backyard or a local green space and watch for these things as the tree goes through its different phases.

Spring

In this season of renewal, the tree buds that have lain dormant for months will begin to burst open—some will become leaves; others, flowers. What's becoming of the buds on your tree? What other signs of new growth can you see? Look for tender green shoots and shiny new twigs as the season progresses. Watch for springtime firsts— first leaf, first flower—and make note of the date you observe them. Also keep an eye out for new inhabitants in your tree, as birds construct their nests and prepare to raise their broods.

Summer

Taking advantage of the abundance of sunlight, trees are dressed in their fullest, greenest foliage of the year. Fruits and berries may begin to appear—can you find any on your tree? Some trees flower late and might only now be displaying their blooms. Find new-growth twigs and compare their bark to older branches. Peel back a bit of bark from the trunk—have any insects made a home in your tree? Don't forget to make yourself feel at home near your tree. Take the time to enjoy sitting in its shade with a picnic lunch or a favorite book.

Fall

This season, of course, is dominated by the turning—and the falling—of leaves. Make note of when your tree's leaves first begin to turn. What color are they? When does the last leaf drop? Some trees drop theirs early, while other trees—such as beech and red oak—cling to their leaves well into the winter, long after others have shed their foliage. Look, too, for trees dropping their fruit—

Spring

Summer

Fall

Winter

cones from pine trees, acorns from oak trees—and dispersing their seeds and seed pods.

Winter

Unless you've chosen an evergreen tree, the most conspicuous feature on your tree most likely will be its buds. Wrapped up tight and packed with potential, the buds will become next year's flowers and leaves. Even in the dead of winter, they provide clues to a tree's identity, distinctive in their shape, color, texture, and their location and arrangement on a twig. As spring approaches, choose a bud from your tree to watch closely, marking it with ribbon or string to help you find it each time you visit. As the bud begins to open, sketch or photograph it each day to document the changes. While your tree is still bare, look for bird or squirrel nests that otherwise might not have been visible.

TAKING NOTES

Since most of the changes a tree goes through will unfold slowly, over time, notes are helpful for tracking its growth and stages. Here are several

Did You Know?

THE SHOWY WHITE PETALS OF THE FLOWERING DOGWOOD—ONE OF THE MOST FAMILIAR AND DISTINCTIVE TREES TO BLOOM IN SPRING—ARE IMPOSTERS, IN A MANNER OF SPEAKING. LOVELY AS THEY ARE, WHAT APPEAR TO BE WHITE FLOWER PETALS ARE *BRACTS*, A SPECIALIZED KIND OF LEAF THAT SERVES TO PROTECT THE ACTUAL FLOWER—WHICH, IN THE CASE OF THE DOGWOOD, IS THE TINY YELLOW CLUSTER IN THE MIDDLE OF ALL THAT WHITE.

ideas for getting to know your tree better by recording your observations and data.

Keep a Tree Diary

Getting to a know a tree—to take the time to really observe and understand how it changes from month to month, from season to season, and from year to year—can be a quietly rewarding experience for children. By recording their observations, measurements, and illustrations in a journal, they will create an interesting living document even as they develop the research skills that will serve them well in school and beyond.

To get started, have your child choose a tree that will be readily accessible throughout the year, whether it's in your backyard, neighborhood, or a favorite local park. For more fun, consider having each member of your family choose a different kind of tree and visit and observe them together. Almost any tree will do, but remember that *deciduous* trees—those that shed their leaves each year—will go through much more dramatic changes as the seasons pass. Also keep in mind that younger trees may be more approachable and will exhibit more noticeable growth over time than older, established trees, especially when viewed from a child's perspective. Don't worry if you can't identify your tree at this point; you'll be gathering information that will help you to do so soon enough.

Begin by finding out firsthand as much as you can about your tree. Start with the basics of its appearance, describing its leaves (if any), branches, buds, and blooms. Touch the bark, and take note of its color and texture. Look at the tree from the ground up. Are the roots visible? If so, what do they look like? Take in the tree as a whole, and describe its general shape—round, oval, V-shaped, A-shaped. Try to sketch it in your journal, or take photographs of both the whole tree and of any details that catch your eye.

Did You Know?

The brilliant reds, oranges, and yellows of autumn leaves may seem to arrive with the season, but these colorful pigments actually have been present in the leaves since springtime. *Chlorophyll*, the pigment that gives leaves their green color, fades with the waning light of the fall season, allowing the other colors to show through and put on a spectacular, if brief, show.

Measuring Trees

To track the growth of your tree, you first will need to record its current size. A tree's circumference, diameter, and height are three good indicators to follow—but they will change slowly, over time.

The *circumference* is a measurement of the distance around the trunk of a tree. It usually is taken at a height of four and a half feet, sometimes called *breast height,* as a way of standardizing the records of arborists and scientists. If a tree grows on a hillside or slope, its circumference is measured at a height of four and a half feet above the ground on the uphill side. Most important is to take your measurement at the same level each time for the sake of consistency. Simply wrap your tape measure snugly around the trunk of the tree to take your reading. If your tape measure isn't flexible enough for this job, wrap cord or twine around the tree. Mark the spot by pinching it carefully and measure it with the tape.

The diameter of a tree is the distance across—that is, straight through—the trunk, and it most easily can be calculated by first measuring the cir-cumference and dividing that figure by pi (3.14). A tree that measures twenty-two inches in circumference, for instance, is approximately seven inches in diameter. Because of its resemblance to a tree's trunk, the empty tube from a roll of paper towels or bathroom tissue can help your child to visualize the concepts of circumference and diameter as they relate to a tree.

Estimating the height of a tree can be a bit trickier. Especially for tall trees, our perspective from the ground can result in some pretty wild guesses. But, with everyday objects and some basic geometry, you and your child can have fun measuring the height of your trees with a fair degree of accuracy.

Here are two different methods you might try.

Shadow Method

What you need:

- a sunny day
- a yardstick
- a tape measure

A tree's height can be measured by its shadow

Finding the ratio between object and shadow

What you do:

1. Place one end of the yardstick on the ground and hold it so that it stands straight up. Find the length of the yardstick's shadow with the tape measure.
2. Compare the length of the yardstick to the length of its shadow. This same ratio will apply to the height of the tree and the length of its shadow.
3. Measure the length of the tree's shadow, and apply the ratio to determine its approximate height. For example: if a three-foot yardstick casts a two-foot shadow, then a tree casting a twelve-foot shadow would be eighteen feet tall.

This method will give you a reasonable estimate of your tree's height, so long as the shadows fall on relatively level ground and the measurements are taken within a few minutes of each other.

Of course, not every day can be a sunny one, and not every tree casts a shadow that can easily or conveniently be measured. Here's another simple approach that requires only a clear line of sight to the top of your tree.

Triangulation Method

What you need:

- a piece of paper or cardboard
- a level
- a tape measure

What you do:

1. Square off a letter-sized sheet of paper or cardstock by folding the top edge over so it lines up perfectly with the left-hand edge. Crease the paper and remove the excess. This creates a *right isosceles triangle* with two sides of equal length. (Cutting a triangle from a piece of corrugated cardboard works even better. The size of the triangle isn't important—that it has two equal sides separated by a right angle is.)
2. Start by standing in a spot that seems to be about as far from the tree as the tree is tall.
3. Hold the triangle so that the two sides of equal length are vertical and horizontal.
4. Looking along the long edge (the *hypotenuse*) of the triangle, move forward or backward until you can just sight the top of the

Using the triangulation method to estimate the height of a tree

Your triangle should have two equal sides separated by a right angle

tree along its length. Use the level to fine-tune your instrument; if the triangle is tipping up or down, your measurement will be inaccurate.

5. Once the top of the tree is lined up, measure the distance from the observer to the base of the tree. Then, add the distance from the ground to the observer's eye level. The total will give you the height of the tree.

If you don't have a level, you can create a self-leveling triangle. Tie a weight—such as a paper clip or a small washer—to a length of string. Tape the end of the string to the top corner of the vertical side of your triangle. As you're sighting the tree, the weight and string should hang parallel to the vertical side of your triangle.

> **TIP:** PUT YOUR FAMILY'S TREE OBSERVATIONS TO WORK IN THE INTEREST OF SCIENCE. TO LEARN ABOUT OR TO TAKE PART IN A PHENOLOGY PROJECT, VISIT PROJECT BUDBURST AT WWW.BUDBURST.ORG OR THE NATIONAL PHENOLOGY NETWORK AT WWW.USANPN.ORG.

More to Explore: Phenology

Keeping an eye on the changes a tree goes through each year makes for some great backyard science. But it also can be helpful to the scientists who are working on some of the biggest environmental challenges we face today.

Observing and studying the timing of recurrent events in the lives of plants and animals is called *phenology*. Things a phenologist would watch for and record might include the appearance of migratory birds or the seasonal emergence of certain kinds of insects. For trees and other plants, easy to study because of their immobility, it might be the opening of the first flower and the appearance of the first leaf in spring—or the dropping of the last one in the fall.

As we learn more and more about the effects of a changing climate, we've been finding out that the timing of many of these periodic events is a bit out of whack. A tree that used to bloom at the end of April, for example, now might begin to bloom at the beginning of the month. Or a songbird species might arrive at its breeding ground several weeks earlier—or begin its fall migration several weeks later—than it did just a few decades ago.

These changes are creating patterns that can give scientists important clues about the effects of climate change on wildlife—and, ultimately, on people. If you'd like to help them tackle the problem, consider joining a citizen science monitoring project and share your family's observations. Most programs are conducted online, provide plenty of background information, and don't require much time or effort—but every bit of data they receive helps.

ATTRACTING BUTTERFLIES

There's probably no more beautiful—or popular—an insect than the butterfly.

Butterflies are no ordinary insects—that's for sure. Brilliantly colored and aerodynamically improbable, these seemingly fragile creatures exhibit a delicate grace that belies their resiliency. And they seem to lead lives as charmed as they are charming. Is there any other insect that, upon landing on a person's hand or head, would not only be tolerated but regarded as a fortuitous symbol of good luck?

To children exploring the outdoors, few living things are more appealing or more approachable than butterflies. Fortunately, these winged wonders can be attracted to almost any backyard, patio, or balcony, and laying out the welcome mat for them is a fun family project that can make

Did You Know?

A BUTTERFLY THAT LANDS ON A PERSON MAY BE ATTRACTED TO THE SALTINESS OF THE PERSON'S SKIN, THE RESULT OF PERSPIRATION.

your space as attractive to people as it is to butterflies.

Tiger swallowtail

ABOUT BUTTERFLIES AND MOTHS

There are more than seven hundred species of butterflies in North America alone, many with names nearly as colorful as they are. Here's a quick look at just some of the more common or familiar butterflies—and a couple of remarkable moths—you might find in your backyard or a nearby green space.

Swallowtails

Unmistakable, these large, striking butterflies get their names from the conspicuous extensions of their hind wings, reminiscent of the forked tails of swallows. Well-known members of this group include the yellow-and-black striped tiger swallowtail, the long-tailed and aptly named zebra swallowtail, the iridescent blue-black pipevine swallowtail, and a familiar visitor to gardens across the continent, the black swallowtail.

Hairstreaks

Smaller than swallowtails, this family of butterflies colored mostly in blues, purples, and tans is named for the small, delicate-looking tails on their hind wings. Long and threadlike enough in some species to resemble antennae, these may provide a defense mechanism for hairstreaks, as predators may be drawn to the wrong end of the butterfly.

Cabbage White

Widespread and very common, the little cabbage white butterfly can be found everywhere from city parks and open fields to gardens and farms—as you might have guessed from its name. Its black spots and wingtips are good field marks, as is the greenish tint to the underside of its wings.

Clouded Sulphur

A cousin to the cabbage white, the clouded sulphur butterfly is similar in size and shape, but with black edges to its clear yellow wings. Look for these butterflies in lawns, fields, and meadows.

Question Mark

This attractive reddish-orange butterfly with black spots has a noticeably irregular shape with odd edges and angles. Its name comes from the silvery-

Cecropia moth

white question mark that can be seen on the underside of its hind wings while it is at rest. Though they will occasionally visit flowers for nectar, question mark butterflies actually prefer to feed on less enticing—to us—choices such as rotting fruit, carrion, or animal droppings.

Monarch

This beautiful species is probably the most beloved of all butterflies. Read more about monarchs in chapter 13.

Mourning Cloak

This familiar and far-ranging butterfly can easily be identified by the wide yellow borders on the outer margins of its dark, nearly black, wings. One of the first butterflies to appear and become active in spring, the mourning cloak also can occasionally be seen on mild winter days, when it will temporarily emerge from its hibernation.

Red Admiral

Like the mourning cloak, its slightly larger cousin, the red admiral also is a widespread butterfly that lives through the winter as an adult. Mostly black interrupted by reddish-orange bars, this common visitor to backyards and parks prefers moist habitats.

Viceroy

This attractive orange-and-black butterfly is an accomplished mimic; its chrysalis resembles bird droppings and, as an adult, it resembles the bitter-tasting and poisonous monarch (more about that, later). Both strategies help to keep it safe from predatory birds.

Luna Moth

Given its size, shape, and color, there's no mistaking the luna moth. Its distinctive green edged in yellow, pink or purple, its transparent eyespots, and its long, curving "tails"—actually parts of its hind wings—are surefire field marks. Look for it near hardwood forests east of the Rockies.

Cecropia Moth

From a subfamily known as the giant silkworm moths, the spectacular cecropia moth is indeed a giant among butterflies and moths, with a wingspan approaching six inches. Its dusky brown wings are adorned by rust-colored bands and crescent-shaped spots, and its furry red body is ringed with white. Adult cecropia moths spend their short lives mating and laying eggs—lacking mouthparts, they don't even eat.

Did You Know?

MANY BUTTERFLY AND MOTH SPECIES HAVE LARGE, COLORFUL EYESPOTS ON THEIR WINGS. THESE CONSPICUOUS MARKINGS MOST LIKELY SERVE THE PURPOSE OF CONFUSING, DISTRACTING, OR DETERRING PREDATORS—AND, POSSIBLY, OF ATTRACTING A MATE AS WELL.

Butterflies and moths are close relatives belonging to the same order of insects and with many obvious similarities. But what's the difference between them?

Here are some characteristics that *usually* hold true for each:

- Most butterflies fly by day, and most moths by night—but there are exceptions to both rules. In fact, some of the most conspicuous day-flying moths are nearly the size of—and sometimes are mistaken for—hummingbirds.
- The bodies of butterflies tend to be smoother and narrower than the thicker, hairier bodies of moths.
- The antennae of butterflies are generally slender and knobbed at the end. Moth antennae can take many forms, including the familiar feathery shape, and are not knobbed.
- While resting, butterflies frequently hold their wings upright and close together, exposing the underside; moths, on the other hand, spread their wings and hold them flat.
- The wings of butterflies typically appear to be smoother than moth wings, which, because of their thicker scales, may appear almost furry.

INVITING BUTTERFLIES

Like many of the insects we met earlier, butterflies *can* be caught for closer inspection—but using the wrong type of net or the wrong technique to do so could possibly harm them. Rather than chase them down for a closer look, why not make your green space a place where butterflies will gladly visit and stay a while?

Start small; think big

MAKE A BUTTERFLY GARDEN

Whether you live in the city, the country, or somewhere in between, you don't need a big space to create a haven for butterflies—but you do need a few essentials to keep them happy.

Sun

Choose a warm, sunny spot for your butterfly garden. Butterflies typically love the sun—and the nectar-rich flowers that love it, too—and naturally will seek out sunny spots sheltered from the wind and rain. Especially early in the day, they will warm and dry their wings by basking in the sunlight. Large, flat garden stones, particularly dark-colored stones that will more readily absorb sunlight, provide them a perfect place for soaking up the sun's rays.

Water

Have you ever noticed butterflies congregating around a puddle or on muddy ground? This behavior is called *puddling,* and it's how butterflies get not only water but also the minerals their bodies need for reproduction. A puddling area for your garden is easy to make. Simply fill a shallow tray or pan with wet sand or stones (or both) and place it on the ground in a sunny location; you may wish to press it into the soil so that the top is flush with the level of the ground. Keep it moist, and refresh the water periodically.

Food

Just as birds will visit feeders for their favorite seeds, butterflies will visit gardens for the nectar of their favorite flowers. No matter where you live, there will be dozens of suitable flowers for you to choose from for your garden, but remember that butterflies are most readily attracted to fragrant, brightly colored blooms, especially purple, pink, orange, or yellow ones. The shape of the flower is important, too—butterflies prefer clustered or flat-topped flowers that offer them a place to land and easy access to nectar. Black-eyed Susan, purple coneflower, and butterfly weed are just some of the nectar plants popular with butterflies and gardeners alike.

As attractive as nectar-rich flowers may be to butterflies, they are an invitation to visit—but not necessarily to stay. To make your garden truly butterfly-friendly, you should consider including not only nectar flowers for adult butterflies, but *host* plants for their caterpillars as well. Fully grown butterflies and their larvae—better known as their caterpillars—differ greatly not only in their appearance but often in their diet, too. The same plants that feed adult butterflies may not necessarily feed their caterpillars, and a host plant, therefore, is the carefully chosen location where adult butterflies lay their eggs; in fact, there are some species of butterflies that rely on a single species of host plant. Including at least a few useful caterpillar host plants, such as milkweed, clover, fennel, or spicebush, will greatly enhance the attractiveness of your garden.

TIPS FOR SUCCESSFUL GARDENS

A few more things to consider when inviting butterflies to your backyard:

Start Small

Many attractive nectar and host plants can be grown successfully in containers. If you have limited space, or simply want to create a manageable garden, try raising them in pots or planters on your balcony, patio, or in a sunny corner of your backyard.

Keep It Green

Herbicides and pesticides should be avoided, as they pose a short-term threat to the butterflies or caterpillars in your garden and a long-term threat to the health of the environment.

Go Native

For your garden, try to choose native plants whenever possible. These naturally occurring species are adapted to the growing conditions of your region, and therefore require less maintenance than exotic, ornamental—and potentially invasive—varieties. These plants also share a mutually beneficial relationship with butterflies, serving as nectar or host plants for the butterfly species that, in turn, pollinate them.

TIP: FOR PHOTOGRAPHS, RANGE MAPS, AND DETAILED DESCRIPTIONS OF THE BUTTERFLIES AND MOTHS OF NORTH AMERICA, VISIT WWW.BUTTERFLIESANDMOTHS.ORG.

TIP: VISIT WWW.NWF.ORG/GARDENFORWILDLIFE AND WWW.WILDFLOWER.ORG FOR MORE BUTTERFLY GARDENING TIPS AND TO FIND NATIVE NECTAR AND HOST PLANTS RECOMMENDED FOR YOUR AREA.

BOOK NOOK

ROOTS, SHOOTS, BUCKETS, AND BOOTS
BY SHARON LOVEJOY
AGE RANGE: 10 AND UP

ATTRACTING BUTTERFLIES IS JUST ONE OF THE MANY DELIGHTFUL GARDENING PROJECTS KIDS AND PARENTS CAN DO TOGETHER. WHETHER YOU'RE A NEWCOMER OR ALREADY HAVE BEEN BITTEN BY THE GARDENING BUG, THIS BOOK IS CHOCK-FULL OF INFORMATION AND RESOURCES TO HELP FAMILIES GET OUTSIDE AND DIG IN. SEPARATE SECTIONS OFFER CREATIVE IDEAS FOR GROWING KID-FRIENDLY PLANTS, FLOWERS, HERBS, VEGETABLES, AND CONTAINER GARDENS.

ON THE TRAIL

ACCORDING TO THE OLD PROVERB, even the journey of a thousand miles begins with a single step. The sentiment it expresses—that no matter the undertaking, you simply must begin where you are—is especially befitting for families seeking to make and to strengthen their connection to the natural world, a lifelong endeavor that begins with the simple action of walking out the door. There's nothing to it but to do it.

And it's hard to imagine anything better to do than walking or hiking outdoors—breathing fresh air, moving through beautiful natural landscapes, and taking the time to be together as a family. The chorus of birdsong, the rustle of leaves, the rush of a stream—the sounds of the trail provide the soundtrack to an experience that can be almost meditative; stress melts away with each breath and with every stride toward a fitter body and a clearer, sharper mind.

But there's another compelling reason to go take a hike—the path brings plenty of adventure, too, with new discoveries always around the bend. The pages that follow feature activities and ideas for finding and making the most of them.

GOING FOR A HIKE

Get up and go, and put your best foot forward.

Colloquially, telling someone to "go take a hike" is to bluntly suggest that his or her presence is unwanted. Taken in a different spirit, it's an invitation to one of the simplest and most enduring of all outdoor activities. Few things are better for mind, body, and spirit than to get your family out on the trail, exercising your legs, filling your lungs with fresh air, and delighting in the sights and sounds of nature.

Whether you're trekking along a stretch of backcountry trail or leisurely following a community path, here are some ideas for making an outing with children a successful one.

PREPARING THE FAMILY

In essence, hiking is nothing more than taking a walk in a lovely outdoor setting, and it might be tempting not to clutter up such a pure endeavor with a pack full of equipment. But as with any outdoor activity— especially those undertaken with children—a bit of preparation goes a long way toward ensuring a safe and enjoyable outing for everyone.

Gear Up

Even for those with a minimalist mindset, some gear is essential for hiking. Here's advice for gearing up your family to remain relatively unencumbered while being ready for the unexpected.

Shoes

A successful hike starts from the ground up—the shoes you wear are more important than any other piece of hiking gear. And more important than having the latest or most expensive hiking boots is simply having the right shoe for the trail. Unless your family is taking on lengthy hikes in the backcountry, rugged, high-topped hiking boots probably won't be worth the extra weight. For most kid-friendly hikes, a sturdy pair of trail shoes or lightweight hiking boots will offer a good compromise between weight, flexibility, and support. A low-cut shoe is fine for easy trails, but longer hikes, heavier backpacks, and rocky terrain all call for better ankle support. And unless you plan to hike in wet conditions or marshy areas, waterproofing—while certainly welcome—may not be necessary. Whichever shoes you choose, be sure to break them in before hitting the trail with them, and consider wearing thin sock liners under a second pair of socks to help prevent rubbing and blisters.

Clothing

The best way to dress for hiking is in comfortable, breathable layers that allow you to warm up or cool off as necessary. Lightweight long pants offer much better protection from itches, scratches, and bites on the trail than short pants, if it's not too hot to wear them. In any conditions, be sure to keep dry by keeping a lightweight waterproof shell in your pack.

Packs

Wearing their own backpacks on a hike allows children to contribute by carrying their own weight. Even if their gear is little more than their own supply of drinking water, snacks, and clothing, packing their personal needs fosters responsibility in the great outdoors. Be careful, however, to fill children's packs carefully; too much weight, or weight carried too high or unevenly distributed, can mean a pain in the back or neck.

Pack for discovery

Pack It Up

To keep your family happy, comfortable, and safe, pack items from the following lists as the length and the location of your outings warrant. Reusable plastic bags or lightweight plastic containers are useful for keeping safety and first aid gear dry.

Did You Know?

THE MAJORITY OF A BACKPACK'S WEIGHT SHOULD BE SUPPORTED BY YOUR HIPS.

Comfort:

- water
- trail mix or energy bars
- sunblock
- sunglasses
- hats
- insect repellant

Safety:

- a whistle
- a flashlight
- ponchos or trash bags
- a lighter or all-weather matches
- a pocket knife
- a compass

First Aid:

- antibiotic ointment
- adhesive bandages
- moleskin for blisters
- tweezers
- rubbing alcohol pads
- analgesic or anti-inflammatory tablets (ibuprofen, etc.)
- over-the-counter antihistamine (Benadryl, etc.)
- elastic wrap (Ace bandage, etc.)
- a bee sting kit for allergic individuals

Discovery:

- a camera
- a magnifying glass
- binoculars
- field guides
- a notebook or journal
- trail maps

FUEL UP

Backpackers have long relied on the old standby known as *gorp*—"good old raisins and peanuts"—to keep them going. And while there are dozens of variations on this theme, it's still hard to beat for on-the-go sustenance while out on the trail.

TIP: THE "LEAVE NO TRACE" ETHIC ENCOURAGES PEOPLE TO GET OUTSIDE AND ENJOY THE NATURAL WORLD—BUT TO TAKE MEASURES TO LEAVE IT JUST AS THEY'D FOUND IT. LEARN MORE ABOUT EXPLORING THE OUTDOORS RESPONSIBLY BY VISITING THE LEAVE NO TRACE CENTER FOR OUTDOOR ETHICS AT WWW.LNT.ORG.

In many ways, trail mix is the ideal food for outdoor activity—each handful is a combination of healthy proteins, fats, and carbohydrates, just sweet enough for a quick energy boost, and just salty enough to help replenish electrolytes lost through perspiration.

Make Your Own Trail Mix

There's no shortage of ready-made products on the shelves of your local supermarket, but half the fun of trail mix is making, and perfecting, your family's own favorite recipes.

What you need:

- nuts, such as peanuts, almonds, walnuts, cashews, hazelnuts, macadamia nuts
- dried fruit, such as raisins, cherries, dates, cranberries, bananas, blueberries, apples, raspberries, apricots
- sweets, such as M&Ms, dark chocolate chips, carob chips, white chocolate chips, yogurt-covered raisins
- grains, such as granola, O-shaped cereal, shredded wheat, whole-grain cereal flakes, whole-grain pretzel bites
- resealable plastic bags or lightweight plastic containers with lids

What you do:

1. As a good starting point, have everyone mix equal parts—about a half-cup or so—of their favorite nuts, dried fruit, sweets, and grains into their containers.
2. Experiment! Try different combinations to create your own signature trail mix. Remember that a well-rounded mix will be a balanced blend of all four groups.
3. Seal the bags or containers and give them a shake to combine the ingredients.

The ingredients listed above strike a fair balance between being delicious and being healthful, but you can make your mix as decadent—everything from mini-marshmallows to chocolate-covered espresso beans is fair game—or as wholesome as you like.

Hike at a child's pace

OUT ON THE TRAIL

Hiking trails so often can lead us to wonderful things we haven't yet seen, or let us glimpse a familiar place more intimately, in all of its moods and seasons. On an ideal outing, your kids will delight in making new discoveries along the way, and you'll have the joy of watching them experience things for the first time. A little forethought goes a long way toward inviting discovery and minimizing difficulties while out on the trail with children.

Advice for Happy Hikes

With a different set of expectations and just a little bit of preparation, hitting the trail with kids can be a delightful and rewarding experience. Here's some tried-and-true advice to help make it a great experience for everyone.

Slow Down

Remember that children will take twice as many strides as you—or more—to cover the same ground. They also may want to stop more frequently, either to investigate new discoveries or simply to rest and refuel. Take your time and enjoy the day at their pace.

Think Small

Choose hikes where the trail itself is the attraction. A destination hike ending at a waterfall or scenic view offers a natural reward, of course, but having a variety of landscapes and features to explore along the way will help to hold children's interest throughout. A leisurely ramble along streams, woods, meadows, and boulders can be just as gratifying as a steep scramble up to an overlook—maybe even more so.

Know Where You're Going

Hiking with kids should be about the fun of exploring and discovering natural places together, not about blazing new trails or deciphering trail maps just to keep from getting lost. Keep the stress level low by choosing a location with which you are already familiar, or an easy trail where navigation isn't a concern.

Stay on Established Trails

This will reduce your family's exposure to off-trail hazards such as ticks, snakes, and poison ivy, and keep children safely away from a potential fall or

Did You Know?

When our bodies are sufficiently hydrated, they work better and more efficiently. During physical activity, such as hiking, regular fluid intake becomes even more important, as dehydration quickly can lead to headaches, cramps, and fatigue.

Packing an adequate supply of drinking water for your children is essential. But how much is enough?

For a quick rule of thumb, divide children's weight by two for a rough estimate of their daily drinking water needs. A child weighing forty pounds, for example, should consume roughly twenty ounces of water per day—more, of course, in hot or dry conditions or during strenuous exercise.

Try to drink plenty of water before hitting the trail, and stay hydrated by taking smaller, more frequent drinks along the way.

injury. And, of course, it can keep you from getting lost. If you're hiking a wooded trail, teach your children to recognize the blazes that mark the path—it's a valuable skill, and something to keep them engaged during the hike. Instruct kids to stay calm—and to stay put—should they become lost, and to blow their whistles as both a signal and beacon.

Review the Troops

Until you've already turned around and headed back toward the trailhead, you're never more than halfway through a hike. Keep tabs on your children's energy level and morale; it's far better to end a hike on a high note, before their tanks are completely empty. As their endurance and confidence grows, your children will be up for increasingly longer adventures.

Bring Along Backup

Portable navigation devices and wireless phones—many of which now have GPS (global positioning system) capability—offer peace of mind should you end up lost or needing emergency assistance. More importantly, always follow the fundamental rule of letting someone know where and when you are hiking, especially in more rugged or remote areas.

TWISTS ON TRADITIONAL HIKES

Anyone who has traveled by car with children knows that games can be a pleasant diversion to help pass the miles. While time spent on the trail together is much more enjoyable, playing games while hiking can be a fun way to open children's eyes and ears to the natural world around them.

Letter Hike

Taking turns, or as a group, look for things that begin with each letter of the alphabet as you hike. Or, as a variation, create a word chain by looking for things that begin with the last letter of whatever preceded it—*acorn, nest, tree,* etc. Younger children can keep an eye out for the shapes of letters themselves hidden among the trees, leaves, flowers, and rocks along the trail.

Sound Hike

Birds singing, frogs croaking, insects buzzing, leaves rustling—these are just some of the sounds you may hear as you hit the trail. Each time players hear a new sound, they share it with the group. While they may be less obvious, smells can be called out, too—whether pleasant, like wildflowers, or less so, like skunk cabbage.

Spy Hike

Best played on breaks, or at least on stretches where the view changes slowly, is a classic game of "I Spy."

REMEMBER: IN THE UNLIKELY EVENT THAT YOU *DO* END UP LOST IN THE BACKCOUNTRY, THE BEST WAY TO BE FOUND IS TO STAY PUT. SEARCHERS WILL LOOK FOR YOU WHERE THEY THINK YOU ARE—NOT WHEREVER YOU MAY HAVE WANDERED TO—AND THE FARTHER YOU ARE FROM THAT POINT, THE HARDER IT WILL BE FOR THEM TO FIND YOU. MOVING EVEN ONE MILE CREATES A SEARCH AREA OF MORE THAN THREE SQUARE MILES.

Night Hike

A familiar trail with safe, even footing makes a great place for a nighttime hike. The silvery light of a bright moon and the chorus of night creatures can give these walks an eerie, almost magical, quality. Bring flashlights for safety, but refrain from using them if possible. Instead, allow your eyes to adjust to the darkness, and keep the members of your group together by having them hold on to the backpack or belt loop of the person in front of them.

More to Explore: From Rails to Trails

Mountains, forests, meadows—wild places and spaces like these are the quintessential settings for a hike. But for most of us, getting to these destinations may take a bit of time and planning. Fortunately, even in urban and suburban areas, there are thousands of miles of trails to be found, many of them passing through areas rich with foliage and wildlife.

Through the efforts of groups like the Rails-to-Trails Conservancy, many old rail corridors that have fallen into disuse have been converted to beautiful trails in communities across the country. These multiuse trails offer a variety of outdoor recreational opportunities and provide attractive green spaces to bring neighborhoods together. They also benefit wildlife by helping to create corridors of habitat in areas where it otherwise might be threatened or fragmented by development.

Because they follow old rail beds, these so-called rail-trails are particularly family-friendly; they are generally flat, wide, and open, offering good visibility and suitable not just for walking and hiking, but often for biking or pushing a stroller as well. Convenient and accessible, they make getting a "green hour" easier for millions of people across the United States.

PICKING UP ON TRACKS AND CLUES

Out on the trail, mystery and adventure await—if you know what to look for.

As young children, we develop a fascination with puzzles, riddles, and mysteries that, fortunately, most of us never seem to outgrow. Hide-and-seek, scavenger hunts—such humble pursuits as these introduce us to the simple pleasures of concealing and revealing secrets and the timeless joys of surprise and discovery.

On the trail, you and your child might find bigger mysteries to solve, some authored by nature, others by people—you may even wish to create a puzzle of your own. Whether you're picking up clues or putting them down, heading into nature with your eyes and mind wide open can make the experience all the more rewarding.

TRACKING

In today's world, many of us are more likely to see tire tracks than animal tracks on a daily basis. But it wasn't all that long ago—and, in some parts of the world it is still the case—that people were keenly aware of the

Did You Know?

DINOSAUR TRACKS ARE FOSSILIZED FOOTPRINTS MORE THAN ONE HUNDRED MILLION YEARS OLD.

comings and goings of wildlife. Being able to read animal tracks could give them the information they would need to have a successful hunt or a warning sign that a threat to their crops, their livestock—even themselves—was near.

For most of us, discovering animal tracks is much less urgent a matter. Still, these signs are clues that pique our curiosity, almost instinctively, and give us plenty to puzzle over.

Every track tells a story. Below are some helpful hints for finding, reading, and saving them.

FINDING TRACKS

While animals of all kinds—including people—are constantly moving across the face of the Earth, we don't always leave tracks behind us. Or, at least, tracks that we can easily detect. Much depends on the medium we move through, and the condition it is in at the time. A mouse might move across the hard, sun-baked clay in a field without leaving a discernible footprint; that same patch after a rainfall would clearly show its footprints—even the track of its tail dragging behind it.

But even a suitable medium won't reveal tracks if there are no animals to leave them. Oftentimes, the best places to find tracks—such as damp woods, shady trails, the banks of rivers and streams—see a lot of animal activity and happen to have a surface that can capture the evidence. Any place where animals feed, drink, bathe, or gather is a good place to look. (It is also quite possible to discover those places by following tracks *to* them.) Even the ground beneath a bird feeder, for instance, probably has plenty of bird and squirrel tracks to be found.

Though they are well-suited for it, mud and damp soil aren't the only places where tracks can be made. Sand—both the wet sand of the seashore and the dry sand of desert areas—can reveal the tracks of birds, reptiles, and more, though the traces left behind here often fade quickly. Dry, dusty soil may not offer the clearest of footprints, but it does show other disturbances to the surface such as drag marks or the sweeping of wing feathers. And, if you happen to live where the winters are cold enough, there is perhaps no better medium for tracking than new-fallen snow.

Squirrel tracks

Raccoon and deer tracks

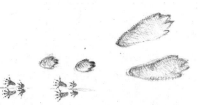

Mouse and cottontail rabbit tracks

READING TRACKS

The shape or form of the tracks you find offers the biggest clues to the identity of the creature that left them. The number, spacing, and orientation of the toes, the size and shape of the pad or foot bed, the presence or absence of claws, the similarity or disparity of the front and hind feet—all are field marks to aid your identification.

Some track shapes, such as those left by birds or deer, are instantly recognizable, while others might take a little practice. At first glance, the tracks left by dogs and cats (and their wild relatives) may look the same, but the typical presence of claws in canine tracks quickly distinguishes them. The tracks of many small mammals have distinctive features of their own: the "thumbs" of raccoon and opossum tracks, the webbing of bea-ver or otter footprints, the mismatched front and back footprints of rabbits.

In much the same way that a still photograph can arrest motion, the arrangement of an animal's tracks creates a snapshot of how it moved through a given space. Look at the placement of tracks in relation to each other for clues to how the animal moved.

- Do the tracks indicate short or long strides? Do the tracks follow a narrow line or are they spread apart? Did the animal walk, run, or hop?
- Do they follow a deliberate course or do they meander? Do they suddenly change direction? What might the animal have been doing?
- Are the toes—or hooves—close together, or spread far apart? What might that tell you about the speed at which the animal traveled? What might it tell you about its footing?
- Are the tracks suddenly interrupted? Do they resume? Are there other clues—food, feathers, fur—nearby?

Tracks also can tell us a lot about the size of the animals that left them. The length and width of its footprints are obvious indicators of size, but the depth of tracks, especially in soft surfaces like mud, soil, or wet sand, correlates well to an animal's weight—especially for walking tracks.

Saving Tracks

Animal tracks are delicate, and often are soon swept away by wind, water, or weather. But preserving a fine specimen can be a rewarding project for young trackers.

What You Need:

- a track
- plaster of paris
- water
- a plastic container
- a spoon
- a wide plastic bottle or yogurt container
- scissors
- petroleum jelly

What You Do:

1. Find an animal track in the soil and gently clear the surrounding area of debris, taking care not to disturb the track itself.
2. With sharp scissors, carefully cut a two-to three-inch cross-section from a large plastic drink bottle or yogurt container to create a ring-shaped mold for your cast.
3. Smear the inside of the mold with petroleum jelly. This will keep the plaster from sticking and allow the cast to slide out easily. Place the mold around the track and press it firmly into the soil.
4. In the plastic container, mix the plaster of paris and water with a spoon, following

---

BOOK NOOK

Wild Tracks! A Guide to Nature's Footprints
By Jim Arnosky
Age range: 8 to 12

This fine introduction to animal tracks reads a bit like a cross between a picture book and a naturalist's notebook, with full color paintings and pencil sketches illustrating the diversity of animal tracks one might encounter—from felines and canines to birds and deer.

Four foldouts present different families of tracks in actual size, allowing the reader to better appreciate the differences between related species. Especially interesting are the comparisons between the tracks of domestic animals and their wild counterparts: a house cat and a mountain lion, a dog and a timber wolf.

Did You Know?

WHILE MOST ANIMAL TRACKS ARE FOOTPRINTS, EVEN ANIMALS WITHOUT FEET CAN LEAVE TRACKS. IF YOU FIND A SERIES OF WAVY IMPRESSIONS IN MUD, SAND, OR DIRT, THEY MOST LIKELY ARE SNAKE TRACKS.

the instructions on the package. Add water slowly, to keep the mixture from becoming too runny; the final consistency should be that of thick yogurt or sour cream.

5. Pour the mixture into the mold, filling the track and covering it with an inch of plaster. Wait for the plaster to harden—thirty to sixty minutes should be enough time—before removing the cast from the mold.

6. Take the cast home and allow it to dry completely overnight. Once the cast has set completely, gently brush away any remaining soil.

If you like, experiment by trying to cast a track in firm or frozen snow. You also may wish to make a cast of your finished cast; this will save the raised track as an impression, just as you'd found it outdoors. Remember to lightly coat the first cast with petroleum jelly to prevent sticking.

More to Explore: Animal Signs

As you explore natural areas, tracks aren't the only evidence of wildlife activity you might find. Keep an eye out for these other animal signs you might encounter on your adventures.

Beavers

Fallen or standing trees with gnaw marks near the base of their trunks are a sure sign that beavers are in the area. Beavers use the trees they fell for the construction of their dams and aquatic homes, called *lodges*. Look for both in the water nearby.

Deer

If you find an otherwise healthy-looking tree or sapling with its bark and twigs scraped away just a couple of feet above the ground, you probably have found a *buck rub*. Male deer, called bucks, will rub their antlers against the trunks of small trees for two reasons: to scrape the itchy "velvet" off of their new antler growth, and to mark their territory—and, perhaps, to attract females—by applying their scent to the tree.

Bears

In certain areas, you may discover tree trunks with parallel grooves scratched into them, usually running vertically, or nearly so. From time to time, both black and brown bears will mark trees by scratching them. Should you find these markings, have your child hold his or her hand up to the claw marks to better appreciate the size of a bear's paw.

Woodpeckers

If a tree is riddled with small holes, chances are that woodpeckers have been there, using their chisel-like bills to hunt for insects and their larvae under the bark or in the wood itself. Neat rows of holes are the work of the yellow-bellied sapsucker, a common woodpecker found throughout North America east of the Rockies. Woodpeckers also create nesting cavities in trees, which oftentimes are used by other birds, or even squirrels, when the woodpeckers are through with them.

Birds and Squirrels

The period between the last leaves of fall and the first leaves of spring is a good time to find animal homes that might have been concealed by foliage. The nests of birds and squirrels, in particular, are easy to spot at this time. Bird nests are incredibly diverse, fashioned from a variety of materials, and are generally much more orderly in their construction than squirrels' nests—which often appear as unruly collections of leaves stuffed in the higher branches of trees.

FOLLOWING OTHER SIGNS

Finding tracks and animal signs lets us peek into the quiet, often hidden, workings of nature. But not all of the signs you might find on the trail have been left by wildlife. Just for the fun and the challenge of it, more and more people have been putting down clues in the great outdoors—and your family might enjoy picking up on them and following them to outdoor discovery.

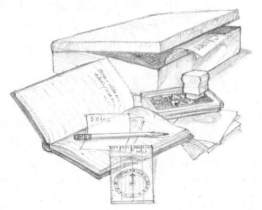

A letterboxer's tools of the trade

LETTERBOXING

Part hike, part treasure hunt, and part mystery, letterboxing is a charming pursuit that has enjoyed a surge of popularity over the past dozen or so years. It's also a wonderful outdoor activity for families to do together.

The concept is simple. Scattered throughout the world, usually in scenic, publicly accessible natural spaces, are hidden a multitude of little treasures known as letterboxes. The person who hides a letterbox composes a series of clues—sometimes straightforward, sometimes puzzling, sometimes on a unique theme—to its location. By following the landmarks, compass directions, and pacing instructions in the clues, the seeker should be able to find the letterbox, which typically consists of a durable waterproof container housing a logbook and a rubber stamp. The seeker carries a rubber stamp and logbook of his own.

For letterboxers, the stamp is both prize and calling card. Almost all letterboxes—and letterboxers—have a uniquely designed, and often hand-carved, stamp. At the end of a successful quest, the seeker marks his logbook with the stamp from the letterbox, and marks the logbook from the letterbox with his personal stamp; it's not unlike collecting the stamps of different destinations in your passport, a reminder of the journey. The logbook and stamp are returned to the letterbox, which is then hidden just as before, ready for the next seeker.

A friendly and far-reaching community has organized itself around this game, and newcomers to letterboxing are always welcome. Getting started is as easy as looking for your first letterbox, and the equipment list is quite reasonable.

What you need:

- a rubber stamp
- a journal or logbook
- a stamping inkpad
- clues
- a compass

Before you know it, you and your child might even be creating letterbox mysteries of your own!

Geocaching

This rapidly growing outdoor game is similar in concept and in spirit to letterboxing, but with a decidedly high-tech twist. If your family has a mobile GPS (global positioning system) device, you might want to give it a try. Written clues are replaced by geographic coordinates and waypoints, and the letterbox is replaced by a *geocache*. Like a letterbox, a geocache usually is a small waterproof container holding treasure; in this case, a logbook for the finder to sign and an assortment of interesting and inexpensive treasures and trinkets. The finder is welcome to take one of the treasures, provided he or she also leaves one behind in its place.

Both letterboxing and geocaching promote a spirit of goodwill and camaraderie, get families outdoors together, and foster a deeper appreciation for the natural spaces that serve as the backdrop to the adventures they inspire. The geocaching community has even created a "Cache In, Trash Out" initiative, encouraging its members to give back by pitching in and cleaning up their local parks and trails.

Tip: Find everything you need to join this high-tech treasure hunt at www.geocaching.com.

BOOK NOOK

THE LETTERBOXER'S COMPANION
BY RANDY HALL
AGE RANGE: 10 AND UP

THIS BOOK IS THE AUTHORITATIVE GUIDE TO LETTERBOXING, COVERING ALL ASPECTS OF THE PASTIME FROM ITS HISTORY AND ETIQUETTE TO FINDING AND CREATING CLUES, STAMPS, AND THE LETTERBOXES THEMSELVES.

TURNING OVER NEW LEAVES

*Looking closely at leaves is a great way to appreciate some grand
living things on an intimate scale.*

Backyard trees are like old friends—familiar, dependable—but out on
the trail, there are new friends to meet. As you venture farther afield, and
as your hikes take you through different environments, you'll encounter
an astonishing variety of trees. This chapter takes a more detailed look at
them—and encourages your family to do the same.

There's an old expression about not being able to see the forest for the
trees. Usually, we use it to describe people who are so concerned about the
details that they end up missing the big picture.

But with the trees themselves, the big picture is pretty hard to miss—
they are, after all, the tallest living things on the planet. And the details
not only are fascinating, they are precisely what gives each tree its unique
character and beauty: bark, buds, flowers, fruit—and, most importantly,
leaves.

No matter how big or small, every tree depends on its leaves. These
seemingly delicate structures perform a most remarkable feat—soaking

up sunlight and turning it into the energy that sustains not just a tree but, ultimately, all of us. Now, *that's* a big picture.

White pine, American beech, sugar maple, and paper birch leaves

ABOUT TREES

In woodlands, parks, and along hiking trails, you'll encounter a rich assortment of trees. Here's a closer look at just a few of the more noteworthy ones you might find.

Pine

For many of us, pine trees are what come to mind when we think of evergreens—handsome, fragrant trees with slender needles for leaves. Several needles grow together in a cluster, usually in pairs or in groups of three or five. Their most interesting feature—to birds, squirrels, and chipmunks, if not to children—is their fruit, the prickly, scaly cones that come in a wide range of sizes and shapes and that give clues to the identity of each tree that bears them. Countless bird feeders and craft projects have been created with pine cones, and no na-

White oak leaves and acorns

ture table is complete without one. Be prepared for sticky fingers and clothes; rubbing alcohol helps to dissolve the messy sap.

Maple

There are many members of this family of trees, but they share a common, familiar leaf shape, fanning out to multiple pointed lobes separated by notches. A closer look reveals that maple leaves always grow in pairs from the same point on a twig, but on opposite sides. Even when the leaves are absent, buds and *leaf scars*—the marks left on a twig when leaves fall or are removed—will show this opposite arrangement. Maples are among the most popular trees, and with good reason. In the summer, they make an excellent choice for shade—or for climbing. Come fall, their colors are eye-popping, ranging from vivid yellows to brilliant reds. In winter, varieties such as the sugar maple and black maple produce the sap from which maple syrup and sugar can be made. And they are prized at any time for their fine wood, often used to make furniture and musical instruments.

Birch

Some of our most distinctive trees are members of this family. Paper birch, a northern tree, is unmistakable for its white bark marked with black, which readily peels off in paper-like strips. Yellow birch has a smooth, sometimes shiny bark with

Sweet gum, redbud, tulip tree, and sassafras leaves

pronounced *lenticels,* the pore-like structures that allow a plant to "breathe." Often found in very wet soils, the river birch has reddish-gray bark that peels away in curls, giving the tree a decidedly shaggy appearance, even from a distance. Another variety, the sweet birch, produces a wintergreen-like oil and sap that can be used to make birch beer, a soft drink similar to root beer.

Oak

The leaves of oak trees often are marked by their numerous lobes—some pointed, others round—though several varieties have no lobes at all. While that may be a bit confusing, one trait they all share is a cluster of buds at the ends of their twigs. But an oak tree's real claim to fame, of course, is its familiar fruit: the acorn. Many kinds of wildlife depend upon acorns for food, and children can't resist picking them up (or stuffing them in their pockets).

Beech

The smooth, gray bark of the beech tree is a sure-fire field mark, as are its sizable buds—decidedly long, reddish-brown, and covered by a dozen or more scales. The somewhat stiff leaves are a tapered, pointed oval, with teeth along the edges. Beech trees often cling to their curled, withered leaves throughout the winter, possibly to help shelter their conspicuous buds. The fruit of the beech tree—a prickly, four-parted casing that opens to reveal the edible nuts inside—is readily eaten by deer, bear, squirrels, and turkey.

Redbud

This small, charming tree often can be found growing in the shade of taller hardwoods. It is best known for its heart-shaped leaves with smooth edges and several pronounced veins radiating from the leaf stem. Look for its clusters of bright pink flowers early in the spring, as redbud is one of the first trees to bloom each year.

Sassafras

Widespread east of the Rockies, sassafras is a small to mid-sized tree that's as useful as it is attractive. Wildlife ranging from birds to bears gobble up the bluish-black fruits hanging from red stems, and

Did You Know?

AN ACORN CAP CAN BE TURNED INTO A SHRILL, HIGH-PITCHED WHISTLE. SIMPLY PRESS THE SIDES OF YOUR THUMBS TOGETHER AND COVER THE CONCAVE SIDE OF AN ACORN CAP WITH THEM, LEAVING A SMALL, V-SHAPED NOTCH. REST YOUR LOWER LIP ON YOUR THUMBS AND BLOW DOWN, AND FORCEFULLY, INTO THE NOTCH. YOU MAY NEED TO EXPERIMENT A BIT WITH THE POSITION OF YOUR LIP AND THUMBS, BUT ONCE YOU'VE GOT IT RIGHT—WELL, LET'S JUST SAY THAT *EVERYONE* WILL KNOW.

people have long made tea from its roots and *filé*—a Cajun seasoning used in foods such as gumbo—from its dried, ground leaves. The smooth leaves are unique in that three separate leaf shapes appear on the same tree: a flattened egg shape, a mitten shape with a small "thumb" on one side, and a three-fingered shape with a large "thumb" on either side. Crush a sassafras leaf and leaf stem between your fingers to release a sweet, almost fruity aroma. Sassafras twigs, smooth and green, also are aromatic, and make exceptional sticks for marshmallow roasting.

Sycamore

At first glance, sycamore leaves bear a superficial resemblance to maple leaves, but are arranged in an *alternate,* not opposite, pattern on the twig. However, to identify this tree, you need look no further than the peeling bark, a striking patchwork of scaly pieces in shades of white, brown, and green. If in doubt, the tightly packed, ball-shaped fruit hanging from long stems should clinch the identification. These stately trees prefer moist soil conditions and are a common sight on flood plains, bottomlands, and near the banks of rivers and streams. Sycamores can grow to a great height and girth, ranking them among our largest broadleaf trees.

Sweet Gum

This fine tree gets its name from the sap that oozes forth from injuries to its bark and hardens into a chewy gum. It has distinctly star-shaped leaves, usually with five points but as many as seven, which often turn deep red or scarlet in the fall. Like sassafras, sweet gum has fragrant leaves; when crushed, they have a pleasant, spicy aroma.

The long-stemmed fruit balls, woody and slightly prickly—they are not nearly as menacing as they appear to be—are fun to collect or play with; break them open to find tiny winged seeds inside.

Tulip Tree

Also known as tulip poplar, yellow poplar, or white-wood, this impressive, fast-growing tree of eastern forests regularly reaches well over one hundred feet in height. Its lobed leaves are distinctive, fanning out into four points, and the greenish-yellow flowers tinged with orange have a tulip-like shape. Its blooms are rich in nectar, making the tulip tree an important honey tree—the honeybees that visit it produce a dark, amber-colored honey. Growing out of the flower is the fruit, a long, cone-like structure comprised of single-winged seeds that ripen and scatter in the wind in autumn.

LEAF WALKS

Leaves really grab our attention twice a year—in springtime, when they reappear in a rising wave of green, and in the fall, when they turn dazzling colors before falling to the ground. But leaves are worth a closer look at any time.

When you're on the trail with your child, look around. Can you find a leaf as big as your hand? As you walk along, pick up a leaf from the ground. Can you match it to the tree it belongs to?

There are many ways to explore the variety of leaves you will find while on the move. Here are several to get you started.

Record your observations

Shapes

Many common trees you might encounter while on the trail have leaves of interesting shapes. Try to find leaves that look like:

- ovals
- hearts
- stars
- eggs
- mittens

Textures

There's great variation in the appearance of leaves, but less apparent may be the variety of textures they can have. See if you can find leaves that are:

- smooth
- rough
- waxy
- fuzzy
- papery

Colors

Autumn is an exhilarating time for a hike, and the colorful display of leaves can be spectacular. While on the trail, look for leaves that are:

- red
- orange
- yellow
- green
- scarlet
- purple
- brown

COLLECTING LEAVES

As you walk or hike your favorite trail, collect several of your favorite leaves and save them in a reusable plastic bag or container. At home, you can prepare them for keepsakes or use them for crafty art projects. Here's how.

MAKE A LEAF RUBBING

The veins do very important work; they transport water and minerals into—and food out of—the leaf. They also can be quite intricate and lovely, and here's a classic activity for capturing their beauty.

WHAT YOU NEED:

- leaves
- paper
- crayons, without wrappers

WHAT YOU DO:

1. Collect fresh leaves from the ground or by gently plucking them from the tree, taking only as many as you need. Old leaves may be too dry or brittle for rubbing.
2. Lay a leaf on a flat surface. For best results, the underside of the leaf, where the veins are more pronounced, should be facing up.
3. Cover the leaf with the paper. Hold a crayon sideways and rub it across the paper. Begin by rubbing lightly and press more firmly until an impression of the leaf appears.

You may wish to collect your leaves and make your rubbings at home. Experiment with several kinds of leaves, different types of paper, and other media such as pastels, charcoals, or chalk.

What else might make a good nature rubbing? Try this with tree bark, seed pods, ferns, or anything else with an interesting texture.

MAKE LEAF PRINTS

WHAT YOU NEED:

- fresh leaves
- newspaper
- nontoxic finger paint, tempera paint, or stamping inkpad

- paper
- tissue paper

WHAT YOU DO:

1. Select a clean, dry leaf and lay it facedown on the newspaper protecting your work surface. Apply finger paint or brush tempera paint evenly on the underside of the leaf. Or, press the underside of the leaf directly onto the stamping inkpad, working in sections if necessary, until it is covered by ink.
2. Lay the leaf onto a clean sheet of paper with the painted or inked side down. Position it carefully; once it's on the paper, moving the leaf will smear your print.
3. Cover the leaf with a sheet of tissue paper. Gently rub the leaf through the tissue paper, taking care not to press too hard.
4. Gently remove the tissue paper, and then the leaf, to reveal your print.

Printing the underside of the leaf will allow the veins to show through more clearly. Experiment by printing the top side of the leaf as well, or by printing both sides of the same leaf onto the same sheet for comparison. Favorite prints make for wonderful wall art or note cards.

Younger children may enjoy the tactile experience of finger painting their leaves before printing

TIP: A GOOD GENERAL GUIDE TO TREE IDENTIFICATION CAN BE FOUND ONLINE AT WWW.ARBORDAY.ORG/TREES. AND, WHILE IT FEATURES TREES THAT MAY OR MAY NOT BE FOUND IN YOUR AREA, THE WHAT TREE IS IT? WEBSITE AT HTTP://OPLIN.ORG/TREE DEMONSTRATES THE PROCESS OF NARROWING YOUR CHOICES BASED ON THE PHYSICAL CHARACTERISTICS OF LEAVES.

them. For older children, or for more realistic leaf prints, an inkpad may work best.

PRESS A LEAF

WHAT YOU NEED:

- freshly collected leaves
- newspaper or paper towels
- thick books

WHAT YOU DO:

1. Make sure your leaves are clean, gently brushing them off if necessary. Place your leaves between two layers of newspaper or paper towels.
2. Carefully place the leaf-and-paper sandwich inside a thick book, such as an old phone book. Add weight by stacking other thick books or bricks on top.
3. Allow the leaves to press for at least five days before checking on them; wait a week or two if possible.

This is the simplest method for pressing leaves and is a favorite way to save brightly colored autumn leaves. If pressed well, your leaves should last for several more months.

PRESERVE A LEAF

WHAT YOU NEED:

- leaves
- waxed paper
- an iron
- an old cloth

WHAT YOU DO:

1. Place one or more leaves on a sheet of waxed paper, arranging them carefully.
2. Place another sheet of waxed paper on top. Cover the top sheet with an old cloth.
3. Apply a dry, medium-hot iron to the cloth and gently press the waxed paper sandwich through the cloth. The sheets of waxed paper will appear less cloudy as they are heated and join together.

This technique will work with most leaves, but if you want to preserve your leaves for a longer time, try pressing them first before sealing them in the waxed paper. Before you begin, be sure to cover your ironing board or work surface with an old towel, cloth, or paper grocery bag to protect it.

More to Explore: Identification

The sheer multitude of tree species and the diversity of their leaves might seem a bit intimidating to someone just beginning to study them. But for children, tree identification is a terrific exercise in recognizing form and pattern, in ordering information and evaluating observations. But, more importantly, it can be a fun and rewarding puzzle that often comes down to a logical process of elimination—sometimes repeated several times over. With each decision, more and more possibilities are ruled out, until you are left with only a few, or even just one.

For example, all *coniferous* trees—we often call them evergreens, though a few of these cone-bearing trees actually drop their leaves in the fall—might, at first glance, appear similar. But a closer look distinguishes those that have true needles for leaves from those that have scaly needle-like leaves.

Those trees then can be differentiated, step by step, and question by question. How large is the tree? How are its branches arranged? What does the bark look like? Feel like?

Taking another look at the needles, what is their shape? Number? Texture? Length? How are they attached to the twig? Each successive question helps to rule species in or out until it becomes clear that a large, evergreen tree with elongated cones and long, thin needles, five to a bunch, most likely is a white pine.

Most of our tree species are *deciduous*, those broad-leafed trees that shed their leaves each year, and there can be a tremendous amount of variation among their leaves. But, with a little patience and a good field guide for reference, you can narrow the leaves you study down to the family, if not the exact species of their tree. Having an understanding of a few fundamental leaf terms makes the job a bit easier, and a little more satisfying, too.

In the most basic terms, a *simple leaf* is a single, complete leaf, attached by its stalk to a twig. A *compound leaf* is comprised of multiple leaflets that share a common stalk—the *midrib*—which in turn is attached to a twig.

Anyone who has done a leaf rubbing knows that the pattern of veins on a leaf can be beautiful. It also can be an aid to identification, as the arrangement of veins emphasizes the general shape of a leaf. *Palmate* leaves radiate from the leaf stem like fingers on a hand; pinnate leaves flow from a central axis, much like a feather.

Both palmate and pinnate leaves can be *lobed*—that is, having several distinct points—such as maples, and many kinds of oak. Another field mark to watch for is whether a leaf's edge—called its *margin*—is smooth, or *toothed* like a saw blade.

BOOK NOOK

Leaf Man
By Lois Ehlert
Age range: 4 to 8

This poetic picture book, with overlapping die-cut spreads, is illustrated by cut-paper collages of color-copied leaves, seeds, and tree fruits. Children will be delighted by the menagerie of creatures formed by leaves, and may be inspired to make leafy creations of their own.

OVER IN THE MEADOW

FIELDS AND MEADOWS are among the quintessential settings of childhood. These sun-kissed open spaces, serene yet brimming with life, give children a sense of possibility and the freedom to do anything—or nothing—from catching fireflies to playing catch.

Even a generation ago, grassy expanses of fields and meadowland—appearing in forms ranging from vacant neighborhood lots to the undeveloped land on the fringes of school or community property—remained a relatively common sight. But such space today is increasingly at a premium, and as the development boom continues, the only fields many children of cities and suburbs know are the manicured playing fields for soccer and other youth sports.

It may be that there's a certain ambiguity to fields and meadows; they often represent the rough or unfinished edges that have been neither completely tamed nor formally preserved. They are Mother Nature improvising, putting down roots and sending up shoots in an almost impromptu display of grasses, wildflowers, butterflies, birds, and bees. But these spaces are an essential part of the landscape of childhood, full of small wonders and simple delights not to be missed.

If you are able to, take the time and make it a point to visit these spaces with your child—many ideas for exploring them can be found on the pages that follow.

10

SEEKING OUT SEEDS

Wherever there are plants, there are seeds. Where there are seeds, there's magic.

In the old story of Jack and the Beanstalk, a poor boy trades away his family's cow for a handful of "magic beans," much to the dismay of his mother, who throws them out the window. As the story goes, those seeds germinate and grow overnight into a magic beanstalk that grows right up to the sky and beckons the boy to unimaginable adventure.

The story, of course, is just a fairy tale, though it wouldn't be much of a stretch to call any kind of seed magic in its own right. When no one is looking—in fact, often long after everyone has forgotten them—those little kernels can take a bit of soil, water, and sunlight and quietly, but surely, come to life.

Little packages filled with great potential, seeds from sunflower to sesame provide food not only for animals but for people as well—and a lot of food, at that. Rice, corn, and beans are incredibly important seed crops, both agriculturally and economically. It has been estimated that rice alone accounts for one-fifth of the calories consumed by humans. And the seeds from the fruit of a shrubby little tropical tree known as *Coffea arabica* are second only to petroleum as the world's most heavily traded commodity. (Perhaps magic beans are real: they also can be roasted and brewed into that hot beverage that is nothing short of spellbinding.)

Most wild seeds, however, simply have the daunting task of scattering, spreading, and perpetuating their species, and taking a closer look to see just how they do it can be both fascinating and fun. The plants of meadows and fields often yield particularly interesting and accessible seeds, making those open spaces a great place to look for them.

HOW SEEDS SCATTER

Have you ever wondered how plants, which are stationary, are able to spread and grow in different places? A seed walk—as we'll see shortly—holds the clues to how some of them do it, but there are several clever ways in which seeds get around.

By Land:

Seeds don't have legs, but many of them get around by attaching themselves to things that do. Burdocks and cockleburs have stiff spines ending in hooks that allow them to stick to an animal brushing past them. Beggarticks, sometimes called tickseeds because they are small, dark, and clingy, have little barbs that allow them to hitch a ride in much the same way. And a number of meadow grasses are topped off by a brushy cluster of spiky seeds—sometimes collectively called foxtails—that readily stick to passersby.

Burdock

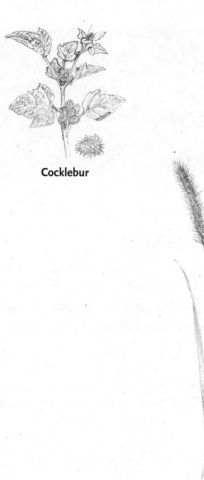

Cocklebur

Foxtail

(Meadow foxtail, a gentler meadow grass, has a softer, bushy top that does indeed closely resemble a fox's tail; its bristles are good for tickling chins and its stem is ideal for chewing thoughtfully.)

By Air:

Some of the most conspicuous seeds are dispersed in a very different manner—they are carried by the wind. Many familiar plants of meadows and fields produce fluffy, lightweight seeds designed to float on the breeze to a new location where they can establish themselves. The so-called parachute seeds of dandelion, thistle, cattail, and milkweed may differ slightly, but all are easily scattered by the wind—or by children—an efficient means of dispersal for plants growing close to the ground. Many trees, on the other hand, take advantage of their height by producing winged seeds that spin and flutter like helicopters to travel sometimes astonishing distances. Tulip tree, maple, and elm are among the trees producing such seeds.

By Other Means:

Many plants disperse their seeds in other, often unexpected, ways. Wild geraniums, violets, and touch-me-nots are among the flowering plants that produce *ballistic* seeds, which, as you might imagine, are launched like little projectiles—sometimes traveling several meters—as the result of tension within the seed capsule suddenly released. Never mind the name; by all means touch them if you happen upon them so that you can

Dandelion, milkweed, cattail, thistle

see, and feel, this interesting phenomenon for yourself.

And, whereas burr-like seeds hitch a ride on animals, still others are spread far and wide by passing *through* animals. This is especially true of fruit seeds such as berries and cherries, which are eaten by animals ranging from birds to bears and then scattered in their droppings. A bit disgusting, perhaps, but further proof that in nature, things might be messy but usually work out in the end.

EXPLORING SEEDS

Seedy science can be a great deal of fun. Here are a couple of ideas for up-close investigation of the ways in which seeds get around, and what happens once they've settled into the right conditions for growth.

TAKE A SEED WALK

Don't toss those ratty old stretched-out socks—use them to take your child on a seed walk.

Did You Know?

- -

THE WIDE, COARSE BLADES OF MEADOW GRASSES ARE IDEAL FOR MAKING GRASS WHISTLES. PRESS YOUR CUPPED HANDS TOGETHER WITH A BLADE OF GRASS STRETCHED TIGHTLY BETWEEN THE FIRST AND SECOND JOINTS OF YOUR THUMBS. THIS WILL MAKE A SIMPLE REED THAT CAN—WITH A BIT OF PRACTICE—PRODUCE SQUEAKY, SQUAWKY, WHISTLING SOUNDS WHEN YOU BLOW IT.

WHAT YOU NEED:

- old cotton tube socks or fuzzy wool socks
- a meadow or field thick with plants
- a magnifying glass

WHAT YOU DO:

1. Slip the socks onto your feet, right over your shoes, and pull them up over your pant legs as high as you can. (Grownups may need to stretch them out a bit, first.) If any of the socks are fuzzier on the inside than the outside, try wearing them inside-out. If you have enough socks, slip your hands and forearms into them, too.

2. Hike through a field or meadow, making sure to walk through or brush up against as many meadow grasses, flowers, and plants as possible, while taking care to avoid thorny brambles and poison ivy.

3. At the end of your walk, carefully remove the socks and examine the seeds that are stuck to them. Use the magnifying glass to get a closer look at the structure of the seeds. Can you see what allowed the seeds to stick to the socks? Is there anything that the different kinds of seeds seem to have in common? If no seeds at all are stuck to the socks, can you guess why not?

4. You can try to grow the seeds you collected by planting your socks in a pan or flower pot filled with a couple of inches of topsoil or potting soil. Moisten the socks and seeds first by spraying them with water, and cover them with an inch or so of soil. Place the planter in a sunny spot, water the soil periodically to keep it from drying out, and see what sprouts.

REMEMBER: CONDUCT A QUICK "TICK CHECK" AFTER YOUR WALK TO MAKE SURE YOU HAVEN'T PICKED UP MORE THAN JUST SEEDS.

SPROUTING SEEDS

With just water, warmth, and soil—and a little bit of patience—your child can watch seeds sprout to life.

WHAT YOU NEED:

- birdseed
- a flower pot
- topsoil or potting soil
- a warm, sunny location

WHAT YOU DO:

1. Put a handful of birdseed in a cup of spring water and allow it to soak overnight. For best results, use a birdseed mix containing a variety of seeds, such as millet.
2. Add the soil to the flower pot. Sprinkle the drained birdseed on top, and cover it with an additional half-inch or so of soil.
3. Place the pot in a warm, sunny location, watering the soil as necessary to keep it moist or damp. A south-facing windowsill makes a good location for trying this activity during the colder months.
4. Monitor the activity in the flower pot for the next couple of weeks.

Encourage your child to record his or her observations in a notebook or journal.

At what point did the first sprouts appear? How many kinds of seeds seem to have sprouted? Did they sprout at the same time?

For a variation on this activity, separate the dif-

More to Explore: Dandelions

Without a doubt, the most common seeds many of us see are the downy white puffballs of dandelions, our most familiar wildflowers—like them or not. But despite the best efforts of homeowners to eradicate them—and their prolific seeds—from their manicured lawns, dandelions keep coming back, able to flourish in even the most unfavorable of conditions. If nothing else, you have to admire their adaptability and their perseverance.

Once you forgive them for being weeds, you might even find them charming again. They are, after all, the quintessential flowers of childhood, with their cheerful yellow crowns and irresistible balls of fluffy seeds, steeped deeply in folklore. You played with them when you were young, so why not have a little dandelion fun with your child?

Make a wish

holding a yellow dandelion crown under some-one's chin on a sunny day, you could determine whether that person liked butter—a bit of yellow color reflected onto his or her skin meant yes. (The same technique also can be tried with the accordingly named buttercups.) It's far from scientific, to be sure, but lots of tickly fun nonetheless.

Make a Dandelion Chain

Like daisies, dandelions can easily be woven into floral chains to be worn as necklaces or crowns. Pick several thick-stemmed yellow dandelions and join them together by making slits in their stems with a penknife or fingernail and then threading the next dandelion through, all the way to its head. (The milky white sap is safe to touch.) For best results, slit each dandelion after you've passed it through the stem of the dandelion before it, and knot the first and last together to complete the chain. Trim the excess stems, or twine the loose ends around the chain as you go.

Make a Meal

If you feel adventurous, harvest the tender young leaves of dandelions for palatable, though slightly bitter, greens suitable for salads or for sautéing. For best results, pick the vitamin-rich leaves before the flowers appear, and be sure to wash them well before eating—but don't eat them at all if they may have been exposed to lawn chemicals. And waste not, want not: even dandelion flowers have epicurean value, and can be turned into a sweet, light-bodied wine with citrus notes.

ferent kinds of birdseed after soaking and plant them in groups; this will make it easier to observe the differences among them. Or, turn it into a science experiment by planting several small containers of seeds, varying the amount of sunlight or water each receives, and recording the results.

Beat the Clock

Another common name for dandelions, *blowballs,* comes from their most distinctive feature, the wispy white ball of seeds—sometimes called a *clock*—that remains after the yellow flower has faded. Every child, at least once, should make a wish on a dandelion clock, puffing extra hard to scatter every last parachute seed—the necessary magic to make the wish come true.

Butter Me Up

Children of previous generations knew that dandelions held great predictive powers. Simply by

GOING WILD FOR FLOWERS

Don't mistake them for mere shrinking violets—wildflowers can be full of surprises.

Of all the names people have used over the years to describe their neighbors in the natural world, some of the most colorful have been given to wildflowers. Names such as shooting star and ironweed, black-eyed Susan and joe-pye weed, bee balm and boneset are steeped in folklore and rich in imagination.

They hearken back to a time when people lived more intimately with nature and held these plants in high regard, not just for their beauty but for their usefulness as well. Before the advent of modern medicine, many were prized for their herbal or medicinal properties. Even today, ordinary meadow flowers such as sunflower, chicory, and purple coneflower—you may know the last one as echinacea—remain important for the various food products and herbal remedies derived from them.

As your adventures take you to meadows, fields, and open spaces, take some time to appreciate the wildflowers you encounter. There's often more to these delicate beauties than meets the eye—and here are some ideas intended to help you discover and enjoy them in new ways.

TAKE A CLOSER LOOK

Wildflowers are amazing in both form and function, with delicate inner workings and intricate details that require closer inspection to fully appreciate them. Try these ideas for seeing the secrets they have to reveal.

MAKING FIELD DRAWINGS

A meadow or field in full bloom is a study in color, shape, and form; it's no wonder, therefore, that artists always have been drawn to them for subject matter and inspiration.

Take a good look at the flowers in a meadow, field, or clearing—or, if it's more accessible to you, a botanical garden. Which is your favorite? Why?

See if you can capture that flower in a sketch—one of the best ways to better comprehend wildflowers is by trying to make an accurate field drawing of them.

WHAT YOU NEED:

- a spiral-bound sketchbook
- lead pencils
- colored pencils

WHAT YOU DO:

1. Find the best angle for viewing and sketching your flower, where the most prominent or distinctive features are clearly visible.
2. Look closely at the flower's petals. How many are there? What shape are they? How are they arranged? Are there noticeable structures between them? Under them?

> **TIP:** WHEN PHOTOGRAPHING WILDFLOWERS UP CLOSE WITH AN AUTOMATIC CAMERA, TRY USING ITS PORTRAIT OR MACRO MODE. EITHER WILL NARROW THE DEPTH OF FIELD SO THAT THE FLOWER REMAINS IN FOCUS, WHILE THE BACKGROUND BLURS AND SOFTENS TO LET THE SUBJECT STAND OUT.

3. Take a good look at the leaves. How many are there? What shape are they? Are their edges smooth? Toothed? How are they arranged on the main stem of the plant?
4. Begin by sketching the outlines of the flower, leaves, and stem—taking care to capture their shapes and proportions accurately—and then adding details, shading, and color.

PRESSING AND MOUNTING WILDFLOWERS

Capturing them in sketches and photographs might be the most satisfying—and least disruptive—way to "collect" wildflowers. But collecting the occasional wildflower specimen to preserve and study can be an engaging way to cultivate your child's interest in nature. It's also a good opportunity to teach responsibility and ethical behavior in the great outdoors.

Remember never to take flowers unless you have permission to do so. Collecting without a permit is forbidden on some public—and all private—

Ready for pressing

lands. Take care to disturb the environment as little as possible, and never take the only flower in any given location; even better, take a flower only if it is one of many.

Like botanists or field scientists, you can try to dry and mount your own wildflower. Here's how.

WHAT YOU NEED:

- sheets of plain newsprint paper
- corrugated cardboard
- heavy books or bricks
- white glue
- a craft paintbrush
- acid-free paper
- waxed paper

WHAT YOU DO:

1. Carefully cut or gently remove the flower, including the stem, leaves, and—if possible, for smaller flowers—the roots. Gently remove any dirt and soil from the roots before pressing.

2. To help preserve it until you get home, keep your flower in a cold lunch pack or cooler.

3. Lay out your flower on a sheet of newsprint paper. Carefully arrange the petals and leaves for display before covering the flower with another sheet of newsprint paper.

4. Sandwich the flower and newsprint sheets between two pieces of corrugated cardboard. Place the flower, sheets of paper, and cardboard underneath or between heavy books. Place additional books or bricks on top to add weight.

5. Allow a week or so for your flower to dry thoroughly. Circulating air from a fan may aid the drying process, but avoid heating the flower, which can cause it to brown.

6. Once it has dried, remove the flower and lightly brush white glue onto its backside before affixing it to a sheet of acid-free paper.

7. Cover the flower with a sheet of waxed paper and return it to the press for a few hours to allow the glue to dry.

A COLORFUL EXPERIMENT

If you happen upon long-stemmed wildflowers with white petals, you may have found subjects for a fun, easy experiment you can do with your child. Look for common, widespread flowers such as Queen Anne's lace or any number of daisies, asters, or fleabanes. If there are many healthy flowers growing together—and if you have permission to do so—cut a few and take them home. If wildflowers aren't available, you can try this same experiment with a store-bought flower such as a carnation or chrysanthemum.

- drinking glasses
- water
- food coloring

WHAT YOU DO:

1. With a sharp knife, carefully trim the end of each flower stem at an angle. Avoid using scissors, which will pinch the stem and prevent water from traveling through it.
2. In a drinking glass, mix about a half cup of water and enough drops of liquid food coloring to dye the water deeply. You may wish to fill several glasses with different colors.
3. Place a cut flower in each glass and wait. Check back after a few hours, and periodically over the next couple of days, to observe the changes.

WHY IT WORKS:

If everything works properly, the white flower petals will begin to take on the color of the water. The colored water is drawn up through the flower stem—through water-conducting tissue called *xylem*—by a process called *capillary action*. The tendency of water molecules to adhere to each other causes them to rise up, in much the same way the corner of a dishcloth or paper towel can wick away a spill.

When you drink through a straw, your mouth creates the negative pressure to draw up the liquid by sucking. In a plant, that force is caused by a process called *transpiration*. Essentially, the evaporation of water in the plant creates the

---

More to Explore: Appreciating Pollinators

When we see a flower, we're not just regarding an aesthetically pleasing part of a plant—we're looking at the part of the plant responsible for reproduction. And for many of these plants, that only can be accomplished by attracting *pollinators*, the creatures that transfer pollen—the dusty grains containing reproductive material—from one flower to another, making fertilization possible.

A flower's vivid color and beautiful shape, its aromatic fragrance, the sweetness of its nectar—each of these can entice a pollinator to visit.

Bees, wasps, butterflies, beetles, and flies all are important pollinators. What do you notice about the flowers that are attractive to each of them? Do you notice any flowers that don't seem to attract any pollinators?

Not all flowers rely on pollinators to spread their pollen and aid their reproduction. Some produce fine pollen that is dispersed by wind, as anyone who suffers from hay fever—an allergic reaction to airborne pollen—could tell you.

Goldenrod, one of the most common flowers of fields and meadows, unfairly gets the blame for causing hay fever in late summer and early fall. But goldenrod is a lovely flower, useful to the bees and other insects that pollinate it. The real culprit is ragweed, which typically blooms at the same time and in the same location as goldenrod, releasing its allergenic pollen. Because ragweed is so inconspicuous, many people wrongly assume that goldenrod is causing their allergies.

TIP: FOR HELP IDENTIFYING THE FLOWERS, SHRUBS, AND TREES YOU ENCOUNTER, CONSULT WWW .WILDFLOWER.ORG OR HTTP:// PLANTS.USDA.GOV FOR DETAILED DESCRIPTIONS, PHOTOGRAPHS, AND RANGE MAPS.

negative pressure to draw more water up from its roots.

You may have noticed that different houseplants require different amounts of water, or that the same plant may seem to need more or less water in different conditions. You can test how the environment might affect transpiration—and therefore how much water a plant draws up from its roots. Try placing one flower in a hu-mid place and another in a dry place. Or place one flower in a hot, sunny location and another where it's cool and shaded. Over time, which flower seems to draw more of the colored water up to its petals?

FINDING A FLOWERY FEAST

Meadow wildflowers have long found their way into our kitchens—from the nutty seeds and oil of sunflower to the soothing tea made from chamomile. But watch for these common wildflowers—they can lead you to tasty treats you can enjoy right in the field.

BERRIES

On springtime walks through meadows, fields, hillsides, and clearings—especially in the thickets, brambles, and fencerows at the edges of these open spaces—keep an eye out for the emergence of small, star-like white flowers clustered together

Did You Know?

THE FAMILIAR FLOWER KNOWN AS QUEEN ANNE'S LACE HAS BECOME SO WIDESPREAD THAT IN MANY PARTS OF NORTH AMERICA IT IS CONSIDERED A WEED. ORIGINALLY BROUGHT TO AMERICA DURING COLONIAL TIMES, IT'S A CLOSE RELATIVE OF WILD CARROT—THE WILD PLANT FROM WHICH OUR GARDEN CARROTS WERE DOMESTICATED.

LIKE MANY FLOWERS, IT HAS A COLORFUL NAME TRACED TO FOLKLORE. THE PREVAILING MYTH LINKS IT TO QUEEN ANNE OF ENGLAND, WHO IS SAID TO HAVE PRICKED HER FINGER WHILE SEWING LACE. THE DELICATE CLUSTER OF WHITE FLOWERS WITH A SINGLE REDDISH-PURPLE FLOWER IN THE CENTER RESEMBLES LACE WITH A DROP OF BLOOD IN THE MIDDLE.

Tip: Learn more about pollinators of all kinds—and the essential role they play in our lives—by visiting the Pollinator Partnership at http://pollinator.org.

Black raspberry

on thorny, cane-like shrubs. Should you find them, remember the spot; before long, the most delicious wild berries will be yours for the picking.

Those white flowers soon will give way to the sweet-tart fruits called *black raspberries,* though you may know them by a number of other names, including *black-caps, thimbleberries,* or *blackberries.* (Black raspberries are related to—and in many ways similar to—the blackberries you can find at the market, but each is a unique fruit unto itself.) Whatever you call them, they are delightful, and finding and picking them is a summertime tradition going back generations.

One never should pick, much less eat, just any old berry, however. Fortunately, black raspberries are easy to identify. Here are some tips to make

sure you've got the right plant before heading out with your kids and filling your berry baskets.

Flowers

Black raspberry flowers are small but conspicuous, with five white, distinctly separate petals arrayed in a manner suggesting a star, appearing in clusters of several individual flowers. The flowers typically appear in May or June, but can be seen as early as April or as late as July in some areas.

Leaves

Look for compound leaves with three, or sometimes five, toothed leaflets, with the leaflet at the end of stem similar to, but larger than, the others. The underside of the leaves is a noticeably paler

Did You Know?

Honeybees and clover—one of the most common wildflowers—are a perfect match. Clover is the most popular honey plant in America. It has been estimated that honeybees are responsible for pollinating the plants that comprise one-fourth of the human diet.

greenish-white and is somewhat fuzzy or hairy; the leaves are darker green and hairless above.

Stems and Twigs

Black raspberry belongs to the rose family and appears as a prickly, tangled shrub. Young stems are pale greenish, while older, thicker canes are purplish-red in color. Both have thorny spines; watch out for them while picking berries. The variation of this plant found west of the Rockies has at least partially white bark, and is commonly known as *whitebark raspberry*.

Fruit

Beginning in early summer, dime-sized black raspberries will appear. The berries themselves, when ripe, are purplish-black, though fruit of different stages—greenish, reddish, purplish—may appear together on the same plant. Ripe berries come off the stem easily with a gentle twist and pull, and reveal a hollow where they had been attached to the plant.

Make a Black Raspberry Parfait

Even a handful of black raspberries is enough to make this sweet, refreshing treat.

WHAT YOU NEED:

- black raspberries
- low-fat vanilla yogurt
- granola
- honey

WHAT YOU DO:

1. Gently wash the black raspberries by rinsing them in cold water and draining them in a colander. Don't wash your berries until you're ready to eat them.
2. In a parfait glass, layer the yogurt, black raspberries, and granola. If you don't have a parfait glass, simply layer the ingredients in a small bowl.
3. Drizzle a spoonful of honey on top, and dig in.

HONEYSUCKLE

In many parts of the country, one of the surest signs that warmer weather has arrived is the sweet fragrance of honeysuckle drifting over fields and woodlots. From late spring into summer, especially on the fringes where developed areas meet undeveloped ones, you can find the small, yellow-white flowers of *bush honeysuckle* in bloom—elongated trumpets with showy, flared ends.

Even children and adults who aren't familiar with wildflowers, trees, and shrubs may know

Extracting nectar from bush honeysuckle

this plant—and the secret for extracting its nectar. Here's an introduction to—or refresher course on—a classic bit of delicious outdoor fun.

WHAT YOU DO:

1. Carefully remove an entire honeysuckle flower from the plant. It should pull free fairly easily.

2. Look for the little bit of green at the narrow base of the flower's tube-like trumpet. Holding the flower petals in one hand, *gently* pinch this green structure—called the *calyx*—between the thumbnail and forefinger of your other hand, and slowly pull it away from the rest of the flower. Pinching too hard will sever the calyx; it may take a couple of tries for you to get the feel of it.

3. As you pull the calyx away, it will reveal a stringy white structure called the *style*. Continue to pull, slowly and gently, until the entire style has been drawn back through the base of the flower.

4. A drop of nectar should appear at the base of the flower petals, ready for you to enjoy.

Did You Know?

ALTHOUGH HARVESTING ITS SWEET NECTAR IS A SIMPLE CHILDHOOD DELIGHT, BUSH HONEYSUCKLE HAS A BITTERSWEET STORY. WHILE ITS FLOWERS ARE BOTH BEAUTIFUL AND FRAGRANT, THAT BELIES JUST HOW PROBLEMATIC THIS PLANT CAN BE. UNLIKE OUR NATIVE HONEYSUCKLES—WHICH TYPICALLY ARE WOODY, FLOWERING VINES USEFUL TO WILDLIFE—BUSH HONEYSUCKLE IS AN *INVASIVE ALIEN*, TAKING OVER AND CROWDING OUT NATURALLY OCCURRING PLANTS, ESPECIALLY IN PLACES WHERE THEIR HABITAT ALREADY HAS BEEN DISTURBED. SO FORGET ANY LINGERING GUILT YOU MIGHT HAVE FELT AT THE THOUGHT OF PLUCKING THESE HEALTHY FLOWERS BY THE DOZEN, AND REST ASSURED THAT YOU'RE DOING NO REAL HARM.

CHASING SUMMER BUGS

Take them or leave them, it's hard to ignore them.

Oftentimes, we don't give insects a second thought. But the warm, wonderful days of summer just wouldn't be the same without them. From the lazy-day din of cicadas and grasshoppers, to the glow of fireflies at twilight, to the sultry nighttime chorus of crickets and katydids, it is the sights and sounds of insects that give the season its very atmosphere.

Get outside, enjoy the show, and try these ideas for revisiting old summer friends—or making a few new ones—with your child.

CAPTURING CRITTERS

Earlier, we learned several simple ways to get a better look at bugs by attracting them to and catching them with different kinds of traps. With many of the bugs of summer, however, the straightforward approach is best—and several ideas for capturing them by hand or by net follow.

Sweep netting in a meadow

Make a Sweep Net

The fields and meadows of summertime are bustling with insect life. One of the best ways to get a closer look is to walk through a grassy area with a sweep net, which you can make from household materials. Here's how to make a simple, but effective, one with your child.

What you need:

- a wire coat hanger
- pliers or metal snips
- an old pillowcase
- scissors
- an old broomstick or wooden handle
- duct tape
- a clear plastic or glass jar with perforated lid

What you do:

1. Straighten the wire hanger by first untwisting it with the pliers or by cutting off the hook with the snips. Bend the hanger into a circular loop, leaving several inches of straight wire at both ends.

2. With the scissors, make a small hole on ei-

ther side of the seam where the pillowcase is hemmed, taking care to cut through only the outer layer of fabric. Thread the wire loop through one hole, through the hem, and back out through the other hole, like the drawstring on a pair of sweat pants.

3. Secure the ends of the wire loop to the end of the broomstick by wrapping them tightly with duct tape. For a stronger connection, fasten cable ties (also known as zip ties) tightly over the tape, and trim the excess. Another alternative is to drill a small hole through the diameter of the broomstick, two or three inches from the end, into which the ends of the wire can be bent and inserted before securing the wire to the handle with duct tape.

4. Head out to a meadow, field, or other grassy area—the higher the grass, the better—and slowly walk through, sweeping through the grass as you go. Experiment with moving the net from side to side or in a figure-eight pattern, but always leading with the mouth of the net.

5. After a few minutes, pause to collect the bugs you've caught in the net. Start by holding the net away from you, open side up,

An insect looking-jar

Catching fireflies

to allow any bees or wasps you may have caught to work their way free and fly away. Shake the net to collect the insects at the bottom and keep them in place by gently pinching the net just above that point with one hand before transferring them to your clear jar for observation.

What have you caught? Sweep netting is a particularly good way to collect beetles (such as ladybugs or click beetles), true bugs (such as stinkbugs or assassin bugs), and even the occasional cricket, mantis, or grasshopper. After you're through studying them, remember to return your bugs to the field where you caught them.

Lightning in a Bottle

If you were to ask a group of adults to reminisce about spending their summer days and evenings as children outdoors, and to distill the wonder of those seasons down to a single memory, chances are that catching fireflies would be near the top of the list.

As well it should be. For as a summer day faded to twilight, the appearance of the dancing, flashing lights of fireflies—perhaps you knew them as lightning bugs—could transform any field, yard, or vacant lot from a mundane space into a place

of enchantment. The fact that you could hold that everyday sort of magic in your own hands made it all the more remarkable.

Unfortunately, the firefly population seems to be on the decline, in large part because people are taking over many of the open fields, meadows, and marshes that comprise their habitat. There are, however, many places where this annual light show still is in full swing, so be sure to catch it with your child, if you can.

Here are a few more ideas for firefly fun:

Patio Lanterns

Catch fireflies by gentling cupping your hand over them. Transfer them to a clear glass jar with a perforated lid—a baby food or jelly jar works well—and watch your fireflies glow. Check out their lanterns by looking through the glass at the underside of the fireflies, and be sure to keep your fireflies for only a little while before releasing them.

Flashlight Tag

Firefly flashing is a form of courtship; male fireflies on the wing flash their signals to the females, who in turn flash back from their hiding places in the trees, grass, or bushes. If a female gives him the "green light," so to speak, the male will make his way to the female and the two will mate. But if you watch closely, you will see that what seems like random flashing actually is a code of light pulses. Some are long, some short, some are fast, some slow; it's not unlike the dots and dashes of Morse code, but with light. With a small flashlight or pen-light, try to emulate the flashes you see—you just might get a response from a lovesick firefly.

Lights Out

The best time to see fireflies is a still, moonless summer night, when there is sufficient darkness for them to send and receive their flashing light signals. But moonlight isn't the only thing fireflies have to contend with. The ever-increasing light pollution caused by people has driven the fireflies in many areas to dim their lights. You can make your backyard or green space more firefly-friendly by turning off outside lights, providing bushes and low-hanging trees for cover, and avoiding the use of lawn chemicals whenever possible.

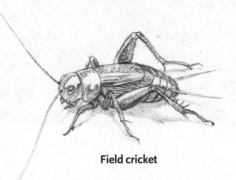

Field cricket

CRICKETS!

Though they prefer the damp, dark habitat of leaf litter, crickets are common meadow insects that can be found almost anywhere, from woods to backyards and around—even inside of—homes. Their unmistakable chirping begins in earnest with the warmer temperatures of summer and typically continues until autumn arrives.

Crickets are among the most popular of insects, appearing as beloved characters in classic films *(Pinocchio)* and books *(A Cricket in Times Square)*. But they also have another, rather unique talent: they can be used as thermometers.

Did You Know?

EVEN THESE GENTLE, SEEMINGLY PEACEFUL BEETLES HAVE A MENACING SIDE. THE FEMALES OF SOME FIREFLY SPECIES WILL COPY THE FLASH PATTERN OF THE FEMALES OF OTHER SPECIES. THEN, WHEN THE MALES OF THAT OTHER SPECIES COME TO VISIT, THE COPYCATS EAT THEM. ALL'S FAIR IN LOVE AND WAR, EVEN FOR FIREFLIES, IT SEEMS.

CRICKET THERMOMETERS

Because crickets, like all insects, are *ectothermic*—that is, cold-blooded—their level of activity rises and falls with the temperature. By counting their chirps and doing some basic math, you can make a pretty good estimate of the current temperature. Here's how:

WHAT YOU NEED:

- a chirping cricket
- a watch or clock with a second hand

WHAT YOU DO:

1. Count the number of cricket chirps you hear in fourteen seconds. You may wish to try this a few times to arrive at a consistent count.
2. Take the number of chirps and add forty to estimate the current temperature in degrees Fahrenheit.
3. If you have access to an outdoor thermometer, compare your calculation to the reading on the thermometer. Are the figures close?

This is strictly a summertime trick; male crickets are chirping to attract mates, and the evenings are generally warm, at that time. Once the mercury dips down into the low fifties, you won't hear much chirping.

More to Explore: Spittlebugs and Froghoppers

Plenty of creatures—such as grasshoppers—protect or defend themselves by spitting in one way or another. Of all the self-defense mechanisms found in nature, that of *spittlebugs* is one of the more interesting ones. As their name implies, these nymphs of the insects known as *froghoppers* produce a lot of spittle—so much so that they make a frothy, bubbly mass in which the spittlebugs can hide from predators and remain in a safe, humid environment while they grow to maturity.

You can find spittlebugs in almost any field or meadow. Simply look for what appears to be a bubbly white glob of saliva on meadow grasses and flowering plants, especially near the stems or at the base of leaves. If you dare, wipe it aside with your finger—or a stick, if you don't—to reveal the little spittlebug hiding within. (Don't worry; both spittle and bug are harmless.)

Spittlebug, by the way, may be a bit of a misnomer. While the bubbles it produces certainly do resemble saliva, the fluid and air it mixes to create them are actually expelled from the creature's rear end.

As adults, spittlebugs have an even bigger claim to fame—the froghopper has been crowned the world's greatest leaper. These widespread insects of grassy areas are less than a quarter-inch long, but can push off so quickly and so forcefully that they can leap well over two feet into the air—the equivalent of a human jumping over a tall office building. By so doing, froghoppers generate a force 400 times greater than gravity. This is an enormous feat, considering that humans jump with a force exceeding gravity by only two or three times, and fleas—amazing leapers in their own right—only 135 times.

Now, that's certainly nothing to spit at.

RAISING MONARCHS

Monarchs and milkweed—they get by with a little help from their friends.

Monarchs are the most familiar, popular, and remarkable species of butterfly—but an ordinary wildflower is the key to getting close to them.

Upon first glance, the butterfly and the plant might seem to make an unlikely couple. The monarch is a regal little creature decked out in vivid orange and black. Milkweed, a rather plain and unassuming flower of meadows, fields, and roadsides, is perhaps most noticeable long after its flowers have faded and its conspicuous pods of fluffy white seeds appear. But the two share a remarkable connection.

Adult monarch butterflies frequently visit milkweed flowers and feed upon their nectar. However, monarchs really rely upon milkweed as their one and only host plant. Their larvae—monarch caterpillars—feed exclusively on the leaves of the milkweed plant, and monarchs therefore lay their eggs only on the underside of milkweed leaves.

One good turn deserves another: the monarch is one of the most important pollinators of milkweed, which relies primarily upon butterflies and bees for pollination. Their interdependence is more than just interesting science; it allows us to take a closer look at one of nature's most amazing transformations.

MAKE A HOME FOR MONARCHS

A long-time favorite activity in elementary school science classrooms, rearing monarch caterpillars and watching them transform into adult butterflies, is a perfect way to share a little natural wonder with your child. It's also a good opportunity to cultivate patience and dedication in young learners, as the project requires daily attention, but for a manageable length of time; monarchs typically grow from larvae to adults in less than four weeks. And, of course, the outcome of caterpillars raised successfully is nothing short of spectacular. All you need is a source of fresh milkweed, a few monarch caterpillars, and a ventilated container or cage.

The following instructions will help you get started.

HARVESTING MILKWEED AND CATERPILLARS

In order to find—and feed—monarch caterpillars, you first need to find milkweed. Fortunately, this plant is common and widespread, easily found in sunny areas at the edges of fields, meadows, road-

A monarch caterpillar

Milkweed

sides, and other open areas. There are many varieties of milkweed suitable for monarchs but the primary one, *common milkweed,* can be identified by its round clusters of small, dull flowers ranging in color from pale green to purplish to pink. Its leaves, broadly oval in shape and with somewhat hairy undersides, appear in alternating pairs on opposite sides of the plant's stem.

While it is possible to raise monarchs from their tiny white eggs—which, with a little luck, can be found affixed singly to the underside of milkweed leaves—it is easier to find, and begin your project with, their larvae. Monarch caterpillars can be found on and around the leaves of milkweed plants, their only source of food. The caterpillars are distinctively colored, striped in black, white, and yellow, and develop black antennae-like filaments at either end as they grow larger. Look for them on milkweed plants with leaves showing signs of damage from hungry little mouths. Handle them very carefully; even better, collect them by simply taking the leaf you found them on.

Did You Know?

MONARCHS ALSO HAVE MILKWEED TO THANK FOR THEIR MOST IMPORTANT DEFENSE MECHANISM. BY CONSUMING MILKWEED PLANTS, MONARCH CATERPILLARS INGEST AND STORE TOXIC CHEMICAL COMPOUNDS THAT DO NOT HARM THEM, BUT THAT MAKE THEM DISTASTEFUL—EVEN POISONOUS—TO PREDATORS, EVEN AS ADULT BUTTERFLIES. BIRDS WILL ONLY TRY TO EAT A MONARCH ONCE; THE CHEMICAL COMPOUNDS TASTE AWFUL TO THEM, CAUSING THEM TO RETCH AND VOMIT.

Unless you are growing your own milkweed in a garden or in a container, locating wild milkweed plants is essential—it not only shows you where you can find and collect your monarch caterpillars, it also provides you a source for the fresh milkweed leaves you will need for the daily feeding of your caterpillars. If possible, harvest the entire milkweed plant and take it home with you. You also can pick fresh milkweed leaves each day, or harvest several days' worth of milkweed at a time, keeping it moist and covered by plastic in the refrigerator.

A Container for Your Caterpillars

Once you have found milkweed and collected your monarch caterpillars, all you will need is a proper—although temporary—home for them. A wide variety of homemade cages and containers will do the trick, so long as they meet a few basic criteria.

A suitable container for rearing monarchs:

- will have a breathable lid or sides to allow proper ventilation

- will provide more than enough room for an adult monarch to spread its wings
- will be easy to open for daily cleaning and feeding

The simplest approach is to take a clear container—anything from a large glass jar to a plastic bin to an aquarium—and to top it off with a flat, breathable, removable cover; mesh screens, netting, or even nylon pantyhose will work. This will allow you a clear view of the action inside, while providing the caterpillars plenty of air flow and a surface from which they can hang their chrysalides.

TIP: TO LEARN ABOUT DIFFERENT KINDS OF MILKWEED AND WHERE TO FIND THEM, VISIT HTTP://PLANTS .USDA.GOV, WWW.ENATURE.COM, OR WWW.WILDFLOWER.ORG.

Caring for Your Caterpillars

Give your caterpillars the best chance of reaching adulthood by following these few simple instructions.

What you do:

1. Keep your monarch container at a comfortably warm temperature. Avoid direct sunlight, excessive heat, and extremes in humidity.
2. Add fresh milkweed to the container each day if possible, every other day at a minimum. Keeping the stems of freshly cut milkweed moist will help it to stay fresher, longer.
3. Every time you add fresh milkweed, clean out the floor of the container as well. The hard little pellets you will find are a kind of debris called *frass*—the proper name for insect poop.

Tip: To see photos of monarch caterpillars and for detailed information on all aspects of rearing monarchs, visit http://monarchlab.org or http://monarchwatch.org.

4. Continue this routine each day, sketching and making note of the changes you observe in a journal, until every caterpillar is snug inside its chrysalis.

What should happen:

The length of a monarch's life cycle, from egg to adulthood, is approximately one month. The egg stage, a tiny white dot laid on the underside of a milkweed leaf, lasts just a few days before

Did You Know?

Even though they seem to have far too many legs to be considered insects, caterpillars are just that. If you look closely, you'll notice that only a caterpillar's first three pairs of legs are jointed. These are true legs, and a caterpillar only and always has six of them. The remaining legs—the stubby, fleshy bumpy ones running along the rest of its body—are known as *prolegs*, which help the caterpillar to move as it ripples along. When a caterpillar completes its transformation into an adult butterfly or moth, the prolegs will be gone, but the six true legs will remain.

the egg darkens and the larval stage—a caterpillar—emerges.

As they grow, monarch caterpillars go through a succession of changes called *instars,* where they molt, or shed their skins. Over a period of two weeks or so, monarch caterpillars go through five instars, each similar to, but larger than, the last.

When the final instar climbs to the top of the container and hangs in a J-shape, it's getting ready for the next stage, and the last stage before it reaches adulthood. A monarch spends one and a half to two weeks as a *pupa,* safe inside its chrysalis. When the chrysalis darkens and becomes translucent, the adult soon will emerge. Though it might appear to be struggling, resist the temptation to help a butterfly out of its chrysalis.

To avoid damaging newly emerged adult butterflies, wait several hours before handling them. Enjoy studying them, handle them very carefully, and be sure to release them into the wild the next day.

More to Explore: Monarch Migration

By relying solely upon milkweed for their continued survival, North American monarchs lead a life with little margin for error. But for monarchs beating the odds, that's only half the story.

Many butterflies hibernate in the winter, sheltering in protected places and waiting out the cold weather. But monarchs undertake a massive migration as the weather cools and the days shorten, and there is nothing else quite like it anywhere in the world. Most of the late summer monarchs in North America—all of them east of the Rockies, save for a fraction of the population along the Atlantic coast that ends up in Florida—make the journey of up to three thousand miles to the mountains of central Mexico. There, as many as one hundred million monarchs congregate in an isolated region of oyamel fir forests, where they huddle together and hang by the thousands from tree branches, riding out the winter in more hospitable climes.

The thought of these delicate beauties making the same sort of physically demanding migration as many of our songbirds is remarkable enough. But unlike their avian counterparts, which make both the southward and northbound journeys individually, oftentimes year after year, the back-and-forth migration of monarchs is guided by instinct and completed over several generations. The monarchs' ability to navigate unerringly to a place they've never been is astounding—the butterflies that make the migration each fall have only their great-great-grandparents' memory of their wintering grounds to guide them. It may not be finding a needle in haystack, but it sure can't be far from it.

Did You Know?

THE BRIGHT, BOLD ORANGE AND BLACK COLORING OF MONARCHS SERVES AS A WARNING SIGN TO BIRDS AND OTHER PREDATORS TO STAY AWAY. TWO OTHER BUTTERFLY SPECIES, VICEROYS AND QUEENS, RESEMBLE MONARCHS; BOTH ARE DISTASTEFUL TO BIRDS AS WELL, AND BY MIMICKING EACH OTHER'S COLORS AND PATTERNS, ALL REMAIN SAFE FROM PREDATORS. EVEN MILKWEED BUGS, COMMON TRUE BUGS THAT CONGREGATE AND FEED IN LARGE GROUPS ON MILKWEED PLANTS, ADVERTISE THEIR MILKWEED-INDUCED TOXICITY IN BRIGHT ORANGE AND BLACK COLORS OF THEIR OWN.

BOOK NOOK

BECOMING BUTTERFLIES
BY ANNE ROCKWELL
ILLUSTRATED BY MEGAN HALSEY
AGE RANGE: 4 TO 8

THIS INFORMATIVE PAPERBACK TELLS THE STORY OF THE MONARCH BUTTERFLY'S LIFE CYCLE BY FOLLOWING THE PROGRESS OF THE CATERPILLARS GROWING IN A SCHOOL CLASSROOM. THE CHARMING ILLUSTRATIONS—LAYERED CUTOUTS FROM PAINTINGS DONE ON ROUGH WATERCOLOR PAPER—STRIKE THE RIGHT BALANCE BETWEEN ACCURACY AND FANCY.

IT'S A SHORE THING

THE PREVAILING SCIENTIFIC WISDOM states that life on our planet had its origins in water, and whatever circumstances brought it into being, this much is certain: water still equals life. Human beings are comprised mostly of the stuff—we're 65 percent water—which is essential to virtually every bodily system and function. Going more than a couple of days without it poses a very serious risk; more than week without it is almost certainly fatal.

We're hardly unique in that regard. Water sustains all manner of life forms, both simple and complex, and not just those that take it internally. Countless species depend upon it to provide them food, a place for reproduction, and their very habitat. It's no wonder, then, that environments with water—both fresh and salt water—teem with life, from microscopic creatures to the largest living thing on Earth.

For the families that explore these places and the creatures that inhabit them, the adventures and discoveries can happen on an intimate scale, whether the setting is as approachable as a pond or stream or as vast as the ocean itself.

In the pages that follow, we'll look at several of them.

EXPLORING PONDS AND STREAMS

If you think there's not much to see in a pond or stream—well, you're all wet.

Ponds and streams are amazing places, brimming with life both above and below. And the point at which the world of water meets the world of air is an incredibly vibrant place; some creatures actually spend the majority of their lives literally walking that razor-thin line. Many others constantly blur the line—from those that begin their lives below the surface and live them out above, to those that hold their breath and take to the water to feed or to mate. Much of this drama plays itself out on a modest scale, requiring a closer look on the part of those who would appreciate it.

You and your child can do so by visiting a stream, pool, or pond near you. You may prefer to try walking on water yourself—by wading at the edges of safe, shallow water—but there's much to be taken in even by those who prefer to stay dry on terra firma.

ON THE SURFACE

Water is wonderful stuff with incredible properties. We're used to seeing its everyday transformations—appearing as ice, steam, rain, and snow—

TIP: FIND LOCAL PARKS AND NATURE
CENTERS WITH STREAMS AND PONDS
AT WWW.NWF.ORG/NATUREFIND.

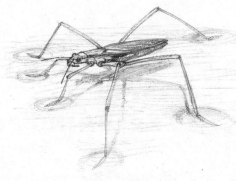

Water strider

but even water at rest can be a force of nature, making life possible for the many creatures that call its surface home.

TESTING SURFACE TENSION

Take your child to virtually any place with quiet, fresh water and you should be able to find and watch some otherwise ordinary bugs doing some extraordinary things. You probably remember watching the most familiar of them—*water striders*—as a child, yourself. Sometimes called *pond skaters,* these thin, spidery insects literally walk across the water, somehow skating with ease on feet that barely dimple the surface.

This seemingly impossible feat is a way of life for water striders, which almost endlessly walk the line between water and air, feeding on insect prey that rises up from below or falls from above. But how do they do it?

The answer lies in the *surface tension* of the water, a scientific concept you can explore with your child and illustrate through an easy experiment.

WHAT YOU NEED:

- water
- a drinking glass
- paper clips
- a fork
- dishwashing liquid

WHAT YOU DO:

1. Fill the glass to the top with water. Then, very carefully and drop by drop, add water until its surface rises above the rim of the glass. Look at the glass from the side for the best view; you should be able to see the curved shape of the water surface hovering above the rim, but not spilling or flowing over the sides. This is called a *meniscus.*

2. Have your child hold a paper clip a few inches above the water before dropping it. Ask him to first predict whether the paper clip will float on the surface of the water when dropped into the glass. (It won't.)

3. Take a second paper clip and lay it across the tines of the fork. Slowly and very carefully, lower the fork into the glass of water. Ask your child to predict whether the paper clip will float on the surface of the water this time. (It should. If it didn't, try it again, lowering the fork into the water with a very slow, smooth motion.) Remove the fork carefully. The paper clip should be floating on the surface of the water.

4. Put a drop of dishwashing liquid on your fingertip and gently touch the surface of

the water. The paper clip should suddenly sink to the bottom of the glass.

Why it works:

Water molecules have a strong tendency to cohere and stick together, an important factor in the capillary action of plants, as we discussed earlier. This cohesive nature is what causes water droplets on a waterproof fabric or a just-waxed car to bead together.

This same quality also causes what is known as *surface tension*. Because the water molecules at the surface layer do not have other water molecules above them to bond with, they hold even more tightly to those below and beside them. It is that surface tension which allows the meniscus to rise above the rim of the glass without spilling over and which allows water striders to stay atop the surface of the water without falling through.

The first paper clip in the experiment, of course, sinks like a stone. But the second paper clip behaves much like a water strider. Even though it is relatively light, it is still heavier than water. However, its weight is spread across a greater surface area, enough so that the force of the water's surface tension is stronger, allowing the paper clip to float as if on a skin atop the water.

By following this same procedure, and with a little patience, you can even make a penny or a dime float atop the surface of the water, too.

Once the drop of dish soap is introduced, the attractive force between the water molecules is diminished and the surface tension is broken.

Water-Walking Bugs

Water striders aren't the only weird and wonderful insects you'll find atop a pond or stream. Here are a few others to watch for.

Whirligig Beetles

Usually seen in large groups on the surface of the water, these shiny, black, oval-shaped beetles get their name from their erratic, unorthodox way of swimming, which often has them spinning in circles. One thing is for sure—it's not because they can't see where they're going. These beetles have specialized compound eyes that allow them to see both above and below the surface of the water at the same time.

Water Boatmen

These aquatic insects of the true bug family are long and flat in shape, not unlike a tiny rowboat. Their long hind legs widen and flatten at the end, making them look and function very much like oars

Did You Know?

WATER STRIDERS AND OTHER INSECTS DON'T ACTUALLY HAVE FEET, AS WE KNOW THEM. THE INSECT EQUIVALENTS ARE KNOWN AS *TARSI*.

Did You Know?

WATER STRIDERS COMMUNICATE WITH EACH OTHER BY CREATING MINUTE VIBRATIONS
THAT RIPPLE ALONG THE SURFACE OF THE WATER, WHICH CAN BE DETECTED BY SPECIAL
NERVE SENSORS IN THE INSECTS' LEGS.

or paddles; they are, in fact, how water boatmen get around—and how they got their name as well.

Backswimmers

At first glance resembling water boatmen with their elongated bodies and long, oar-like legs, backswimmers can be distinguished by their most unusual way of swimming: upside down. A back-swimmer's top side—the "up" side that usually is down—is contoured like the underside of a boat, giving it a hydrodynamic shape. Though they're interesting insects, give backswimmers the right of way, as they've been known to nip people wading or swimming near them.

Diving Beetles

Even though they spend much of their time diving below the surface in search of food, diving beetles still need to come up for air. They surface by poking their abdomens above water, collecting air bubbles that they store under their specialized forewings. The largest of these sleek, football-shaped beetles are nearly two inches long.

DOWN BELOW

Still waters run deep, the old saying goes, and in ponds and slow-running streams, there's certainly much more than what first meets the eye. Below the surface, a whole world waits to be discovered—and here are some ideas for taking a closer look at it with your child.

Look out, below!

MAKE A WATER SCOPE

What better way to check out the action in a stream or pond than with a water scope? To help you see clearly below the surface of the water, try making this homemade water scope with your child and put it to the test in the great outdoors.

WHAT YOU NEED:

- a milk jug or coffee can
- clear plastic kitchen wrap

- scissors
- a can opener
- rubber bands
- duct tape

What you do:

1. Carefully cut off the bottom of the milk jug. Remove the top (above the handle), as well, to create a larger viewing hole. If you're using a coffee can, use a can opener to remove the bottom of the can to create an open cylinder.
2. Stretch a piece of plastic wrap across the bottom of the container, holding it in place with rubber bands. Pull the plastic wrap taut and secure it tightly to the sides of the container with a band of duct tape. Make sure to circle the container with the duct tape to create a watertight seal.
3. In a lazy stream or at the edge of a pond, push the scope down into the shallow water. Look through the top for a clear view of the features and creatures below the surface.

Get the Scoop

If you and your child would like to get up close and personal with the myriad of creatures to be found

Tip: Make sure your scope is watertight by testing it in the sink or bathtub before taking it to a pond or stream.

in a pond or the pools of a slow-flowing stream, try dipping for them. This timeless activity never disappoints, giving children a glimpse into, and an appreciation for, this little universe apart. Minnows, tadpoles, snails, crustaceans, worms, and insect nymphs and larvae all can be caught with a net or strainer—and so can dozens of busy little creatures so small you will need a magnifying glass just to get a look at them.

What you need:

- a wire mesh strainer, sieve, or dipping net
- a shallow plastic tray
- small white plastic containers
- plastic spoons
- a magnifying glass

Did You Know?

Dragonflies and damselflies, those large iridescent insects with needle-like bodies, are a familiar sight near ponds, where they hover above or near the water, feasting on flies and mosquitoes. Tell them apart by their bodies (damselflies are generally more slender) and their wings (damselflies fold theirs while at rest but dragonflies do not).

Pond dipping

WHAT YOU DO:

1. Fill the shallow tray and white plastic containers with clear water from the pond or stream.

2. With the net, skim and scoop the water—at the surface, near the bottom, close to rocks, near aquatic plants, or anywhere in between.

3. Empty the net into the tray. Use the plastic spoons to transfer the creatures you've caught into individual containers.

4. Observe each one, using the magnifying glass for a detailed look or to see creatures otherwise too small to notice.

5. Return all the creatures to the water when you're through studying them.

PLAY IT SAFE

Here's some common sense caution for making all your pond and stream adventures safe ones:

- Follow the buddy system; avoid exploring aquatic places alone.
- If possible, dip from the sides of the pond. Stay along the edge of the water, entering only where the water is shallow and the bottom is visible and firm.
- Protect your feet by wearing wading boots or ratty old sneakers. Flip-flops or other sandals will likely result in unsure footing and banged up toes, or worse.
- Don't put your hands or feet somewhere you can't see; something you'd rather not meet could be seeking shelter there.
- There are lots of interesting insects around streams and ponds; others, like mosquitoes, will just plain bug you. Remember to use repellant, and sunscreen, too.
- Avoid handling the creatures you catch in your net or strainer. Most will be harmless, but a few may be able to pinch or bite.
- Never drink from streams or ponds.

Did You Know?

LEAVE NO STONE UNTURNED (WELL, AT LEAST SOME OF THEM) WHILE EXPLORING A STREAM. CRAYFISH, THOSE MINIATURE LOBSTERS OF PONDS AND STREAMS, SEEK SHELTER BENEATH THEM DURING THE DAY. AND THE RIFFLES OF A SHALLOW STREAM, WHERE WATER WASHES OVER ROCKS AND STONES, ARE GREAT PLACES TO FIND THE NYMPHS OF AQUATIC INSECTS SUCH AS MAYFLIES, STONEFLIES, AND CADDISFLIES.

More to Explore: Leaf Boats

You and your child can put your knowledge of the water's surface tension to good use by creating leaf boats to float and race on the water—a wonderful way to have some old-fashioned, lazy-day fun at the edge of a pond or stream.

Almost any kind of leaf can be used, but several of the plants commonly found near fresh water—such as skunk cabbage, pickerelweed, or certain varieties of dock—may have broad, tapered leaves with a strong central rib, making a suitable keel for a leaf boat.

Gently fold up the sides of the leaf into a boat shape, using whatever is available to secure the structure. There's really no wrong way to construct one; if it floats, it's a leaf boat—and creativity wins the day. Small twigs can be used to join and brace a leaf's upturned sides. Narrow, reedy stems or even pine needles can be used to stitch or pin a leaf boat into shape. A leaf's stem can even be folded up into a mast, hoisting a smaller leaf as a sail; small pebbles, acorns, or the ball-shaped fruit of sweet gum and sycamore can serve as ballast. Even if your creations aren't entirely seaworthy, they still will be a lot of fun to design and build.

And, of course, you always can have the simplest of leaf races—where each participant chooses a leaf from a nearby tree, floats it on the water, and cheers it on to a finish line downwind or downstream.

HAVING FUN WITH FROGS AND TOADS

Give a second look—and listen—to frogs and toads.

It's hard to imagine places marked by the presence of fresh water—ponds, streams, pools, and marshes—without the frogs and toads that fill them with sound. The voices of these curious little amphibians are to those places what birdsong is to the woods, the chorus of background music that defines them, even if the singers never set foot in the spotlight.

All of which is not to suggest that these are necessarily shy and retiring beings—many of them are quite visible, and therefore have long been the irresistible quarry for children who delight in catching and handling them. Even to children who have never seen them, they are familiar animals, populating countless songs, books, and fairy tales of childhood. But don't let the charm of their fictional counterparts suffice—these are gentle, approachable creatures children can get to know by sight, by sound, and even by touch.

Spring peeper

IDENTIFYING FROG SONG

As spring approaches each year, even before the last of winter's snows have melted, frogs awaken from their slumber to ring in the season with the sound of their songs and mating calls. It's a chorus that continues through the summer, with different species carrying the tune—from the tiny wood frogs and spring peepers that kick off the festivities to the bullfrogs that wind them down. The concerts go into full swing each evening, especially after a rainfall, but you can catch occasional matinee performances as well.

Ponds, marshes, and stream banks all make

American toad

excellent places to take in the show, but any low-lying depression where rainfall and snowmelt collect in the springtime—a *vernal pool*—should have plenty of singers to entertain you.

Head out to these places with your child to listen for frog sounds—simply to appreciate them, or even to challenge yourselves by trying to identify them.

Here's a look at just some of the stars of the show.

Wood Frog

These little frogs of moist woods and grasslands have special adaptations that allow them to literally freeze solid without harm each winter. They thaw and revive with the rising temperatures and are often the first to sing as spring nears, congregating around vernal pools to mate and breed. Listen for their low, quacking sounds.

Spring Peeper

One of the surest signs of the arrival of spring is the chorus of these little frogs, which sounds like the musical jingling of sleigh bells from a distance. Individuals call with a clear, whistled "peep," usually ascending in pitch; you will be more likely to hear than to see them.

Leopard Frog

Spring is usually in full swing when leopard frogs begin to sing—a long, low rattling purr from the northern species, a series of almost bird-like croaks from the southern species.

Cricket Frog

As the name might suggest, the song of these frogs ranges from a high-pitched cricket-like sound to a wooden clicking.

Gray Tree Frog

As spring turns to summer, listen for the nighttime song of gray tree frogs: a clear, short trill.

Green Frog

You can hear these common frogs near ponds, streams, and swamps through the spring and summer. Their call, a distinctive *glunk,* is often and accurately described as the sound of a very loose banjo string being plucked.

American Bullfrog

With a bass voice befitting its size, the low resonant sound and *jug-o-rum* call of this aquatic frog are unmistakable. The call of the American bullfrog can be heard up to a quarter of a mile away.

American Toad

You don't need to be near water to hear the sound of these toads, a very long, high-pitched musical trill on spring and summer evenings.

GETTING UP CLOSE

Frogs and toads can be enjoyed, by ear, from a distance. But if you can hear frogs and toads, you can approach them for a closer look—even hold them in your hands. Here's some advice for telling them apart, handling them safely, and attracting them to your backyard or garden.

FROG OR TOAD?

Frogs and toads are closely related and share many common characteristics. So what's the difference? While there are no hard and fast rules, the following generally hold true:

- Frogs have smooth, moist, shiny skin while toads have dry skin that usually appears warty or bumpy.
- Because of their long, powerful hind legs, frogs are excellent jumpers. Toads use their shorter legs to walk and are hoppers instead of leapers.
- With their longer, sleeker bodies, frogs look well suited for the life aquatic. Toads, on the other hand, are more squat and chunky in shape.
- Frogs have eyes that bulge conspicuously from their heads, while toads' eyes are not quite as bulgy.
- Both frogs and toads need a body of water for reproduction and for their young to grow to maturity. Once grown, frogs typically remain close to the water, while toads can live quite successfully away from water.
- Most frogs and toads lay eggs in or on the surface of the water. Frogs typically do so in a big

Did You Know?

BULLFROGS ARE NOT ONLY OUR LARGEST FROGS, THEY'RE ALSO THE SLOWEST TO MATURE, TAKING UP TO TWO YEARS TO COMPLETE THEIR TRANSFORMATION INTO ADULTS.

clustered mass, while toads lay their eggs in long strings or strands.

HANDLING FROGS AND TOADS

Few children can resist the temptation to catch and hold a frog or toad. With a few common-sense precautions, it can be a lot of fun and safe for both child and animal.

Frogs are more difficult to catch than toads, being generally faster, better leapers, and often residing near the water's edge where they can escape by simply jumping in. But frogs on land (such as wood frogs and tree frogs) or those approached from shallow water (such as green frogs and bullfrogs) can be caught by approaching them slowly and quickly cupping your hands over them. Take care to handle frogs gently and only with clean hands—their permeable skin readily absorbs chemicals from lotions, sunscreens, and insect repellants—and to wet your hands occasionally if you hold them for more than a few minutes.

REMEMBER: ALWAYS WASH YOUR HANDS AFTER HANDLING FROGS AND TOADS.

Toads, on the other hand, are much easier to catch, and often will allow you to simply pick them up. Approach them slowly and gently grasp them between your thumb and fingers, just behind their forelegs. Be careful not to touch the raised bumps that appear behind the eyes of most toads—these are glands that secrete a toxic substance that can irritate skin or harm pets.

MAKE A TOAD ABODE

Because they need to be near a body of water only for breeding, toads live most of their lives in more terrestrial locations, including lawns, parks, and gardens—anywhere they can stay damp, keep cool, and feast upon slugs and insects. If your family would like to lay out the welcome mat for the toads near you, try making them a toad abode by

A pleasant abode for a toad

using old, or even cracked, flower pots turned up-side-down in your yard or garden.

WHAT YOU NEED:

- an old terracotta flower pot with saucer
- a pencil
- a cordless drill
- a hammer
- safety glasses
- acrylic paints

WHAT YOU DO:

1. Wipe clean an old flower pot or, if it's very dirty, rinse it clean with a garden hose.
2. If your pot is already cracked or chipped along the rim, carefully enlarge that spot into an opening more or less the size of a baseball. If your pot cracks all the way

through, don't worry; you can create your toad abode by laying the pot on its side.

3. Otherwise, pencil in the outline of a door shape along the rim of the pot. Use a small bit on the cordless drill to perforate the terracotta along the line and gently hammer the piece to remove it. If your pot has a chip or crack in the rim, you may prefer to draw a door around it and use this technique as well.
4. If you wish, decorate the toad abode with paint and allow it to dry thoroughly.

BOOK NOOK

GROWING FROGS
BY VIVIAN FRENCH
ILLUSTRATED BY ALISON BARTLETT
AGE RANGE: 5 TO 8

THIS CHARMING BOOK CAPTURES THE WONDER OF THE LIFE CYCLE OF FROGS WITH A NICE MIX OF FACT AND FANCY. THE NARRATIVE, WHICH RECOUNTS HOW A YOUNG GIRL AND HER MOTHER RAISE FROGS FROM THE EGGS THEY COLLECT IN A NEARBY POND, IS SUPPLEMENTED BY INFORMATIVE SUBTEXT THROUGHOUT, OFFERING USEFUL INFORMATION TO THOSE WHO WOULD LIKE TO TRY GROWING (AND THEN RELEASING) FROGS OF THEIR OWN.

5. Place the toad abode in your yard, garden, or flower bed, choosing the coolest, dampest, shadiest location available, preferably under the cover of a bush or other plant. The saucer can remain on top to cover the hole in the bottom of the pot.

Did You Know?

A HEALTHY TOAD THAT MANAGES TO ELUDE PREDATORS CAN LIVE AS LONG AS FORTY YEARS.

More to Explore: Life Cycles

Frogs and toads don't have many secrets when it comes to, well, making more frogs and toads. Every step of the way—from the courtship to the egg-laying to the transformation of tadpoles—is on display for all who care to see, or hear, it.

It's a fascinating process, and one you can observe with your child as it unfolds over the course of the warmer months.

Courtship

Male frogs are not at all shy about advertising their presence to potential mates, calling out for the whole world to hear, with the loudest and most persistent singers receiving most of the attention from the females. This is much like the melodic courting ritual of birds, though it also can be reminiscent of insects; the males of some frogs, such as spring peepers, will sing in a chorus to attract mates, creating a high-pitched, musical din.

Mating

For many animals, once willing partners have found each other, mating takes place in at least some semblance of privacy. Not so with frogs and toads, for whom this delicate moment is all very much out in the open. In or near the water's edge, the male clasps the female, fertilizing the eggs as she releases them into the water. The egg masses, known as spawn, are laid upon the surface of the water, in clusters for frogs and strands for toads. It's not uncommon for a pond or pool to be bustling with the activity of many frogs or toads mating at the same time.

Transformation

Perhaps most remarkable of all is the transformation of frogs and toads after the egg stage, in which they undergo a fundamental change from gilled, water-breathing tadpoles to air-breathing adults with lungs. And unlike the dramatic transformation from caterpillar to butterfly or moth—which remains shrouded in the secrecy of a chrysalis or cocoon—this process can be observed over time in almost any pond, pool, or slow-moving stream.

The stages of the transformation are as follows:

- Egg: Round and gelatinous, with a dark spot in the center that will develop into a . . .
- Tadpole: More fish than frog and fully aquatic, with a long

tail, gills, and—at first—no legs. Over time, rear legs appear, followed by front legs, as the tadpole becomes a . . .

• Froglet: More frog than fish and less aquatic, its gills give way to lungs and its tail shrinks until it leaves the water as an . . .

• Adult: Fully developed, air-breathing, insect-eating frogs and and toads grow to maturity and repeat the cycle.

Did You Know?

FROGS AND TOADS LAY NUMEROUS EGGS BECAUSE SO MANY OF THEM—AND THE TADPOLES THAT DEVELOP FROM THEM—WILL BE EATEN BY PREDATORS. A SINGLE FEMALE FROG CAN LAY AS MANY AS TWENTY THOUSAND EGGS.

HEADING TO THE SEA

It's amazing what a little sand beneath the toes can do for your soul.

There's a wonderful moment that occurs with every visit to the seaside—that point where you first draw near enough to notice the end of the trees, houses, or buildings sprouting up from the land and glimpse the expanse of ocean commanding your view to the far horizon.

For those of us who do not live near the coast—and who never outgrow the anticipation of swimming, racing the waves, finding seashells, and building sand castles—it's always a special thrill, almost like stepping into another world. And in many ways it is a world unto itself, defined by the meeting of land and sea; a realm of sun, sand, and surf swept clean by ocean breezes and inhabited by a bewildering array of shorebirds and sea creatures.

But above all, the seaside is alive. The endless cycle of waves and tides is the pulse of our planet, an elemental force that sustains life yet is powerful enough to break rock down into the very sand on which we walk, play, or relax. Just to be in its presence is invigorating, and alluring enough to draw us back to the sea, season after season, year after year.

BEACH FINDS

One of the magical things about the seashore is that it is always in motion, ever-changing and endlessly new. The tireless waves and the ebb and flow of the tides deposit a veritable bounty on the seashore—only to sweep it clean again as the cycle repeats itself.

Sand dollar, shells, and mermaid's purse

TREASURES IN THE SAND

Few children—or adults—can resist walking along the water's edge, looking for the natural treasures washed ashore by the sea. Especially at low tide, or after the passage of a storm, keep an eye out for seaside finds such as these, some of which make perfect keepsakes from time spent at the shore.

Seashells

The bounty of choice for beachcombers drawn to their intricate, delicate beauty, seashells appear in a seemingly infinite variety of sizes, shapes, and colors. Inside every shell you find, there once lived a mollusk that created the marvelous structure that served as both its shelter and its skeleton; by the time the shell washes ashore, its inhabitant is usually dead and gone. The works of sea art that remain come with befittingly colorful names: conchs and bonnets, whelks and trumpets, spindles and tulips, cockles and cowries, just to name a few.

Pebbles

For children who collect rocks and stones, a walk along the shore brings the opportunity to find just the perfect pebble—if not a dozen of them. Rounded, worn smooth, and polished by the surf, ocean pebbles are a delight to touch and often display the interesting lines and striations of sedimentary rock seen in cross-section.

Sand Dollars

Flattish discs with five conspicuous pores arranged like flower petals, sand dollars are the skeletons of little marine creatures related to sea urchins. Bleached to a sandy color and smooth by the time they wash up on shore, they are covered by fine, reddish-colored spines while alive, giving them an almost velvety texture.

> **TIP:** THE NATIONAL PARK SERVICE MAINTAINS MANY NATIONAL SEASHORES ALONG THE ATLANTIC, PACIFIC, AND GULF COASTS OF THE UNITED STATES. LEARN MORE ABOUT THEM AT WWW.NPS.GOV.

Mermaid's Purse

One of the more unusual natural objects to commonly wash ashore is the mermaid's purse, which looks like a small, dark sack with tendrils trailing from all four of its corners. While it is actually the egg case for fish such as sharks, skates, and rays, it does resemble a purse or handbag—perhaps making a perfect place for a mermaid to keep her sand dollars.

Seahorse

The population of these fantastic fishes, which look like miniature scaly dragons with horse-like heads, has been in decline, making a seahorse an uncommon—and very special—find. Despite their distinctive appearance, seahorses are true fish; should you find one on the shore, it has almost certainly already expired.

Driftwood

Driftwood is simply a piece of wood that has washed ashore and been weathered by the sand, sun, and sea, often bleached, worn smooth, and twisted into unusual shapes. Artists and crafters often seek out driftwood for use in sculptures.

Sea Beans

Earlier, we explored several ways in which seeds can spread and disperse. One additional way is by water, which can carry seeds for surprising distances. Sea beans, also called drift seeds, are the hard-bodied, buoyant seeds of mostly tropical plants that have worked their way to the ocean and drifted to a distant shore. Look for them in late summer among the lines of seaweed washed ashore by the tide.

Sea Glass

Colorful pieces of smooth, frosted sea glass can be so pretty that it's hard to believe they began as trash. Though they look like jewels from the sea, they are simply pieces of glass—mostly from old bottles—that were discarded or which otherwise ended up in the ocean, where the sand and the surf smoothed their sharp edges and gave them their finely etched surface.

Always handle sea stars gently

SEASHORE CREATURES

Not all of your seaside finds will be inanimate. Some of the most interesting of all are the unique creatures that call the seashore home; here are just a few to watch for.

Horseshoe Crabs

With their sleek, spiky armor and fearsome tail-like structure, horseshoe crabs seem to have come from either the distant future or the long-forgotten past. In actual fact, these "living fossils" have remained essentially unchanged for several hundred million years. Despite their bizarre appearance, they are harmless—even helpful—to people, as their blood, which turns blue when exposed to oxygen, has been widely used by medical researchers. And that dangerous-looking spine at its rear is actually used by the horseshoe crab to right itself should it be upended by the surf. But it doesn't always work; if you find one upside down, do a good turn and gently flip it over.

Sea Stars

These unmistakable sea creatures are sometimes called starfish, even though, as relatives of sand dollars, they are not actually fish. They feed on mollusks such as clams and oysters and have a most unusual way of getting a meal—a sea star will actually eject its stomach from its body, retracting it once it has surrounded its prey. Most of the sea stars you happen upon probably will be alive and therefore should be handled very gently, but not collected.

Ghost Crabs

By day, you will be more likely to hear than to see these fascinating little crabs that spend most of their days in burrows in the sand. And, even if you should happen to spot one of them, it can disappear again in the blink of an eye. As darkness falls on the shore, however, the sand comes alive with ghost crabs, scuttling about and along the water's edge with surprising speed. Their emergence at night—and their elusive nature—gives them their colorful name.

"SEA" FOR YOURSELF

The seas and oceans are mysterious forces of nature that have given rise to their share of folk wisdom

MOST OF YOUR SEASIDE FINDS CAN SIMPLY BE RINSED IN CLEAN WATER AND ALLOWED TO DRY. TO PRESERVE THE REMAINS OF THE SAND DOLLARS, SEA STARS, OR SEAHORSES YOU FIND, PLACE THEM IN A CONTAINER FILLED WITH RUBBING ALCOHOL FOR FORTY-EIGHT HOURS AND ALLOW THEM TO DRY COMPLETELY IN THE SUN.

over the centuries. Are those colorful old sayings true? While many are not, others do have a basis in scientific fact.

Here are three common seashore myths your children can investigate and put to the test.

Is Every Seventh Wave Larger?

Sometimes. Many conditions—from the wind to the geography of the shoreline—affect the formation and breaking of waves. It is true that a larger than average wave will arrive at more-or-less regular intervals, which you can determine by observing the waves as they roll in. It could be—but isn't necessarily—every seventh wave.

There's little variation in the height of waves out at sea, where the water is deeper. As the waves approach the shore, however, the sea bottom gradually rises, giving them less vertical space and forcing them to rise and swell as they move toward land. When one wave "catches up" to the wave preceding it, they combine to create that larger wave.

Can You Hear the Ocean in a Seashell?

Not really. But if you hold a seashell to your ear, especially a large shell such as a conch, you can hear a rushing, roaring sound that might remind you of the sound of the surf.

What you're actually hearing are waves of ambient sound being captured by—and echoing throughout—the shell. The shell's spiral shape and intricate interior provide those sound waves plenty of surfaces for reverberation, but even an ordinary drinking glass can produce a similar effect.

Is It Easier to Float in the Sea?

Yes. The salt water of the seas and oceans is denser than fresh water, and this greater density makes it much easier for people and objects to float in it. In especially salty or mineral-rich water—such as the Great Salt Lake or the Dead Sea—the effect is

REMEMBER: AVOID HANDLING ICE-CREAM-CONE-SHAPED SHELLS WITH LIVE OCCUPANTS. THE CONE SNAILS THAT CREATE THESE PARTICULAR SHELLS CAN DELIVER A VENOMOUS STING.

Did You Know?

- -

WHEN THE GOING GETS TOUGH, THE TOUGH GET RE-GROWING. SOME SEASIDE CREATURES HAVE THE AMAZING ABILITY TO REGENERATE LOST BODY PARTS SUCH AS LEGS OR CLAWS—BUT NOTHING TOPS THE SEA STAR, WHICH, IF CUT IN TWO, COULD GROW INTO TWO COMPLETE INDIVIDUALS.

so pronounced that a person may have no choice but to float.

You can demonstrate this principle anywhere with everyday kitchen items. Fill a tall drinking glass halfway with fresh water and gently lower an egg into the water with a spoon. You should find that the egg sinks to the bottom. Remove the egg and begin to stir in ordinary table salt, a spoonful at a time. Add the egg to the water after each spoonful of salt, and watch it gradually rise higher until it is suspended in the salty water.

PLAY IT SAFE

Here's some common-sense caution for keeping your family safe at the seaside:

- Follow the buddy system; avoid exploring the seashore alone.

- Remember that both sand and water can reflect the ultraviolet rays of sunlight. Protect your eyes and skin by wearing sunglasses, hats, UPF-rated clothing, and sunscreen as appropriate.
- Stay off of rocks and jetties, where footing can be treacherous and where breaking waves at high tide can be extremely dangerous.
- Never turn your back to the ocean. Big waves, or waves carrying debris, can come at any time.

TIP: LEARN MORE ABOUT INTERNATIONAL COASTAL CLEANUP AND HOW YOUR FAMILY CAN HELP, AT WWW.COASTALCLEANUP.ORG.

More to Explore: Coastal Cleanup

The bits of broken bottles that in time turn into sea glass are the exception to the rule. Most of the trash that ends up in our oceans never turns into something useful or beautiful; at best, it remains trash, and at worst, it presents a hazard to both wildlife and people. And, unfortunately, there is a lot of it.

Each year, during International Coastal Cleanup, hundreds of thousands of volunteers around the globe remove millions of pounds of trash from beaches, coastlines, and waterways *in a single day*. According to a report from the Ocean Conservancy, the organization behind International Coastal Cleanup, much of the trash polluting the oceans is caused by nothing more than human carelessness—cigarette butts, plastic bags, and food wrappers top the list of trash items—and is therefore easily preventable.[2]

Whether you're spending time at the seaside, a lakeshore, a pond, or a stream, consider taking a few minutes to pitch in by cleaning up any trash you might find there.

Did You Know?

EVEN THE SALTY WATER OF THE OCEAN HELPS TO PRODUCE FRESHWATER RAIN. AS OCEAN WATER WARMS IT EVAPORATES INTO THE ATMOSPHERE AS FRESH WATER VAPOR, WHILE THE DISSOLVED SALTS REMAIN BEHIND.

WHATEVER THE WEATHER

UNLESS AND UNTIL it has taken a turn for the worse, we tend not to think much about the weather. Yet, almost without fail, it is that one enduring topic of conversation that can break the ice between strangers in virtually any setting.

The fact that it can is a bit comforting; it demonstrates that we really are, on some level, tuned in to the daily atmospheric changes—or, in some cases, the lack thereof—in our environment, even if we spend much of our days sheltered from them. And in light of the connection between the weather we observe and the larger trends affecting our global climate, paying attention to it now may in part help to secure our future.

Watching the weather is a way for all children—whether they live in the heart of the city or in the heartland—to connect with the natural world and some of its most powerful and mysterious forces. Neither snow, nor rain, nor gloom can keep them from exploring—and ideas for doing just that, whatever the weather, follow.

BLOWING IN THE WIND

Any way the wind blows—it doesn't really matter to me.

Everyone is familiar with wind. Even though we can't see it, we can feel it, hear it, measure it, and even observe it, though indirectly. In that regard, it's an interesting phenomenon for children to investigate, to consider that not all causes and effects may be obvious ones; where science is concerned, reasoning and observation together often can do what either, alone, cannot.

Wind is a constant reminder that our planet is a living, moving, ever-changing place. It also is an incredibly powerful force of nature, beneficial when harnessed, and potentially destructive when unleashed.

But wind also has the gentler power to refresh and uplift us—so when it comes, enjoy it. Let it flow through your hair and caress your face. Let it flutter your flags, spin your pinwheels, and scatter your bubbles.

Here are several ideas for making the most of a windy day.

PLAYING WITH THE WIND

Long before battery power, people came up with many clever toys and amusements that harnessed the power of wind. Kites, pinwheels, wind chimes, and whirligigs all take advantage of moving air to create motions or sounds to delight us. In that same spirit, here are several ideas for homemade fun that require little more than a windy day to power them.

Maple seeds in flight

HAVE A WIND RACE

There are lots of ways to make your own outdoor fun on a breezy or blustery day, and having a wind race is one you can do almost anywhere. You may come up with variations of your own, but here are a few to get you started.

Whirlybird Race

Many of the trees we see every day produce spinning, helicopter-like seeds designed to stay aloft in even the slightest breeze. Of these, maples are probably the most familiar and most common, but other trees, from ash to tulip tree, also produce winged seeds suitable for a wind race. Collect some of these seeds and toss them up to race them, seeing which seed reaches a downwind finish line first. Or, switch it up by seeing whose seed can travel the farthest from the starting point, or stay aloft the longest.

Leaf Race

Turn your driveway, sidewalk, or patio into a drag strip for leaves. Have each player select a leaf—fallen leaves that have dried and curled up work best—and release them at the same time. The leaf that scurries to the finish line first is the winner.

Cloud Race

On a breezy day when the sky is dotted with clouds, try having a cloud race. Take note of the direction in which the clouds are drifting, then have each player choose a cloud to race. The first cloud

A fun wind sock

to reach a predetermined finish line, such as an overhead wire or the edge of a house, wins.

Make a Wind Sock

Your child may have seen windsocks before. These tubes of lightweight fabric can be found mounted to poles at airports and airfields, where they billow or droop to indicate the relative speed and direction of the wind—important information for pilots to know. Even the place kicker on a football team takes his cues from the windsocks that dangle from the goal posts.

Making a windsock is a fun craft project you and your child can do together. Hang it in a place where it can flutter in the breeze, and watch it rise and fall with the velocity of the wind.

> **Tip:** Find the local forecast and current atmospheric conditions for your zip code at www.weather.gov.

What you need:

- a cylindrical oatmeal box
- a hole punch
- thick twine or string
- ribbon or crepe paper
- construction paper
- craft glue

What you do:

1. Remove the lid and bottom of the oatmeal box to create an open cardboard cylinder.
2. Decorate a sheet of construction paper and cover the oatmeal box with it by gluing it into place.
3. Punch four evenly spaced holes along the top edge of the oatmeal box, about one-half inch in from the edge.
4. Cut two even lengths of string, of about eighteen inches. Knot the end of one string. Pass the other end of the string through two opposite holes, and tie another knot at the other end of the string. The knots should be big enough so that they can't pass through the punched holes. Repeat this process for the second length of string and the remaining holes.
5. Create streaming tails for your wind sock by punching several holes along the bottom edge of the oatmeal box and tying lengths of ribbon to them. If you prefer, you can glue crepe-paper streamers along the inside of the bottom edge.
6. Hang the crisscrossing strings at the top of your wind sock from a hook on your porch or deck. Or, tie them together with a longer length of string and use that string to hang

the wind sock from a tree branch or other breezy location.

MEASURING THE WIND

As unpredictable as the wind might seem at times, it moves in larger cycles and patterns that help scientists to understand both our local weather and our global climate. One of the most important characteristics of the wind is the direction from which it is blowing. Knowing that allows us to better harness its energy, to travel more safely and efficiently, or to prepare for the weather heading our way.

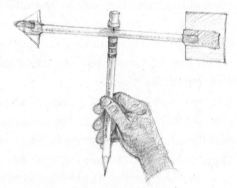

A homemade weather vane

MAKE A WEATHER VANE

Long before people had ready access to the weather forecasts made by meteorologists, they kept a close eye on the atmospheric conditions near them with homemade instruments. Weather vanes are one of the oldest and simplest weather instruments, turning freely in the wind to show its direction. They indicate not only the prevailing winds for a given area, but also the sudden changes in wind direction that might mean a change in the weather.

To illustrate how they work, you and your child can easily make a handheld weather vane from items you can find in almost any kitchen or desk drawer.

WHAT YOU NEED:

- a new pencil with an eraser
- a drinking straw
- a straight pin or long push pin
- index cards or cardstock
- scissors
- tape
- paper clips
- a compass

WHAT YOU DO:

1. Poke the pin all the way through the straw at its midpoint, and gently wiggle the pin to enlarge the holes a bit. The straw should be able to spin freely around the vertical pin.

2. Make a half-inch vertical slit in either end of the straw by flattening it and carefully snipping it with the tip of the scissors.

3. From the cardstock or index cards, cut a square and a pointed triangle with sides roughly two or three inches in length.

4. Insert the triangle and square shapes into the vertical slits in the straw, fastening them with tape, to create an arrowhead and tail, respectively.

5. Push the pin into the eraser to hold the straw loosely in place, making sure it can spin freely. Add one or more paper clips to the arrowhead to balance the straw, as necessary.

6. Take the weather vane outside on a windy day and hold it upright. If you have one, use the compass to determine which direction the arrow is pointing—this is the current wind direction.

Keep in mind that truly accurate readings are taken from locations well above ground level and away from buildings or other structures that might interfere with the flow of wind. For that reason, weather stations and observatories often are located atop ridges or on the roofs of buildings. But, for the purpose of illustrating the concept, this simple handheld vane works just fine.

Can your child figure out why the weather vane works? What would happen if the arrowhead were much larger, the same size as the tail? What might happen if the weather vane were not balanced?

More to Explore: The Beaufort Scale

In 1805, Sir Francis Beaufort, a British naval officer, devised a method for standardizing the descriptions of wind speed based on observation. Originally used to describe the winds at sea, land conditions eventually were added to broaden its usefulness. Some two hundred years after its creation, the wind force scale that bears Beaufort's name is still in use, by meteorologists, sailors, and anyone else concerned with the ways of the wind.

The names and descriptions it assigns to different wind speeds are as follows:

- Calm: No discernible movement in the air. Smoke or steam will rise vertically.
- Light air: Wind speeds of 1 to 3 miles per hour. Smoke will drift in the direction of the wind, but weather vanes remain still.
- Light breeze: Wind speeds of 3 to 7 miles per hour. At this point, you can feel the breeze on your face. Leaves will rustle and weather vanes will begin to move.
- Gentle breeze: Wind speeds of 8 to 12 miles per hour. Leaves on the trees will remain in motion, and flags may begin to straighten.
- Moderate breeze: Wind speeds of 13 to 17 miles per hour. The breeze will kick up dust, leaves, and loose paper. Small branches on the trees will begin to move.
- Fresh breeze: Wind speeds of 18 to 24 miles per hour. Moderately sized branches and small trees with leaves will begin to sway.
- Strong breeze: Wind speeds of 25 to 30 miles per hour. At this point, the wind whistles in the wires overhead and sets large branches in motion.
- Near gale: Wind speeds of 31 to 38 miles per hour. Whole trees will be in motion, and it will take some effort to walk against the wind.

These describe the mildest, and most common, wind conditions, but the scale continues, increasing in intensity from gale to hurricane-force winds.

What is the wind doing near you? Head outside with your child to make and record observations of your own. Compare your assessment of the wind speed with the measurements made by meteorologists.

MAKING THE MOST OF GRAY SKIES

Into every life, a little rain must fall.

For most of us, a perfect day to be outside means clear blue skies and plenty of sunshine, making clouds, when they come, rather unwelcome visitors. But while they can put a damper on our plans, clouds—and the rain they sometimes bring—are nonetheless parts of the grand cycle that endlessly recycles our planet's fresh water. Though we might wish for them to go away—perhaps to come again another day—they are essential to a process that makes life as we know it possible.

And clouds are amazing in their own right, seemingly defying gravity, if not description; sometimes wisps of white brushed high across a canvas of blue sky, sometimes sheets of steely gray looming low and ominous, conjuring rain—almost literally—out of thin air.

Like everything, they, too, shall pass. In the meantime, here are some ideas for appreciating these underappreciated marvels with your child.

Tip: See an animation explaining the water cycle at http://epa .gov/ogwdw/kids/flash/flash_ watercycle.html

ABOUT CLOUDS

Cloud spotting probably has been around as long as people have. All it takes is a day dotted with clouds and an idle imagination to turn the sky into a gallery of truly unique, if ephemeral, works of art; beauty, in this case, truly lies in the eye of the beholder. If you haven't played this game lately, grab a blanket or lawn chair and head outside with your child to while away the time in one of the most relaxing ways imaginable.

At first glance, clouds might seem to be more or less the same, but a closer look reveals subtle differences in shape, altitude, and color. Learning to distinguish among them—and the weather they bring—can hone children's powers of observation and keep them in tune with the changing elements of their environment.

The atmospheric scientists who study clouds divide them into three groups based on the altitude at which those clouds form and appear. Logically enough, there are high-level, mid-level, and low-level clouds, each with different characteristics and associated with different kinds of weather.

High-Level Clouds

If you like fair weather, you will be glad to see the thin, wispy, white clouds known as *cirrus* clouds in an otherwise blue sky. These clouds form four or more miles above us, where temperatures are so cold that they are comprised not of water droplets, but of ice crystals.

Mid-Level Clouds

At altitudes ranging from 1¼ to 4 miles overhead, you can find the mid-level clouds known as *alto-cumulus* and *altostratus*. Altocumulus clouds appear as whitish or gray puffy clouds, often with some blue sky between them, whereas altostratus clouds form a uniformly overcast layer above us. Both types often mean that rain soon may be on the way—warm-weather thunderstorms in the case of altocumulus clouds, steady rain when altostratus clouds appear.

Low-Level Clouds

With their bases hovering no more than 1¼ miles above us, these clouds loom low in the sky—and that usually means rain. *Nimbostratus* clouds appear as a layer of heavy, gray, low-hanging rain clouds and typically bring steady precipitation. But not all low clouds necessarily mean rain; *cumulus* clouds resemble puffy cotton balls and often are short-lived, forming and dissipating, only to be replaced by more cumulus clouds. But on warm summer days with moist, rising air, you can watch cumulus clouds grow into the *cumulonimbus* clouds that produce thunderstorms.

Multi-Level Clouds

Billowy cumulonimbus clouds are unique in that they stretch vertically, sometimes for tens of thousands of feet. The bases of these towering thunderclouds can hang as little as one thousand

Did You Know?

- -

CLOUDS MAY SEEM TO HAVE MIX-AND-MATCH NAMES, BUT KNOWING THE MEANINGS OF THE LATIN ROOTS THAT MAKE THEM UP MAKES THINGS A BIT CLEARER. *STRATUS* MEANS "LAYER," *CUMULUS* MEANS "HEAP," AND *NIMBUS* (OR *NIMBO*) MEANS "RAIN." NIMBOSTRATUS, THEREFORE, IS A LAYERED RAIN CLOUD, WHILE *CUMULONIMBUS* IS A HEAPED RAIN CLOUD.

feet overhead, while their tops can climb to more than seven miles above the ground.

UNDERSTANDING THE WEATHER

When we talk about the weather, we're really referring to all of the observable day-to-day changes in the atmosphere. As you might imagine, our planet is not warmed evenly by the sun, creating differences in temperature. The combination of those differences, fueled by the atmospheric elements of air and water, results in instability and gives rise to phenomena such as the blowing of wind, the formation of clouds, or the falling of precipitation. Fortunately, for those interested in understanding the weather, many of these phenomena are easily observed and measured—even re-created.

MAKE A CLOUD IN A BOTTLE

It only takes a minute to demonstrate the conditions that cause clouds to form. Here's a quick and easy experiment, using readily available materials, to do just that.

WHAT YOU NEED:

- a large, clear plastic water or soda bottle
- water
- matches

WHAT YOU DO:

1. Add a bit of water to a clear, clean plastic bottle, then cap the bottle and shake it vigorously. Pour out the remaining water.
2. Strike a match and blow it out. Stick the match in the opening of the bottle for a moment to collect a bit of smoke.
3. Place the cap back on the bottle. Quickly squeeze and release the bottle ten or twenty times. Then squeeze the bottle as hard as you can and hold it for a long moment.

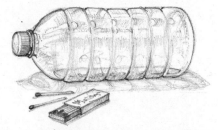

You can make a "cloud" using everyday objects

4. Release the pressure to see a cloudy mist—your "cloud"—appear inside the bottle. Squeeze hard again and hold to watch it disappear.

WHY IT WORKS:

In nature—and in simple terms—clouds form when moist air rises, cools, and its moisture condenses onto tiny particles such as dust, smoke, or salt.

By adding a bit of water to the bottle and shaking it, you introduce water droplets into the air inside the bottle.

By collecting a bit of smoke, you introduce particles onto which the water vapor can condense.

By squeezing the bottle, you change the air pressure within it. When the pressure is greater, so is the temperature. Likewise, when the pressure is lower, so is the temperature. By squeezing and holding the bottle, the air within is under greater pressure and temperature. When you suddenly release your grip, the temperature and pressure fall again, causing the water vapor in the air to condense onto the tiny particles of smoke.

If you have a rubber stopper and a bicycle or ball pump, you can conduct a more sophisticated version of this experiment to see more dramatic results. Follow the first two steps as above, but instead of using the lid, seal your bottle with the rubber stopper—the kind used to reseal wine bottles might work if the seal is tight enough. Push the inflating needle through the stopper and pump air into the bottle until it becomes difficult to do so. Pull out the stopper to release the pressure and watch the cloud form inside the bottle. If you try this, remember to cover your eyes with goggles or safety glasses first.

Measuring precipitation with a simple gauge

Make a Rain Gauge

Not all clouds bring rain, but when they do, it can range from a sprinkle to a downpour. Making a rain gauge is a simple project to let you see just how much precipitation the clouds bring your way.

What you need:

- a jar or can with straight sides
- a ruler

What you do:

1. Place your container outside in a relatively open area, away from trees, houses, or other structures that might interfere with the rainfall.
2. After the rain, dip the ruler into the jar so that it rests on the bottom and stands straight against the side before taking your measurement.
3. Empty your gauge so it will be ready for the next rainfall.

For greater accuracy, rainfall totals are usually calculated on a daily basis. You may wish to measure the precipitation over a longer period of time, but remember that the collected rain will begin to evaporate.

Keep a Weather Journal

By using simple instruments and making a few observations of the conditions outside, you and your child can compile enough information to keep a basic weather journal.

Make an entry for each day, and include as much of the following information as possible:

- date
- time
- temperature (using an outdoor thermometer)
- wind direction (using a weather vane)
- wind speed (based on your observations)
- cloud type and cover (based on your observations)
- precipitation type and amount (using a rain gauge, which also works for snow)

Even if you don't keep a separate weather journal, this sort of data can be interesting and useful when collected in a nature journal or for science fair projects. Your child may begin to notice connections between weather conditions and natural events such as the opening of flowers, the appearance of birds, the emergence of insects, and the singing of frogs—and you may begin to notice his or her observation and research skills flourishing.

Did You Know?

WHILE IT'S NOT QUITE LIKE HOLDING A CLOUD IN YOUR HAND, THE MOST FAMILIAR EXAMPLE OF CONDENSATION—THE PROCESS WHERE WATER VAPOR TURNS TO LIQUID BY COOLING—ARE THE DROPS OF WATER THAT FORM ON A COLD BOTTLE, GLASS, OR CAN ON A WARM DAY.

More to Explore: Timing Thunder

Even rainy days still can be good times to be outside, but not when thunderstorms are present. Those are best appreciated from a sheltered location; when a thunderstorm nears, always be sure to get inside fast. But, while you're waiting for a storm to pass, you can have fun calculating its distance with your child. And for younger children who might find thunder and lightning a bit frightening, counting down their approach and departure can be a reassuring activity.

Light travels so incredibly fast that for most earthbound instances—including lightning—it reaches our eyes almost instantly. Sound, on the other hand, takes much longer to move through the air. If you've ever watched a baseball game from the outfield bleachers and heard the crack of the bat a split second after seeing the hit, you've already noticed the difference in speed, and it is this difference that allows us to estimate the distance of the lightning strokes that occur during a thunderstorm.

At about 1,115 feet per second, on average, sound travels roughly one mile every five seconds. In actual fact, it's closer to four and three-quarters seconds, but it's a small grain of salt to take for convenient seat-of-the-pants science.

As soon as you see a flash of lightning, start counting the seconds on your watch, clock, or timer until you hear the rumble of thunder. Each second that passes represents approximately one-fifth of a mile between you and the lightning. Successively shorter intervals between flash and boom indicate a storm drawing closer, longer intervals one moving farther away. And a flash and thunderclap that seem to happen at the same time, of course, mean lightning that is *very* close.

PLAYING IN THE SNOW

Nature reveals a multitude of everyday wonders, but few of them have the power to transform the world like a snowfall. From the time those first flakes begin to drift earthward, everyone—young and old alike—bristles with the anticipation of a landscape eerily hushed and blanketed in white, bringing an almost otherworldly beauty right to our own backyards.

There's simply something magical about the snow, something that calls the child inside all of us to come out and play. Forget about traffic and travel delays, plowing and shoveling—they can wait. For those of us lucky enough to receive it, a snowfall brings the fleeting chance to put adulthood on hold for a day, and to laugh and play with our children as though we were all the same age—and that's as good as gold.

STUDYING SNOWFLAKES

Nature's wonders often hide in plain sight, waiting to reveal themselves to those willing to take the time—and a closer look—to discover them.

Such is the case with falling snowflakes, whose delicate, crystalline structures shimmer like jewels for a few brief moments before they become hopelessly lost in the crowd. Sneaking a peek at one before that happens is a little like sharing a secret with the universe. And snowflakes are perhaps more than just a little bit like us—unique individuals, each beautiful in its own right; just one in a million, yet one of a kind.

Sneaking a peek at snowflakes

Snow crystals, close up

How to Catch a Snowflake

Every snowflake is a wonder of natural design. The best way to get a closer look at the intricate beauty of snowflakes is to catch them before they reach the ground. Here's how.

What you need:

- a snowy day
- black construction paper
- a magnifying glass

What you do:

1. Place the construction paper in the freezer, for several hours if possible. (Black felt, tacked with craft glue onto a piece of cardstock for stiffness, also works well.) This will become your snowflake landing pad.
2. Bundle up and take the construction paper out of the freezer just before heading outside. For best results, the paper should remain frozen.
3. Use the paper to catch snowflakes as they fall. Because they are landing on a frozen surface, the snowflakes won't melt, and the contrast of white snowflakes on black paper will make it easier to see them. Take a close look at the flakes with the magnifying glass, noting the fine details and the unique shape and structure of each one.

What do you notice about the snowflakes you've caught? Are any of them symmetrical? While some snowflakes do appear as perfect six-sided crystals with branching arms, most snowflakes actually form irregular crystals. The number and variety of shapes they take—from needles and columns to plates and rosettes—is nothing short of amazing.

> **Tip:** See examples of the different types of snowflake crystals, and download a chart to help you identify them, at www.snowcrystals.com.

SNOW-PACKING FUN

For as marvelous as each individual snowflake is, the real joys of a snowfall come from putting those flakes together. Skiing, snowshoeing, snowball-making—all require packing these delicate crystals together into the wonder stuff of winter time, as do these ideas for more outdoor fun.

MAKE BLOCKS

Even a modest snowfall yields a generous supply of building material for young architects

TIP: Watch a virtual snowfall of Kenneth Libbrecht's microphotographs of snowflakes at http://images .amazon.com/media/13d/01/ snow2.swf

and engineers. Forming the snow into blocks first makes the most of the available snow—and makes it much easier to work with. Create them by packing snow into a rectangular plastic box or bin—storage containers, minus their lids, work well—before turning it over and lifting it away to reveal a block of snow. Wetting the inside of the container first will help to prevent snow from sticking to it; if all else fails, you can even use a bit of cooking spray to make your block form nonstick. In this manner you can create the walls of a respectable snow fort in no time, offsetting the blocks like bricks with each additional row. For an extra touch, use a large canister or a plastic bucket to create cylindrical blocks for corner turrets to give your fort a castle-like appearance.

If you're up for a greater challenge, and have plenty of nicely packing snow, try building your own igloo with your child. Stackable plastic storage bins that narrow at the base can be used to create blocks well-suited to igloo construction because the sides, instead of being parallel, will be set at a slight angle, a bit like a keystone. Lay each block on its side, with the shorter base—the surface formed by the bottom of the bin—facing inward. The angles should allow you to create a circular course for the base of the igloo and, more importantly, should allow each successive course to arch slightly inward to create a domed shape. (Even better—once they are in place, cut the first several blocks you lay on a long diagonal; this will create a "ramp" for the second tier of blocks and allow you to proceed in a spiral all the way to the top of the dome.) Use additional snow as mortar to strengthen the joints between the blocks, especially to help join the upper courses of the igloo, but don't worry about leaving gaps and cracks between the blocks—these will provide a way for air to flow in and out of the igloo. Without such cracks, your igloo would need air holes for breathing, should you be able to successfully complete the dome.

MAKE TRACKS

There may be no better medium for tracking than fresh snow. Birds, squirrels, rabbits, foxes, and

Did You Know?

In traditional igloos, a section of clear ice sometimes was used as a "window" to allow light into the interior of the structure.

Did You Know?

THOUGH YOU MIGHT NOT THINK OF IT AS SOMETHING TO KEEP YOU WARM, FRESH SNOW IS A GOOD INSULATOR. MUCH LIKE GOOSE DOWN, SNOW CRYSTALS TRAP AND HOLD AIR BETWEEN THEM, AND THAT TRAPPED AIR LIMITS THE TRANSFER OF HEAT.

deer—these are just some of the animals that leave clues to their passing by leaving their tracks behind in packed snow. If no animal tracks are present, try tracking your pets—or your family—by playing hide-and-seek in the snow. And if you've got waterproof snow gear, don't forget to flop onto your back and make those uniquely human tracks: snow angels.

But hills, if you have access to them, provide the opportunity to make the best snowy tracks of all—those left by sleds, toboggans, and saucers. Nothing compares to an exhilarating run down a good sledding hill. Keep these things in mind to make sure your downhill adventure is as safe as it is fun:

- Always ride feet first. Flopping downhill headfirst—as many of us did when we were children—may be thrilling, but it invites serious head and neck injuries.
- Never sled on streets or roadways, and avoid runs that end on or near them.
- Choose clear, open hills free of stationary hazards such as trees and rocks.
- Avoid plastic sheets or other materials that could be punctured and that cannot be steered or controlled by the rider.
- Consider visiting a ski area with dedicated runs for family snow tubing.

MAKE SNACKS

Building a snowman is the quintessential backyard activity for a snowy day. For a change of pace, try making a snowman your local wildlife can enjoy long after your family has headed inside to warm up with some hot cocoa. Instead of, or in addition to, the usual decorations for a snowman, try using dried fruit, sunflower seeds, peanuts, and popped corn, all of which will be appreciated by winter birds, and dried corn on the cob, a favorite snack of squirrels.

A snowy day can be a great time to make a unique snack for people, too. Those syrup-

A wildlife-friendly snowman

sweetened balls of shaved ice known as snow cones may be a classic summertime treat, but you might enjoy making your own natural, homemade version after a snowfall. Simply scoop up some clean, freshly fallen snow into small plastic cups and drizzle it with fruity syrups like those used to flavor coffee and other drinks. Or, for a more healthful alternative, allow some frozen fruit juice concentrate to thaw and pour a little bit over each cup of snow.

More to Explore: Reflection and Absorption

On the first clear, sunny day after a snowstorm, look around you. Can you see where the snow is beginning to melt?

Places receiving direct sunlight, of course, will warm more quickly; a snowman built in the shade stands a much better chance than one in an open, sunny spot.

But that's not the whole story.

You may have noticed, on sunny summer days, the temperature difference between the dark-colored blacktop of parking lots and streets and the comparatively light-colored surface of sidewalks. (The same comparison can be drawn between black and white shirts.) Both feel hot, but in each case the darker material absorbs more of the sun's rays and gets hotter, faster.

This same principle can easily be demonstrated after a snowfall. White snow reflects most of the sunlight that hits it—a property known as *albedo*—while the dark trunks of trees absorb the sun's light and heat and help to melt the snow around them. This exposes more grass and soil, dark surfaces, which in turn absorb more of the sun's energy—perpetuating, and eventually speeding, the melting process.

EYES ON THE SKIES

WHILE ORBITING THE MOON on Christmas Eve, 1968, astronaut William Anders of the Apollo 8 mission snapped a photograph that forever changed the way we think about our place in space and time. The image, popularly called *Earthrise,* captures a soul-stirring sight that had never before been witnessed by mankind: our home planet, as seen from another world. Visible above the barren gray surface of the moon in the photo's foreground, the half-lit Earth is a tiny swirl of color and life in the blackness of space, looking at once astonishingly vibrant and fragile. One needn't travel to the moon to reach that conclusion but, once regarded from a vantage point a quarter-million miles away, it becomes clear that the Earth is, indeed, just that.

For almost all of human history, of course, our knowledge of the heavens—and our rightful place in them—came from earthbound observation. Even the ancients—who saw the sun and planets as gods, and the firmament as full of heroes and mythical creatures—understood intuitively that these were powerful forces at work. Though they didn't have the science to explain the rising and setting of the sun, moon, and stars, they were incredibly keen observers of them, living their lives in step with these celestial cycles—even revering them.

Though we might look at these heavenly bodies today with a more analytical eye, it doesn't diminish the wonder of them. The sun gives us nothing less than life and light, day and night; the moon fills our nights with mystery and light and gives rise to the tides of our oceans; the stars capture our imagination and, from their impossible distances, orient us and herald our seasons as surely as any earthly guide.

To introduce children to these celestial objects is as easy as looking up, looking around, and becoming aware of the grand, elemental—almost mystical—rhythms we might easily overlook or take for granted. And to help children to discover, know, and appreciate them is to share an awe-inspiring yet humbling experience that may stay with them for a lifetime—the quiet reassurance that while we are infinitesimally small, we are inexorably linked to something almost unimaginably great. In considering the astronomical scale and the vastness of the space we inhabit, they may come to understand just how improbable, how impermanent, and how imperative life on this small, blue, wonderful planet truly is.

The ideas that follow can help to point the way.

INVESTIGATING THE SUN

Is there anything more reliable than the daily rising and setting of the sun?

The sun is the closest star to the Earth. And it's not just any star—it's *our* star, the center of our solar system, radiating the light and heat that make life on our planet possible.

The sun's closeness, of course, is relative. It's still very far away from us, at a distance of roughly ninety-three million miles. But, compared to the closest stars we can see in the night sky, it's our next-door neighbor; those stars are some twenty-five million *million* miles away.

For most of human history, people held fast to the belief that the sun, moon, planets, and stars revolved around the Earth, with many early cultures even revering the sun as a deity who traveled through the sky each day. It's an easy conclusion to make—after all, we don't *seem* to be moving, and those heavenly bodies do *appear* to be moving across our skies.

But in the early 1500s, a Polish astronomer named Nicolaus Copernicus turned everything upside down. He suggested that the sun, not the Earth, was the center of the universe. The Earth, he said, was in motion, spinning daily on its own axis like a top, while also moving yearly in orbit around the sun.

Copernicus was mostly correct—the sun isn't the center of the universe, but it *is* the center of the solar system—and his assumptions provided the foundation for modern astronomy and much of our everyday understanding of space and time.

Investigating the light, heat, and motion of the sun can be done almost anywhere. Here are several ideas for you and your child to try.

MEASURING THE SUN ON THE MOVE

Imagine for a moment that our planet did not spin on its axis, and always turned the same side toward the sun. Never mind the broader implications for those of us who call the Earth our home—for now, let us just consider how it would fundamentally change our perception of time. Our understanding of hours and days, of the passage of time itself, is rooted in the perceived motion of the sun across the sky—and indeed all of nature seems to run according to this incredible solar clock. Fortunately for all of us, it's the most reliable timepiece there is.

SUNRISE, SUNSET

The sunrise that greets us each morning and the sunset we see each evening are the result of the Earth's rotation on its axis. Imagine a slow carousel ride spinning into, and then out of, the glow of a stationary sun.

In which direction does the sun rise? Set? Even if your child has already memorized these facts, proving it can be a fun exercise. Head outside and use a compass to determine the direction of the sunrise and the sunset. And consider this: Earth rotates from west to east. What if it rotated in the opposite direction? In which direction would the sun rise and set? (These concepts can be reinforced by using a globe and flashlight.)

Though our distance from the sun remains essentially the same throughout the day—easily

Did You Know?

IT TAKES JUST OVER EIGHT MINUTES FOR SUNLIGHT TO REACH THE EARTH. THE LIGHT OF THE NEXT NEAREST STAR—PROXIMA CENTAURI IN THE CONSTELLATION CENTAURUS, "THE CENTAUR"—TAKES MORE THAN FOUR YEARS TO REACH US.

illustrated by holding a ball at arm's length and moving it over your head in a slow arc from horizon to horizon—the angle at which its light strikes us changes dramatically. Ask your child to predict whether and how your shadows might demonstrate this change.

While it happens on a grand scale, the geometry itself is simple. Use a tape measure to take measurements of your shadows throughout the day—or stand in the exact same spot and mark the length of the shadows on the ground. What happens from morning until noon? What happens from afternoon until evening? What happens at midday, when the sun is directly overhead?

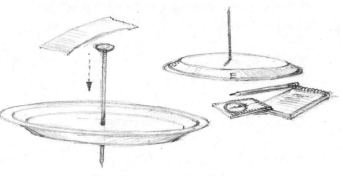

Creating a simple sundial

MAKE A SUNDIAL

Here's a fun and easy way to explore how the sun's daily course relates to the way we keep and measure time.

WHAT YOU NEED:

- a sunny day
- a paper plate
- a long nail with a flat head
- tape
- a marker

WHAT YOU DO:

1. Gently push the nail through the center of the top side of the paper plate.
2. Tape the head of the nail to the paper plate to secure it in place. Turn the plate over so the nail stands straight up. (A pencil or straw could be substituted for the nail, but it might not be as stationary as the nail.)
3. Take the plate outside and place it in a spot that gets sunlight throughout the day. Choosing a picnic table or patio table will keep your sundial safely off the ground and allow you to tape or pin it in place. If you have a compass, you may wish to find and mark north on your sundial. Should you need to move the sundial, you'll be able to orient it properly the next time.
4. Beginning in the morning, check your sundial at the top of each hour. Find the end of the nail's shadow on the plate. Make a line or hash mark to indicate the position of the nail's shadow and label it with the hour of the day (11, 12, 1, etc.).

When was the nail's shadow shortest? Longest? Where was the space between the hour marks biggest? Smallest? How is your sundial similar to a clock? How is it different?

SEEING THE SUN AT WORK

The sun is our planet's primary source of light, but it provides us with more than just illumination. The electromagnetic rays of sunlight that bathe our planet contain enormous energy—they are, in fact, the source of energy that ulti-

THE MOST FAMOUS SHADOW OF ALL MAY BE THAT OF PUNXSUTAWNEY PHIL, THE GROUNDHOG THAT EMERGES EACH GROUNDHOG DAY TO MAKE A WEATHER FORECAST. ACCORDING TO LEGEND, THERE WILL BE SIX MORE WEEKS OF WINTER WEATHER IF HE SEES HIS SHADOW ON THAT DAY, AND AN EARLY SPRING IF HE DOESN'T.

FOR AS LONG AS RECORDS HAVE BEEN KEPT—WELL OVER A CENTURY—PUNXSUTAWNEY PHIL HAS SEEN HIS SHADOW ABOUT SEVEN OUT OF EVERY EIGHT TIMES, BRINGING IN SPRING RIGHT ON SCHEDULE.

mately sustains all life on Earth. Its complexity had puzzled scientists for centuries, but we now generally accept the dual nature of light—it has the properties of both waves and particles alike. Here are two simple activities to help you see it at work.

MAKE YOUR OWN RAINBOW

We've all seen orange sunrises, red sunsets, and the yellowish glow of the afternoon sun, so it might be odd to think of sunlight as white light. But it is—sunlight contains the full spectrum of visible light. And, just as a musical chord is comprised of several distinct notes, sunlight can be broken into many individual colors.

In nature, the best-known example of this, of course, is a rainbow. Right after it rains—or even during a sun shower—water droplets in the atmosphere act as a prism, separating the sunlight into a spectrum of familiar colors: red, orange, yellow, green, blue, indigo, and violet.

Spotting a rainbow stretching across the sky is always an awe-inspiring sight, but you don't have to wait for a rainy day for the chance to see one.

WHAT YOU NEED:

- a sunny day
- a garden hose
- a spray nozzle with a mist setting

WHAT YOU DO:

1. Stand so that the sun is at your back or over your shoulder.
2. With the nozzle, make a mist of water droplets. If you don't have a spray nozzle, try placing your thumb over the end of the hose to create a fine spray.
3. When your viewing angle and the mist are just right, a bright rainbow will appear before your eyes.

If you don't have access to a hose, you may be able to accomplish the same effect with mist from a spray bottle. Rainbows also can be found in places that create their own mist, such as waterfalls and fountains.

Making sun prints

MAKE A SUN PRINT

There is enormous energy—both light and heat—in the rays of the sun. Leafy green plants are able to turn that energy into a source of food, which in turn helps to feed most of the life on our planet. People are able to absorb vitamin D—also called the sunshine vitamin—directly from sunlight. But too much sunlight can cause big changes in whatever absorbs it. A fun way to demonstrate this is by making sun prints.

WHAT YOU NEED:

- a bright, sunny day
- construction paper of different colors
- several leaves with interesting shapes
- craft glue

WHAT YOU DO:

1. Position each leaf on a sheet of construction paper. Use a glue stick or a few dabs of glue to hold each leaf in place, using as little glue as possible.
2. Place the sheets of paper in a location where they will receive plenty of direct sunshine. Tape or pin down the sheets of paper, or use rocks as paperweights to hold down the corners and keep them in place.
3. Allow the sheets of paper to remain in the sun for as long as possible. Remember that the rays of the sun are strongest from late morning to mid-afternoon. At the end of the day, remove the leaves and look for their shapes printed onto the paper. Compare the color of the paper that was hidden beneath the leaves to the rest of the sheet.

The results will be most dramatic when you try this in the summertime, but an alternative for any time of the year is to tape your sheets of paper to a window where they can face the sun for several days.

When human skin is exposed to the sun, it darkens over time because the sunlight causes our bodies to produce more melanin, the pigment that gives color to our skin, hair, and eyes to differing degrees. When the construction paper, which gets its color from dyes, is exposed to the sunlight, it creates chemical changes in those dyes that cause them to fade.

To see the effects of sunlight happen more quickly and more dramatically, try using photo-sensitive paper, available from almost any retailer that carries educational or scientific supplies. Within minutes of exposure to bright sunlight, the sharp sun prints of leaves—or even more intricate shapes and patterns such as feathers, ferns, or flowers—will appear on the specially coated paper, which is similar to that used for blueprints. The resulting prints can be striking in their detail, and make wonderful pieces of nature art.

More to Explore: Fire from Light

There is probably no better demonstration of the sun's power—and, as far as kids are concerned, no more compelling one—than to create fire with its light. Virtually every child of bygone years, given a magnifying glass and a sunny day, could conjure up the unmistakable smell of leaves smoldering on the sidewalk in a matter of minutes. While it may be somewhat of a lost art today, it is nonetheless useful knowledge worth sharing with your child—if for no other reason than to demonstrate safe and proper form. (Or so you may choose to tell them.)

The rays of the sun, as anyone who has suffered from sunburn already knows, are strong; when focused, they can pack a wallop sufficient to burn combustible materials. Like any lens, a magnifying glass focuses light to a fixed point, called the *focal point.* By focusing the energy of all the sunlight passing through it to that single point, a magnifying glass can create temperatures high enough to cause paper, leaves, or wood to burn.

Remember to try this on a safe surface such as brick, stone, sand, or dirt, well away from any other flammable materials. Be sure to protect your eyes with sunglasses; you are focusing not just the sun's heat, but its light as well.

Hold the magnifying glass so that the sun's rays pass through directly and fall on the object. The shadow of a circular magnifying glass also should appear circular; if the shadow is elliptical in shape, tilt the glass until the shadow rounds out. Then slowly move the glass closer to or farther away from the object until the bright dot of focused sunlight becomes as small and as bright as possible. Ignition could happen almost instantly or it might take a moment, depending upon the strength of the sun's rays, the shape of the lens, and temperature at which the material burns.

This technique can be useful for more than just starting a fire. Get creative by doing a little *solar pyrography*—a type of woodburning that uses the sun's rays instead of a heated tool to burn an image into wood. Small pieces of wood—even ice cream sticks or craft sticks—make a good medium for trying your hand at creating words or designs in this way.

Did You Know?

THE AMOUNT OF TIME IT TAKES THE EARTH TO MAKE ONE COMPLETE ROTATION ON ITS AXIS IS ONE *DAY*. THE AMOUNT OF TIME IT TAKES THE EARTH TO MAKE ONE COMPLETE REVOLUTION AROUND THE SUN IS ONE *YEAR*.

21

WATCHING THE MOON

In the evening sky, there's nothing more magnificent—or mysterious—than the moon.

You could make the argument that the moon is one of the first elements of the natural world we come to know. From a tender age, we find it in our lullabies, nursery rhymes, and bedtime stories, and it is almost certainly the first thing any of us beholds in the evening sky. Generations of children have raced the moon, marveled at its silvery light, and traced the benevolent visage hidden in its features.

But the fascination doesn't end there. With its timeless allure, the moon has long captured our imaginations, inspiring the world's greatest thinkers, artists, and composers and captivating romantics and scientists alike.

Our planet's only natural satellite, the moon is a world apart, yet tantalizingly close; a little more than a second away at the speed of light, yet nearly three days away by rocket ship. It is the brightest object in the night sky, but its light is borrowed, reflected, from the sun. It moves in cycles that are as familiar and reassuring as they are seemingly unpredictable, drifting through the skies at its own pace against a backdrop of stars, or the clear blue daytime sky. It shows us a multitude of faces, all without ever averting its luminous gaze.

These different faces—literally, different phases—of the moon are its most obvious and bewildering charm, and the key to understanding our relationship with it.

New moon   **Waning crescent**

Waxing crescent   **Last quarter**

First quarter   **Waning gibbous**

Waxing gibbous   **Full moon**

THE PHASES OF THE MOON

The moon's cycle begins with a phase called *new moon,* though at this time there is actually no moon visible to us. At this point, the moon rests between the Earth and the sun, rising in the morning and setting in the evening.

Within a couple of days, a thin sliver of moon will be visible in the western sky shortly after sunset. This is the *waxing crescent* moon, which grows larger and climbs higher with each successive evening. During this phase, but especially early on when the crescent moon is still quite narrow, you may notice the dark remainder of the moon glowing dimly. This phenomenon is known as *earthshine.* What you are seeing is actually the Earth's light being reflected back to us; the moon's bright silvery light, in any of its phases, is itself directly reflected sunlight. The fuller the moon grows, the less visible earthshine becomes.

By the seventh or eighth day of the cycle, the moon is said to be in its *first quarter* phase, even though to the eye it clearly presents a half-moon in shape. The name refers not to its form but rather to where it falls in sequence: the moon at this point is one-fourth of the way along its journey around the Earth, from new to full and back again. Look for the first quarter moon high overhead at nightfall.

Next comes the *waxing gibbous* moon, which becomes even fuller—and shines for longer—each night for several days.

Halfway through the cycle is the familiar *full moon,* which is opposite the new moon in every way: the moon now presents its fully lit face to us, rising with the twilight and setting with the break of day.

The full moon is followed by the *waning gibbous* moon, which rises later and later each evening, becoming less and less full.

Just over three weeks into its cycle, the moon reaches its *last quarter.* Like the first quarter, this phase is a half-moon in shape. The two are mirror images of each other. In its first quarter, the right side of the moon is lit; in its last quarter, the left. And, where the first quarter rises early and shines for the first half of the night, the last quarter rises late and shines for the second half.

Unless you're a night owl—or a very early riser—you'll be more likely to see the waning *crescent* moon in the morning following its rise. Just like the waxing crescent, it presents a narrow, curved slice of moon; unlike the waxing crescent, which grows each night, the waning crescent slowly fades away, until the moon slips out of sight altogether and returns to its new moon phase.

Keep a Moon Journal

One terrific way to introduce children to the phases of the moon is by having them sketch their own observations of them. While one can be kept at any time of year, a moon journal makes an excellent project for wintertime, when the long, early nights offer ample opportunity for viewing the moon and its changes.

What you need:

- a spiral notebook or notepad
- a pencil
- a large coin or small lid
- a flashlight or lantern

What you do:

1. Each evening, go outside and try to find the moon in the sky. Try to choose a vantage point giving you a wide view of the sky from east to west. Begin by making your observations at approximately the same time, and in the same location, each evening.

2. Use the coin or lid to trace a circle in your notebook for each day. Within the circle, carefully sketch the shape of the moon as you observe it. Pay particular attention to representing the areas where the moon is bright, and where it is dark, as accurately as possible. Gently shade in the dark areas with the pencil.

3. For each observation, record the date, time, and—if you're able—the direction where you found the moon. It's helpful to number each observation (Day 1, Day 2, etc.) as well. If weather conditions keep you from observing the moon, or there's no moon to be found, make note of that, too, and leave the circle blank.

Did You Know?

THE WORD *LUNACY* COMES FROM *LUNA*, THE LATIN NAME FOR THE MOON. IT ONCE WAS THOUGHT THAT THE PHASES OF THE MOON—PARTICULARLY THE FULL MOON—HAD THE POWER TO INFLUENCE THE BEHAVIOR OF PEOPLE, AND EVEN TO DRIVE THEM MAD. A PERSON WHO HAD BEEN DRIVEN INSANE, THEREFORE, MIGHT BE CALLED A *LUNATIC*. TODAY, WHEN WE TALK ABOUT LUNACY OR LUNATICS, WE'RE USUALLY JUST REFERRING TO WILDLY FOOLISH PEOPLE OR IDEAS.

4. Try to make and record an observation every evening, for thirty days or more.

Though it's not necessary to do so, this activity works best if you start your moon journal just after the new moon phase. At that time, a thin sliver of moon will be visible shortly after (and just above the) sunset, and the dramatic changes in the moon's appearance and location will become readily apparent over the first week of observation. (Consult a calendar, almanac, or website for the timing of the moon's phases to find a suitable start date.)

Remember that while the moon follows the same approximate path across the sky as the sun, it may rise very early or very late, depending upon its current phase. When the moon no longer appears in the nighttime sky, try looking for it early the next morning instead.

What do you notice about the position of the moon in the sky when making your observation at the same time each evening? For a variation on this theme, you may wish to find a landmark along the moon's path—a tree, a flagpole, a roofline—and make note of the time, each evening, that the moon reaches it. What do you notice on each successive evening?

A *lunar month*, in the simplest terms, is the time between like phases of the moon (for instance,

TIP: TAKE A VIRTUAL WALK IN THE FOOTSTEPS OF THE APOLLO ASTRONAUTS BY VISITING WWW .GOOGLE.COM/MOON.

from one full moon to the next full moon). Based on your observations, approximately how many days long is a lunar month? What do you notice about the time and direction you recorded each time the moon appeared to be at the exact same phase?

THE MOON IN MOTION

We have long regarded the moon as romantic, and it may be for reasons beyond its enchanting, silvery glow. Perhaps it's because in a firmament that often seems to turn with great order and precision, the moon is a bit of a vagabond, moving in mysterious, wonderful ways.

A solar eclipse   A lunar eclipse

ECLIPSES

The Earth, of course, revolves around the sun, and the moon in turn revolves around the Earth. But the paths they take—their *orbits*—do not lie in the same plane. Think of it this way: if the orbits of the Earth and moon each were a flat disc, they wouldn't stack neatly like plates; there would be a slight wobble, tipping up one of the discs and keeping them both from lying perfectly flat.

This may not seem particularly important, and it has little effect on either Earth or moon the majority of the time. But despite their slightly

TIP: Find out where and when the next lunar eclipse can be seen by visiting http://eclipse.gsfc.nasa.gov/lunar.html.

off-kilter orbits, there are two points where the orbits of the Earth and moon intersect; imagine a Hula-hoop offset within a Hula-hoop to visualize it. Should the moon happen to be either a full or new moon when its orbit crosses one of those two points, something extraordinary happens: an *eclipse.*

A *solar eclipse*—that is, an eclipse of the sun—happens when a new moon passes precisely between the Earth and sun. For a brief period, the moon—which, being a new moon, appears completely dark to us—slips in front of the sun, blocking its light and bringing temporary darkness to those observers lined up just so to see it. Because it requires the perfect alignment of sun, Earth, and moon—not to mention being in the right place on Earth and having fair weather for observation—getting to experience a solar eclipse is a rare treat.

A *lunar eclipse*—an eclipse of the moon—occurs when a full moon wanders squarely into the Earth's shadow. A lunar eclipse is a spectacular sight, and it is quite easy and rewarding to observe with nothing but the naked eye. Over the course of a couple of hours, the moon slowly dims as a shadowy disc covers it—even turning it deep shades of coppery red or orange—before gradually returning to its normal hue and brightness. Though uncommon, lunar eclipses typically occur at least once per year, and are very much worth seeing and sharing.

Imagine for a moment that the orbits of the Earth and moon were not slightly off-kilter and instead were perfectly aligned. What do you suppose would happen at each new moon? At each full moon?

Lazy Moon

The sun moves through our sky in very predictable patterns. Its daily journey through the heavens

Did You Know?

Because of the Earth's gravitational pull, the same side of the moon always faces us—no matter what phase it happens to be. The so-called dark side of the moon was never seen by mankind until the advent of satellites and space travel. (It's not actually dark, either.)

The moon, by the way, exerts its own gravitational force on the Earth, though to a much lesser degree. Still, the force is significant enough that we can see its effect every day—in the rising and falling tides of our oceans.

is the result of the Earth's own rotation; the sun seems to rise as we spin toward it, and to set as we spin away from it. The same is true, as we will see, of the stars.

Things with the moon are a bit different. Like the sun and stars, the moon does appear to rise in the east and move across the sky before setting in the west. But unlike the sun and stars, the moon also is revolving around the Earth—from west to east, as we see it. To the earthbound observer, the moon therefore seems to drift along lazily, falling behind those other celestial bodies.

A carousel illustrates this concept well. Imagine riding the merry-go-round as two friends watch from the ground; with each rotation, the friends will come into view at the same time. But what if one friend begins to slowly walk around the carousel, in the direction of its spin? With each rotation, he would seem to lag farther behind the stationary friend. Eventually, the friend in motion would circle the carousel and end up where he had started, and, as with the moon, the cycle would begin again.

You and your child can easily observe the moon's unique pace among the sun and stars. Try spotting the moon at the exact same time of day for three successive nights and note its location. What do you notice about its position in the sky on the second night? The third? If the moon is not far from the horizon—such as a waxing crescent moon

Did You Know?

WE'VE ALL SEEN THIS BEFORE: A FULL MOON RISING, JUST ABOVE THE HORIZON, SEEMS MUCH LARGER THAN THAT SAME FULL MOON SEEN HIGH IN THE SKY A FEW HOURS LATER. BUT THE MOON, OF COURSE, DOESN'T ACTUALLY CHANGE ITS SIZE IN THE SPAN OF AN EVENING.

THIS PHENOMENON IS KNOWN AS THE *MOON ILLUSION*, AND IT REALLY IS JUST THAT—A TRICK PLAYED ON US BY OUR SENSES. WHILE SCIENTISTS HAVE YET TO EXPLAIN DEFINITIVELY HOW IT OCCURS, IT ALMOST CERTAINLY HAS TO DO WITH THE WAY OUR BRAINS PERCEIVE AND PROCESS THE APPEARANCE OF OBJECTS IN THE DISTANCE. WHATEVER THE REASON, IT IS PERHAPS NATURE'S GRANDEST OPTICAL ILLUSION. AND, EVEN BETTER, IT MAKES A FULL MOON SEEM EVEN MORE SPECTACULAR.

NOT CONVINCED? SEE FOR YOURSELF. HOLD A SMALL ROUND OBJECT, SUCH AS A TINY BUTTON, BREATH MINT, OR MEDICINE TABLET, AT ARM'S LENGTH AND COMPARE IT TO THE SIZE OF THE FULL MOON ON THE HORIZON. SEVERAL HOURS LATER, COMPARE IT TO THE SIZE OF THE FULL MOON OVERHEAD.

setting, or a nearly full moon rising, early in the evening—the effect may be more noticeable, with trees, houses, or buildings serving as convenient markers. This will work, however, during any visible phase of the moon.

With a little patience, you can see the moon fall behind the stars in the course of just one evening. For best results, try this on a clear night when the moon is in its waxing crescent or first quarter phase; a moon much fuller than that might drown out the stars with its own light. As soon as the sky is dark, find the moon and look for one or more stars close by, the brighter the better, especially stars that seem to lie ahead of or behind the moon on its westward path. Make note of their arrangement, sketching it if you like. Measure the distance between the moon and your stars with a hand held at arm's length: the width of one thumb, three fingers, and so forth. Come back every hour or so to check the relative position of the moon and stars. What do you find?

More to Explore: Full Moon Names

In our hurried modern world, it's sometimes easy to lose track of just which day it is, much less what the current phase of the moon might be. But for the people who came long before us, living in tune with the cycles of the moon and the progression of the seasons often was a matter of survival. For those who depended on the land to provide them every essential, knowing when to plant, to pick, to hunt, or to harvest was of the utmost importance.

This connection to—and respect for—the natural world is evident in the names they gave the different full moons occurring in each of the months of the year, names dating back to the Native American tribes of North America and the English settlers who followed them.

Some of the names—Snow Moon, Flower Moon—seem fitting and obvious. In which month do you think the Worm Moon, Strawberry Moon, Harvest Moon, and Beaver Moon occur? Why do you suppose they were given those names? What names might your family give to the full moons you observe together?

GAZING AT THE STARS

Stargazing is a great year-round family activity, perfect for lazy summer nights or chilly winter evenings when daylight fades early.

There's something magical about the night sky. The stars seem like they've always been there, and always will be. Yet at the same time, the stars appear to be constantly changing, from season to season—even hour to hour—giving order to the heavens, marking time, and showing us the way. Like falling leaves and migrating birds, the stars are part of nature's great rhythms, and to know them is like having old friends you can look forward to seeing year after year.

Best of all, introducing children to these distant wonders couldn't be easier; all you need is a clear, dark night. A star chart or guide is helpful for finding and tracing the constellations, but anyone, young or old, can appreciate the simple beauty of the stars themselves. The farther away you are from bright city lights, of course, the more rewarding your experience will be—but we will focus here on heavenly bodies visible even in the near-dark skies of towns and suburbs.

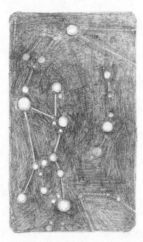

Orion is the finest winter constellation

ABOUT CONSTELLATIONS

In much the same way we can find familiar forms in the clouds, people have long gazed at the stars and, with just a little imagination, have seen pictures there. Unlike those fleeting images in the clouds, the pictures drawn in the stars—we know them as *constellations*—are much more dependable, with many dating back centuries, or even thousands of years.

The ancients who drew imaginary lines between the stars to create the earliest constellations were astute observers of the heavens, even if they didn't understand the science behind them. They often believed that the things they saw in the stars—heroes and maidens, animals and beasts— were placed there by the gods, making the connection, which endures to this day, between the constellations and the mythologies of ancient civilizations. The stories and legends lend that much more charm to these already magical sights, which have remained essentially unchanged for thousands of years.

Each season brings new constellations for your family to find, and a good star guide provides help with tracing their shapes. Here's a look at just a few of the constellations to look for, by season.

Winter

Bundling up on a chilly winter evening is worth the effort. The colder, drier air makes for clearer skies, and the most splendid part of the night sky is on display. Seven of the seventeen brightest stars in the sky—including the brightest star of all—can be found in close proximity to each other.

In the midst of them stands Orion the Hunter, easily the most impressive of all the constellations. Orion is unmistakable, with a row of three bright stars in his belt and even brighter stars marking a foot and shoulder; they are the bluish star Rigel and the reddish star Betelgeuse, respectively. Two bright stars near Orion's right shoulder and foot belong to Canis Minor and Canis Major—the Little Dog and the Big Dog—the constellations that depict his hunting dogs. The star nearer his foot, in the Big Dog, is noteworthy; it is the brilliant bluish-white Sirius, the brightest star in the night sky.

Spring

While there may not be a tiger among them, springtime stars bring a lion and a bear—oh my! Leo the Lion is a regal constellation that stands most high and proud at this time of year. Look for it by first finding the sickle-shaped group of stars—really more of a backward question mark— that marks its front end.

You may already know the Big Dipper (more about that, soon), which is actually just part of the larger constellation Ursa Major, the Great Bear. As fall turns to winter, the Great Bear, like its earthly counterparts, lays low—to rise again as winter turns to spring. As the days grow warmer and longer, look for this large constellation in the northern sky at night.

Summer

Even though warm summer nights can mean somewhat hazy skies, there's still plenty for stargazers to see. High overhead by the middle of the season is the so-called Summer Triangle comprising three of the twenty brightest stars in the sky—Altair, Deneb, and Vega—each belonging to a different constellation—Aquila the Eagle, Cygnus the Swan, and Lyra the Lyre, respectively. Three stars in a tight little row mark the Eagle's head, and the Swan is easily traced by finding the bright Northern Cross within it; the long part of the cross is actually the Swan's neck.

Autumn

Several constellations joined by a common mythology can be seen overhead in the autumn sky. Cassiopeia was an ancient queen whose familiar W shape can be seen on almost any night; however, it resembles an M when this constellation is at its highest. According to legend, Cassiopeia's boasts of

Did You Know?

ON VERY CLEAR, VERY DARK NIGHTS, YOU MIGHT NOTICE THE HAZY, SILVERY BAND THAT MEANDERS BETWEEN THE STARS. THIS IS THE MILKY WAY, WHICH IS AT ITS SHIMMERING BRIGHTEST DURING THE SUMMER MONTHS—ESPECIALLY LATE SUMMER, WHEN HUMID NIGHTS GIVE WAY TO CRISP, DARK SKIES AND THE BRIGHTEST PART OF THE MILKY WAY IS HIGH OVERHEAD. EVEN SO, IT NEVER APPEARS VERY BRIGHT, AND UNLESS YOU CAN GET AWAY FROM THE LIGHTS OF THE CITIES AND THE SUBURBS, YOU MAY HAVE TROUBLE SPOTTING IT. IF YOU ARE ABLE TO SEE THE MILKY WAY, CONSIDER THIS: YOU WILL BE LOOKING EDGEWISE AT OUR OWN GALAXY, A FLATTENED DISC FULL OF STARS SOME ONE HUNDRED THOUSAND LIGHT-YEARS IN DIAMETER.

BOOK NOOK

FIND THE CONSTELLATIONS
BY H. A. REY
AGE RANGE: 7 TO 12

THE STARS: A NEW WAY TO SEE THEM
BY H. A. REY
AGE RANGE: 12 AND UP

THE AUTHOR AND ILLUSTRATOR H. A. REY IS BEST KNOWN AS THE CREATOR OF CURIOUS GEORGE, ONE OF THE MOST ENDEARING CHARACTERS IN CHILDREN'S BOOKS. PERHAPS NOT AS WELL-KNOWN, BUT EVERY BIT AS ENDURING, ARE REY'S BOOKS *FIND THE CONSTELLATIONS* AND *THE STARS: A NEW WAY TO SEE THEM*.

SIMPLY BY RECONNECTING THE STARS OF EACH CONSTELLATION INTO MEANINGFUL, RETRACEABLE SHAPES, REY REVOLUTIONIZED THE WAY WE LOOK AT THE NIGHT SKY. THESE CHARMING VOLUMES MAKE STARGAZING FUN AND ACCESSIBLE, AND ARE THE PERFECT INTRODUCTION TO ASTRONOMY FOR KIDS—AND FOR KIDS AT HEART, AS WELL.

her daughter's beauty angered the gods and caused the princess—named Andromeda—to be chained to a rock by the sea, where she was to be sacrificed to a sea monster. Fortunately, the hero Perseus came along to slay the monster and rescue Andromeda, whom he married. Perseus rode a most famous steed: the winged horse, Pegasus. Perseus, Andromeda, and Pegasus can be found close to Cassiopeia, and all of the constellations—easily traced with the aid of a guidebook —lie within, or near to, the Milky Way.

CONNECT THE DOTS

Tracing the constellations in the night sky is a grand game of "connect the dots." But even when the skies or the weather aren't cooperating, you still can have fun finding them. Refer to a star guide and sketch the stars of your favorite constellations on a sheet of paper. Using your book, trace their shapes with your child. See if you can remember and find the constellations on your sheet without looking at the book.

You can also make your own constellations.

Cover a sheet of paper with a random assortment of dots. See what shapes you and your child can find among the "stars" on the paper. Don't forget to give names to your constellations. Or, like the people of ancient civilizations before us, tell stories about the animals, people, and objects you see—and explain why they've been placed in the sky for all of eternity.

NAVIGATING BY THE STARS

Just as the sun and moon appear to rise and set, so too do the stars. As the Earth spins on its imaginary axis like a globe on a stand, celestial objects seem to rise in the east, move across the sky, and set in the west.

But some stars—such as those of the Big Dipper—never seem to set at all, at least for observers in the Northern Hemisphere. Instead of big, sweeping arcs across the sky, they move in tighter, circular paths.

Do you know the Big Dipper? Chances are that it's the first pattern you'd learned to spot in the night sky. And if you don't know it yet, rest assured; it's one of the easiest groups of stars to learn and find. All of its seven stars are at least fairly bright, making it visible even in semidark skies, and they very clearly form the shape of a ladle with a curved handle—though the legends of various cultures have described it as a plow, wagon, or cart, among others.

For most observers in the Northern Hemisphere, this most famous group of stars never dips below the horizon (though it sometimes will appear upside-down or sideways, depending upon the hour and the time of year). This means that on any clear night, anyone north of the equator should be able to trace at least part of the Big Dipper. However, the farther north you are, the easier the Dipper is to see.

That's because the stars of the Big Dipper are *circumpolar*. They, along with several constellations, are situated close to Polaris, the Pole Star—sometimes called the North Star—the one star in the night sky that seems fixed in place while the other stars move in circles around it. Because it rests almost precisely on what is called the *north celestial pole*, that point around which all stars appear to move, Polaris is as clear and reliable a marker for north as any compass. It is just by fortunate happenstance that Polaris, a fairly bright star, happens to occupy that particular spot in the heavens, as we see it.

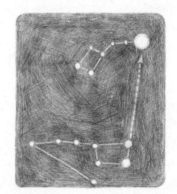

By finding the Big Dipper, you can always find north

FIND NORTH

The Big Dipper's proximity to Polaris makes this group of stars as useful as it is impressive. For hundreds of years, it has been a dependable means of navigation for travelers, and it remains so today. Quite simply, if you can find the Dipper, you can find north.

WHAT YOU DO:

1. On a clear night, look for the familiar, ladle-like shape of the Big Dipper: a curving handle ending in a wide, nearly rectangular bowl.
2. The two bright stars at the end of the bowl—the ones farthest from the Dipper's handle—are known as the Pointers, as they point directly to Polaris, the North Star.
3. Simply imagine a line connecting these two stars, and extend it in the direction of the Dipper's open end to the next bright star. Your imaginary line from the Pointers to Polaris will be about five times as long as the distance between the Pointers themselves.

No matter how the Big Dipper appears—upside-down, right-side-up, or sideways—this trick for finding north will always work.

FIND YOUR LATITUDE

Polaris has another interesting characteristic—it always appears in the northern sky at an elevation equal to the latitude of the observer. For example, if you live at latitude 40° north, the angle from the horizon to Polaris (as you see it) also will be 40°. Therefore, stargazers in Beijing, Madrid, and New York City all would see Polaris at roughly the same position in the night sky, provided the lights of the city didn't obscure it from view.

Why not see for yourself? Try this little bit of backyard navigation with your child.

WHAT YOU NEED:

• a protractor
• a yardstick
• a globe or map with latitude markings

WHAT YOU DO:

1. Trace the Big Dipper and find Polaris.
2. Rest a protractor and one end of a yardstick on a level outdoor surface such as a picnic table or deck railing.
3. Raise or lower the other end of the yardstick until you can sight Polaris along its length, and hold it steady.
4. Use the protractor to make an approximate measurement of the angle between the horizon and Polaris by measuring the angle between the yardstick and the level surface.
5. Check a globe or map to find your latitude and compare it to your measurement. Are the two figures close?

Think about this: Where would you see Polaris if you were standing at the North Pole? Just north of the equator? Anywhere in the Southern Hemisphere?

ABOUT SHOOTING STARS

When you catch a glimpse of a shooting star, you can't help but feel that you've just seen something

> **TIP:** WANT TO KNOW WHAT'S IN THE SKY THIS EVENING? YOU CAN FIND AN INTERACTIVE SKY CHART, INCLUDING ALL VISIBLE STARS AND PLANETS, BY VISITING WWW.SKYANDTELESCOPE.COM/OBSERVING/SKYCHART.

special. Seemingly out of nowhere, a bright flash streaks across the night sky, and then—as quickly as it came—it's gone.

While shooting stars—you may know them as falling stars—may not be magic, they certainly do feel mysterious and wonderful, a simple delight we never seem to outgrow. No wonder people through the ages have whispered their secret wishes to the night upon seeing them. After all, what could be more wish-worthy?

In actual fact, shooting stars can and do happen at any time; many simply go unseen because they happen during daylight hours or because they occur at an instant when nobody is observing. However, the more time you spend watching the skies at night, the greater your chances of seeing them.

Though we casually refer to them as "shooting stars," these celestial events are more properly called *meteors.*

Our solar system is a busy place, with planets, asteroids, and comets all on the move. And drifting in the space between them are *meteoroids*— solid objects as small as grains of sand or as big

as boulders. When a meteoroid enters the Earth's atmosphere at great speed, it becomes heated, and sometimes burns so brightly that it leaves a visible streak across the sky—a *meteor.* Usually, the solid object disintegrates as it passes through the atmosphere, but sometimes it survives the fall and the impact with the ground. When that happens, it's called a *meteorite.*

CATCH A METEOR SHOWER

Many of the meteors you might see are a matter of good luck and good timing. But, luckily, there are several times throughout the year when we know exactly where and when to expect them. These events are called *meteor showers,* and they occur when Earth passes into the stream of debris and fragments shed by a comet. The result is a brief concentration of meteors that appear with great frequency—oftentimes as many as a meteor per minute—and seemingly streaming from a single point in the sky.

There are about a dozen significant meteor showers that recur each year, some more spectacular

Did You Know?

- -

FROM TIME TO TIME, A METEORITE LARGE ENOUGH TO LEAVE A MARK WILL REACH THE SURFACE OF THE EARTH. THE FAMOUS METEORITE THAT FELL NEAR CANYON DIABLO IN ARIZONA LEFT A VERY BIG MARK: ITS IMPACT CRATER IS SOME 4,000 FEET WIDE AND 570 FEET DEEP!

than others. Although the peak times and viewing conditions will vary somewhat from year to year, the following meteor showers are among the most observable and usually can be counted on to put on a good show.

Perseids

The Perseids are the most well-known meteors, offering a consistently reliable shower at a convenient and comfortable time of year to be out at night: late summer. Though some meteors can be seen in the days leading up to and following the peak, the greatest number of them typically is clustered around August 12 and 13 each year.

These meteors are named for Perseus, the constellation from which they seem to radiate; the meteors themselves can be seen across the sky as it rises. Early in the evening, position a lawn chair

Meteor Shower	Peak	Parent Comet
The Perseids	Mid-August	Swift-Tuttle
The Leonids	Mid-November	Tempel-Tuttle
The Geminids	Mid-December	3200 Phaethon

so that it faces east, and recline as the night progresses until the wee hours, when Perseus will be overhead. Because the Earth will be rotating into the direction of its orbit around the sun at the time—and therefore picking up more space debris along the way—the predawn hours often produce the best meteor displays.

Observers far from city lights can expect to see as many as sixty meteors per hour on dark nights with little interference from the moon. The brightest Perseids still will be visible from suburban, even urban, areas, but the number of visible meteors will of course be much lower.

Leonids

The Leonids are famous for producing the most memorable meteor shower in recorded history. Like the Perseids, the Leonids are named for the constellation from which they radiate—in this case, Leo the Lion. On the night of November 12, 1833, the Leonids erupted in a display so spectacular that people were awakened from their sleep by it. Eyewitness accounts report seeing thousands of meteors per minute on what became known as "the night the stars fell."

While we may never again see such a dramatic display from them, the Leonids are highly variable and do become unusually active every thirty-three years. During those periodic showers, hundreds, if not thousands, of meteors can be seen per hour. Most years, however, you can expect to see ten or twenty fast-moving meteors per hour during the peak, which usually falls around November 17 or 18.

Geminids

The Geminids are perhaps the most impressive of all the meteor showers, but because they typically peak around December 13 or 14 each year, the conditions for observing them can be cold and uncomfortable. But if you don't mind bundling up, you may find it worthwhile: the wintry air often means clearer, drier skies that can make for splendid viewing conditions and meteors that seem even brighter than usual.

The Geminids—can you guess how they got their name?—are widely regarded as the most reliable and active meteor shower of the year, offering as many as two or three meteors per minute at its peak, under ideal viewing conditions. But there are two other characteristics that make the Geminids a unique display: they are conspicuously long and colorful. Because they approach Earth at a modest speed compared to other showers, Geminids tend to create lengthier—and more persistent—trails, making them easier to spot. And, while most of them appear white, fully one-third of Geminids have a noticeable hue; yellow is the most prevalent color, but blue, red, and even green meteors can be seen.

TIPS FOR METEOR VIEWING

Whichever meteor shower you try to catch, follow these general tips to help you see as many meteors as possible:

- Choose a viewing location far from light pollution and with an unobstructed view of the horizon, if possible.
- Give your eyes at least fifteen minutes to fully adjust to the darkness—especially before heading out for cold-weather meteor viewing.
- Avoid sources of white light once your eyes have adjusted. A flashlight covered with red plastic film or construction paper shouldn't affect your night vision.
- Sit or recline to watch meteor showers. Standing

Did You Know?

COMETS ARE THE "DIRTY SNOWBALLS" OF OUR SOLAR SYSTEM, AND WHEN THEIR ORBITS BRING THEM CLOSE ENOUGH TO THE SUN, THEY TAKE ON THEIR CHARACTERISTIC SHAPE: A SOLID *NUCLEUS*, COMPRISED MOSTLY OF DUST AND ICE, SURROUNDED BY A CLOUD OF GASES CALLED A *COMA* AND FOLLOWED BY A LONG, STREAMING *TAIL* OF GAS AND DUST THAT ALWAYS POINTS AWAY FROM THE SUN.

Did You Know?

ONE OF THE BIG DIPPER'S STARS JUST MIGHT HAVE YOU SEEING DOUBLE. TAKE A CLOSER LOOK AT THE MIDDLE STAR OF THE DIPPER'S HANDLE. IF THE SKY IS CLEAR AND DARK ENOUGH, AND IF YOUR EYES ARE SHARP ENOUGH, YOU MIGHT NOTICE THAT THIS BRIGHT STAR (NAMED MIZAR) HAS A FAINT, TINY COMPANION (NAMED ALCOR).

SOMETIMES CALLED HORSE AND RIDER, MIZAR AND ALCOR FORM THE BEST KNOWN DOUBLE STAR VISIBLE TO THE NAKED EYE. MIZAR'S EASY TO SPOT, BUT CAN YOU SEE ALCOR? BE SURE TO CHECK THEM OUT WITH FIELD GLASSES OR BINOCULARS, IF YOU'VE GOT THEM.

and craning your neck will quickly become very uncomfortable.

- Face the section of sky from which the meteors will radiate, but try not to narrow your focus on a single point. Let your gaze drift among the stars and, if possible, let your peripheral vision cover a wide section of sky from zenith to horizon.
- Keep tabs on the phase of the moon. Unless the moon is full, there should be at least a small

window of opportunity to view meteors without interference from its glow.

Just as with stargazing, clear, dark nights with little or no moonlight offer the best scenario for viewing meteors. If a meteor shower peak falls during such conditions, get ready for a great show.

The ideal setting will give you a wide, unobstructed view of the sky, and if you can get away from the glow of city lights, all the better—they'll wash out many of the meteors you otherwise might see in a dark sky.

But these just might be the best viewing conditions of all: from your sleeping bag.

To conjure up a little family magic, camp out with your kids—even in your own backyard—on the night of a meteor shower. No matter how many, or how few, meteors you see, chances are you'll be making memories you won't soon forget. And someday, when their childhood has streaked by like a shooting star fading in the night, those are the only things that will matter.

TIP: FOR DETAILED INFORMATION ABOUT METEOR SHOWER PEAKS AND VIEWING TIMES, VISIT WWW .EARTHSKY.ORG AND SEARCH FOR "METEOR SHOWER GUIDE" TO FIND THE CURRENT YEAR'S GUIDE.

More to Explore: The Planets

Though the stars at first glance seem white, you may have noticed by now that some of them actually have a very noticeable hue. Many of the brightest and most well-known stars have a distinctly yellow, blue, red, or orange tinge. But be forewarned: some of those very bright, colorful "stars" aren't stars at all—they're planets. (If you think you've spotted a planet, remember one easy way to tell the difference: stars will twinkle or shimmer, while planets will shine with a steady, even light.)

The brightest planets—Venus, Mars, Jupiter, and Saturn—all can easily be seen with the naked eye, typically outshining even the brightest stars around them. And unlike the stars, which rise and set like clockwork, the planets seem to chart their own course through the night sky. A given planet may be visible—or may slip from view—for months on end. One clue to their whereabouts is that they, like the sun and moon, seem to follow more or less the same path across our skies.

Venus is our close neighbor, relatively speaking, and very similar in size to our own planet. Venus, however, is blanketed by a thick atmosphere of carbon dioxide, contributing to its incredibly hot surface temperatures. While this might make it inhospitable to life, Venus glows with a brilliant yellowish-white light and is nothing short of dazzling in our skies. After the sun and moon, this second planet from the sun is the brightest natural object we can see.

Venus always and only appears as a so-called morning star or evening star. When it is visible, you'll find it either in the western sky shortly after sunset or in the eastern sky shortly before sunrise—but not for long, and never very high overhead. Why do you suppose this is true? Think about its location in our solar system for a clue.

Mars is our other next-door neighbor, the fourth planet from the sun. Because of its proximity to us, the ebb and flow of its orbit are more noticeable than for the more distant planets. Therefore, it varies from moderately to very bright in our night skies. There is, however, one characteristic of Mars that remains constant: its deep reddish tint.

Jupiter is named for the mythological king of the gods, and it could rightly be called the king of the planets as well. It is far and away the largest of the planets in our solar system, and only Venus appears brighter in our skies. To the naked eye, Jupiter shines with a brilliant, yellow-orange light, but be sure to take a look through binoculars, if you've got them: you might be able to see one or more of Jupiter's primary moons—Io, Europa, Callisto, and Ganymede.

Saturn, of all the planets in our solar system, has the most spectacular appearance. Its enormous orbital rings are its defining feature, but you would need at least a small telescope to fully appreciate them. While not as bright as Jupiter, Saturn still can readily be seen with the naked eye—it is the most distant planet easily observed without aid—typically shining as brightly, or more so, as the stars around it. But even at its most luminous, Saturn can't match one star: Sirius, the brightest star in the night sky.

NOTES

PREFACE

1. Julie Henry, "Words Associated with Christianity and British History Taken Out of Children's Dictionary," *Telegraph.co.uk* (December 8, 2008), http://www.telegraph.co.uk/education/3569045/Words-associated-with-Christianity-and-British-history-taken-out-of-childrens-dictionary.html.

INTRODUCTION

1. Rhonda Clements, "An Investigation of the Status of Outdoor Play," *Contemporary Issues in Early Childhood* 5, no. 1 (2004): 72.
2. Sandra L. Hofferth and Sally C. Curtin, "Leisure Time Activities in Middle Childhood," Indicators of Positive Development Conference (March 12–13, 2003): 5, http://www.childtrends.org/Files/HofferthCurtin-Paper.pdf.
3. Oliver R. W. Pergams and Patricia A. Zaradic, "Evidence for a Fundamental and Pervasive Shift away from Nature-Based Recreation," *Proceedings of the National Academy of Sciences* 105, no. 7 (2008): 2295–2300.
4. Andrew Balmford et al., "Why Conservationists Should Heed Pokémon," *Science* 295, no. 5564 (2002): 2367.
5. Stephen R. Kellert, "Nature and Childhood Development," in *Building for Life: Designing and Understanding the Human-Nature Connection* (Washington, D.C.: Island Press, 2005), 64.
6. Victoria Rideout, Donald F. Roberts, and Ulla G. Foehr, *Generation M: Media in the Lives of 8–18 Year-Olds* (Menlo Park, Calif.: Henry J. Kaiser Family Foundation, 2005): 6.
7. Marcella Nunez-Smith, et al., *Media and Child and Adolescent Health: A Systematic Review* (San Francisco, Calif: Common Sense Media, 2008): 3.
8. Victoria J. Rideout, Elizabeth A. Vandewater, and Ellen A. Wartella, *Zero to Six: Electronic Media in the Lives of Infants, Toddlers, and Preschoolers* (Menlo Park, Calif.: Henry J. Kaiser Family Foundation, 2003): 4.
9. Ibid, 7.
10. Victoria Rideout, Donald F. Roberts, Ulla G. Foehr, *Generation M: Media in the Lives of 8–18 Year-Olds*, 6.
11. Robert Weisman, ed., "Commercializing Childhood: The Corporate Takeover of

Kids' Lives," *Multinational Monitor* 30, no. 1 (2008): 32.

12. Ibid.

13. Marcella Nunez-Smith, et al., *Media and Child and Adolescent Health: A Systematic Review*, 4–7.

14. Colleen Cordes and Edward Miller, eds., *Fool's Gold: A Critical Look at Computers in Childhood*, Alliance for Childhood (September 2000): 3, http://drupal6.allianceforchildhood.org/fools_gold.

15. Ibid, 35.

16. Teri M. McCambridge, et al., "Active Healthy Living: Prevention of Childhood Obesity through Increased Physical Activity," *Pediatrics* 117, no. 5 (2006): 1834–1842.

17. National Center for Health Statistics, "Obesity Still a Major Problem" (2006), http://www.cdc.gov/nchs/pressroom/06facts/obesity03_04.htm.

18. Steven Reinberg, "Restricting TV and Computer Time Helps Kids Lose Weight," *U.S. News & World Report* (March 4, 2008), http://health.usnews.com/usnews/health/healthday/080304/restricting-tv-and-computer-time-helps-kids-lose-weight.htm.

19. Teri M. McCambridge, et al., "Active Healthy Living: Prevention of Childhood Obesity through Increased Physical Activity."

20. S. Jay Olshansky, et al., "A Potential Decline in Life Expectancy in the United States in the 21st Century," *New England Journal of Medicine* 352, no. 11 (2005): 1138–1145.

21. Janice F. Bell, Jeffrey S. Wilson, Gilbert C. Liu, "Neighborhood Greenness and Two-Year Changes in Body Mass Index of Children and Youth," *American Journal of Preventive Medicine* 35, no. 6 (2008): 547–553.

22. Leonard H. Epstein, et al., "A Randomized Trial of the Effects of Reducing Television Viewing and Computer Use on Body Mass Index in Young Children," *Archives of Pediatrics and Adolescent Medicine* 162, no. 3 (2008): 239–245.

23. Terrance Woodworth, Drug Enforcement Administration Congressional Testimony before the Committee on Education and the Workforce: Subcommittee on Early Childhood, Youth and Families (May 16, 2000), http://www.usdoj.gov/dea/pubs/cngrtest/ct051600.htm.

24. Ibid.

25. Dimitri A. Christakis, et al., "Early Television Exposure and Subsequent Attentional Problems in Children," *Pediatrics* 113, no. 4 (2004): 708–713.

26. Carl Erik Landhuis, et al., "Does Childhood Television Viewing Lead to Attention Problems in Adolescence? Results From a Prospective Longitudinal Study," *Pediatrics* 120, no. 3 (2007): 532–537.

27. Frances E. Kuo and Andrea Faber Taylor, "A Potential Natural Treatment for Attention-Deficit/Hyperactivity Disorder: Evidence From a National Study," *American Journal of Public Health* 94, no. 9 (2004): 1580–1586.

28. Andrea Faber Taylor and Frances E. Kuo, "Children with Attention Deficits Concentrate Better after Walk in the Park," *Journal of Attention Disorders* 12, no. 5 (2009): 402–409.

29. Nancy M. Wells and Gary W. Evans, "Nearby Nature: A Buffer of Life Stress among Rural

Children," *Environment and Behavior* 35, no. 3 (2003): 311–330.

DISCOVER TOGETHER

1. Colleen Cordes and Edward Miller, eds., *Fool's Gold: A Critical Look at Computers in Childhood*, Alliance for Childhood (September 2000): 19, http://drupal6.alliance forchildhood.org/fools_gold.
2. Ibid.
3. Stephen R. Kellert, "Nature and Childhood Development," in *Building for Life: Designing and Understanding the Human-Nature Connection* (Washington, D.C.: Island Press, 2005), 83.
4. Office of the United Nations High Commissioner for Human Rights, Convention on the Rights of the Child, General Assembly Resolution 44/25 of 20 November 1989, http://www.unhchr.ch/html/menu3/b/k2crc.htm.
5. Kenneth R. Ginsburg, et al., "The Importance of Play in Promoting Healthy Child Development and Maintaining Strong Parent-Child Bonds," *Pediatrics* 119, no. 1 (2007): 183.
6. The National Center on Addiction and Substance Abuse, *The Importance of Family Dinners IV* (New York: Columbia University Press, 2007): 5.
7. Rhonda Clements, "An Investigation of the Status of Outdoor Play," *Contemporary Issues in Early Childhood* 5, no. 1 (2004): 74.
8. Nancy M. Wells and Kristie S. Lekies, "Nature and the Life Course: Pathways from Childhood Nature Experiences to Adult Environmentalism," *Children, Youth and Environments* 16, no. 1 (2006): 1–24.
9. Susan S. Lang, "Camping, Hiking and Fishing in the Wild as a Child Breeds Respect for Environment in Adults, Study Finds," *Chronicle Online* (March 13, 2006), www .news.cornell.edu/stories/March06/wild .nature.play.ssl.html
10. Louise Chawla, "Learning to Love the Natural World Enough to Protect It," *Barn*, no. 2 (2006): 71–72.
11. David Sobel, *Beyond Ecophobia: Reclaiming the Heart in Nature Education* (Great Barrington, Mass.: Orion Society, 1996).

SAFETY FIRST

1. Centers for Disease Control and Prevention, *West Nile Virus Fact Sheet* (2005), http://cdc.gov/ncidod/dvbid/westnile/resources/WNV_factsheet.pdf.
2. Centers for Disease Control and Prevention, "Protect Yourself from Tick Bites," www .cdc.gov/ncidod/dvbid/lyme/Prevention/ld_Prevention_Avoid.htm.
3. National Institute of Allergy and Infectious Diseases, "Common Cold," www3.niaid.nih .gov/topics/commonCold/cause.htm.
4. Environmental Working Group, "Sunscreen Summary—What Works and What's Safe," www.cosmeticsdatabase.com/special/sunscreens2008/summary.php.

CHAPTER 4. DISCOVERING DETAILS IN THE DIRT

1. University of Bristol, "Getting Dirty May Lift Your Mood" (April 2, 2007), www.bristol .ac.uk/news/2007/5384.html.

CHAPTER 16. HEADING TO THE SEA

1. Victoria Lambert, "Be Beside the Seaside" (November 8, 2008), www.telegraph.co.uk/health/dietandfitness/3355947/Be-beside-the-seaside.html.

2. *A Rising Tide of Ocean Debris* (Washington, D.C.: Ocean Conservancy, 2009), http://www.oceanconservancy.org/pdf/A_Rising_Tide_full_lowres.pdf.

RESOURCES

BOOKS AND MAGAZINES

The following works offer valuable information, inspiration, and assistance to families seeking meaningful connections to the natural world—and to each other.

BOOKS FOR PARENTS

Bloom, Benjamin S. *Taxonomy of Educational Objectives*. New York: Pearson Longman, 1977.

Cornell, Joseph Bharat. *Sharing Nature with Children*. Nevada City, Calif.: Dawn Publications, 1979.

Gardner, Howard E. *Frames of Mind: The Theory of Multiple Intelligences*. 1983. 10th ed. New York: Basic Books, 1993.

Louv, Richard. *Last Child in the Woods: Saving Our Children from Nature-Deficit Disorder*. Rev. and expanded ed. Chapel Hill, N.C.: Algonquin Books, 2008.

Montessori, Maria. *The Absorbent Mind*. New York: Macmillan, 1995.

Montessori, Maria. *The Montessori Method*. New York: Frederick A. Stokes, 1912.

Sobel, David. *Beyond Ecophobia: Reclaiming the Heart in Nature Education*. Nature Literacy Series. Vol. 1. Great Barrington, Mass.: Orion Society, 1999.

Wilson, Edward O. *Biophilia: The Human Bond with Other Species*. Cambridge, Mass.: Harvard University Press, 1984.

FIELD GUIDES AND INSTRUCTIONAL BOOKS FOR PARENTS AND CHILDREN

Appelhof, Mary. *Worms Eat My Garbage: How to Set Up and Maintain A Worm Composting System*. 2nd ed. Kalamazoo, Mich.: Flowerfield Enterprises, 1997.

Arnosky, Jim. *Wild Tracks! A Guide to Nature's Footprints*. New York: Sterling, 2008.

Aston, Diana Hutts. *A Seed Is Sleepy*. San Francisco: Chronicle Books, 2007.

Bial, Raymond. *A Handful of Dirt*. New York: Walker Books, 2000.

Chichester, Page. *The National Wildlife Federation Book of Family Nature Activities*. New York: Henry Holt and Company, 1997.

Danks, Fiona and Jo Schofield. *Nature's Playground: Activities, Crafts, and Games to Encourage Children to Get Outdoors*. Chicago: Chicago Review Press, 2007.

Diehn, Gwen and Terry Krautwurst. *Nature Crafts for Kids: 50 Fantastic Things to Make with Mother Nature's Help*. New York: Sterling Publishing, 1992.

Hall, Randy. *The Letterboxer's Companion*. Guilford, Conn.: Falcon Guides, 2003.

Leahy, Christopher. *Peterson First Guide to Insects*. 2nd ed. Boston: Houghton Mifflin, 1998.

Libbrecht, Kenneth. *The Little Book of Snowflakes*. McGregor, Minn.: Voyageur Press, 2004.

Lovejoy, Sharon. *Roots, Shoots, Buckets, and Boots: Gardening Together with Children*. New York: Workman Books, 1999.

Mizejewski, David. *National Wildlife Federation: Attracting Birds, Butterflies, and Other Backyard Wildlife*. Upper Saddle River, N.J.: Creative Homeowner, 2004.

Peterson, Roger Tory. *Peterson First Guide to Birds*. 2nd ed. Boston: Houghton Mifflin, 1998.

Petrides, George A. *Peterson First Guide to Trees*. 2nd ed. Boston: Houghton Mifflin, 1998.

Rey, H. A. *Find the Constellations*. Boston: Houghton Mifflin, 2008.

Rey, H. A. *The Stars: A New Way to See Them*. Boston: Houghton Mifflin, 1976.

Russo, Monica. *The Tree Almanac: A Year-Round Activity Guide*. New York: Sterling Publishing, 1983.

Silver, Donald, M. *One Small Square: Backyard*. New York: McGraw-Hill, 1993.

Williams, Ernest H., Jr. *The Nature Handbook: A Guide to Observing the Great Outdoors*. New York: Oxford University Press, 2005.

BOOKS FOR CHILDREN

Elhert, Lois. *Leaf Man*. New York: Harcourt, 2005.

French, Vivian. *Growing Frogs*. New York: Walker Books, 2008.

Martin, Jacqueline Briggs. *Snowflake Bentley*. Boston: Houghton Mifflin, 1998.

Rockwell, Anne. *Becoming Butterflies*. New York: Walker Books, 2004.

Sidman, Joyce. *Song of the Water Boatman, and Other Pond Poems*. Boston: Houghton Mifflin, 2005.

Silverstein, Shel. *The Giving Tree*. New York: HarperCollins, 1964.

MAGAZINES FOR CHILDREN

Wild Animal Baby
Your Big Backyard
Ranger Rick

WEBSITES

A wealth of online resources can help your family make the most of the time you spend unplugged and outdoors. As a starting point for further exploration, the websites mentioned in this book are collected here.

BIRDS

Audubon Christmas Bird Count: www.audubon.org/Bird/cbc/

The Cornell Lab of Ornithology's searchable bird guide: www.allaboutbirds.org/guide/search

The Cornell Lab of Ornithology's Project Feeder-Watch: www.birds.cornell.edu/pfw/

The Great Backyard Bird Count: www.birdsource.org/gbbc/

CITIZEN SCIENCE AND SERVICE PROJECTS

Leave No Trace Center for Outdoor Ethics: www.lnt.org

Ocean Conservancy's International Coastal Cleanup: www.coastalcleanup.org

Project Budburst: www.budburst.com

U.S.A. National Phenology Network: www.usanpn.org

GAMES AND ADVENTURES

Atlas Quest, a letterboxing community: www.atlasquest.com

Geocaching: www.geocaching.com

Letterboxing North America: http://letterboxing.org

Rails-to-Trails Conservancy's trail finder: www.traillink.com

GENERAL RESOURCES

Children & Nature Network: www.childrenandnature.org

National Wildlife Federation's Green Hour website: http://greenhour.org

National Wildlife Federation's website for finding nature activities in your community: www.nwf.org/naturefind

Nature Rocks, a family nature planner: www.naturerocks.org

U.S. National Park Service: www.nps.gov

Website devoted to the wild animals and plants of the United States: www.enature.com

INSECTS

Butterflies and moths of North America: www.butterfliesandmoths.org

An interactive bug identification guide: http://bugguide.net

Journey North: www.learner.org/jnorth/monarch

University of Kansas Monarch Watch: http://monarchwatch.org

University of Minnesota Monarch Lab: http://monarchlab.org

PLANTS AND TREES

Arbor Day Foundation's tree website: www.arborday.org/trees

Lady Bird Johnson Wildflower Center: www.wildflower.org

Ohio Public Library's website on treeidentification: http://oplin.org/tree

Pollinator Partnership: http://pollinator.org

United States Department of Agriculture's plant database: http://plants.usda.gov

SAFETY

The Centers for Disease Controls website on Lyme disease prevention: www.cdc.gov/ncidod/dvbid/lyme/Prevention/ld_Prevention_Avoid.htm

Environmental Working Group's Cosmetic Safety Database: www.cosmeticsdatabase.org

Summary of findings from the Environmental Working Group's sunscreen study: www.ewg.org/cosmetics/report/sunscreen09/investigation/summary-of-findings

STARS AND PLANETS

EarthSky science podcasts: www.earthsky.org

Google moon: www.google.com/moon

Interactive sky charts from *Sky & Telescope:* www.skyandtelescope.com/observing/skychart

NASA's eclipse website: http://eclipse.gsfc.nasa.gov/lunar.html

WEATHER AND WEATHER PATTERNS

Environmental Protection Agency's water cycle website for kids: http://epa.gov/ogwdw/kids/flash/flash_watercycle.html

An interactive "snowfall" of Kenneth Libbrecht's snowflake photographs: http://images.amazon.com/media/i3d/01/snow2.swf
National Oceanic and Atmospheric Administration's National Weather Service: www.weather.gov
Photo gallery of snowflakes and snow crystals: www.snowcrystals.com

ABOUT THE AUTHOR

AMY HUGHES

TODD CHRISTOPHER is a writer, educator, and producer who celebrates wonder whenever he finds it. He was the creator of the National Wildlife Federation's Green Hour website and served as director of online media for its award-winning publications, including *Ranger Rick, Your Big Backyard,* and *Wild Animal Baby.* He resides with his family near Washington, DC, where they make a green hour part of their daily routine. You can find more of his writing on kids and nature at www.toddchristopher.com.